Harry Swanson

THE BLENDING OF RACES

THE BLENDING
OF RACES

MARGINALITY AND IDENTITY
IN WORLD PERSPECTIVE

Noel P. Gist

Anthony Gary Dworkin
University of Missouri

WILEY-INTERSCIENCE

a Division of John Wiley & Sons, Inc.
New York • London • Sydney • Toronto

Library of Congress Cataloging in Publication Data:

Gist, Noel Pitts, 1899–
   The blending of races.

   Bibliography: p.
   1. Race problems—Addresses, essays, lectures.
2. Miscegenation—Addresses, essays, lectures.
3. Minorities—Addresses, essays, lectures.
I. Dworkin, Anthony Gary, joint author.   II. Title.

HT1523.G57   301.45   72-5122
ISBN 0-471-30253-8

Printed in the United States of America

10 9 8 7 6 5 4 3 2 1

Dedicated to

The Racially Mixed Peoples of the World

BIOGRAPHIES

Noel P. Gist, professor of sociology at the University of Missouri, Columbia, has held two Fulbright Awards in India, where he did research on the Anglo-Indians. He holds a Ph.D. degree from Northwestern University.

Anthony Gary Dworkin is an assistant professor of sociology at the University of Missouri, Columbia, and Associate Editor of *The Sociological Quarterly*. He received his Ph.D. from Northwestern University and has published several articles and chapters on Mexican-Americans and Mexican-American stereotypy.

H. F. Dickie-Clark was formerly professor of sociology at Natal University, Durban, South Africa. His book, *The Marginal Situation*, is concerned with the Coloured people of Durban. In 1971 he joined the sociology staff of the New University of Ulster, Northern Ireland.

Tissa Fernando is presently assistant professor at the University of British Columbia. A lecturer in sociology at the University of Ceylon from 1963 to 1971, he has a Ph.D. degree from Oxford University.

Elizabeth P. Wittermans, who was born in the former Dutch East Indies, is a representative of the Eurasian minority. Educated in Indonesia, the Netherlands, and England, she holds degrees in Indonesian studies and anthropology. Presently she is associate professor of human development at the University of Hawaii.

Dennis Hilary Gouveia, a native of Guyana, belongs to the Colored minority he discusses in his chapter. He holds a master's degree from the University of Missouri.

Betty H. Watts is Reader in Education at the University of Queensland, Brisbane, Australia. She holds a Ph.D. degree from the University of Queensland.

Richard Slobodin, who holds a doctorate from Columbia University, is professor of anthropology at McMaster University, Hamilton, Ontario. He is the author of a research monograph on the Metis people, the subject of his chapter in this book. Beginning in 1936, he spent several years in research among the people of the Canadian and Alaskan subarctic.

Brewton Berry, professor of sociology at Ohio State University, holds a doctorate from Edinburgh University. He has done extensive research on racially mixed peoples in the United States and is the author of a well-known text on race relations.

Bernhard L. Hormann is professor of sociology at the University of Hawaii. He holds a doctorate from the University of Chicago and has taught at Lingnan University, Canton, China, Chung Chi College of the University of Hong Kong, and the University of Chicago.

Donald Pierson received his doctorate at the University of Chicago. He was professor of sociology and social anthropology at the Escola de Sociologia e Politica in São Paulo, Brazil, from 1939 to 1959, and dean of the graduate division from 1943 to 1957. He was a Guggenheim research fellow in Portugal and Spain in 1963–1964 and a Fulbright lecturer in Portugal in 1966. Among his published works are *Negroes in Brazil*.

Peter A. Munch is professor of sociology at Southern Illinois University, Carbondale. He has long been interested in the Tristan da Cunha islanders and has conducted field research on this group in the South Atlantic. His book, *Crisis in Utopia*, deals with the people on the island.

PREFACE

This symposium had its origin in a series of conversations in 1969 between the senior editor and Dr. Elizabeth Wittermans at the East-West Center in Hawaii. At that time an outline was formulated for the development of a symposium on racially mixed peoples in various societies. Later Dr. Wittermans found it necessary to withdraw from editorial responsibilities but agreed to continue as one of the contributing authors. In the summer of 1969 Dr. Anthony Gary Dworkin assumed responsibility as coeditor of the planned volume.

Anyone who has been involved in editing a symposium represented by numerous authors is aware of the difficulties in orchestrating the contributed papers by persons who may differ in interpretations and theoretical perspectives, not to mention the practical problem of persuading them to observe deadlines and keep their contributions to manageable length. In this case the problem was compounded by the widespread geographical distribution of the authors and consequent difficulties in communicating with some of them. Yet each chapter author fruitfully and painstakingly complied with our wishes. Several helped to find possible contributors and supplied some of the positive affect needed to maintain high morale during the three-year effort.

As far as we know this is the only cooperative study of racially mixed peoples on the world scene. Some of the contributors are themselves members of the racially mixed minorities discussed in this book. All of them have conducted systematic research on the groups about which they write and from many personal contacts with these peoples are familiar with their social lives, their values, and their problems. As might be expected, each author has emphasized those aspects of the group that represent the major point of his or her interest. Hence there is considerable variation in the analyses. Some have emphasized the theoretical aspects of marginality as applied to the group under consideration; some have provided a detailed historical account of the group's origin and evolution; others have been concerned primarily with such matters as the organization of social life and the relations of the group with others differing in racial composition or even in culture. Taken together, the essays represent a contemporary study of racially blended peoples widely distributed geographically.

We are indebted to Dr. Donald O. Cowgill, chairman of Missouri's Department of Sociology, who authorized some of the expenditures necessary for the completion of the symposium; the clerical staff—Jeanie Slagle, Ann S. Wright, Mary Grace Burroughs, and Edith Pinet—who demonstrated in a most salutary manner their secretarial expertise; and Dean Robert Culpepper, who funded the indexing of the book. Finally, we should like to express our appreciation to our wives: to Rosalind J. Dworkin, a sociologist herself, who critically evaluated some of the writings, and to Mabel Gist, whose assistance was invaluable in the field work involved in her husband's research in India.

NOEL P. GIST
ANTHONY GARY DWORKIN

Columbia, Missouri
May 1972

CONTENTS

THE BLENDING OF RACES

Noel P. Gist and Anthony Gary Dworkin

University of Missouri

CHAPTER ONE

INTRODUCTION

Racial "purity" is a myth accepted by mankind in many civilizations. The converse of a belief in racial purity is race "mixture" about which have clustered various notions concerning the consequences of biological blending. A formidable body of evidence exists that *all* peoples represent an admixture of hereditary traits in varying degrees and forms but in which the fusion is more visible in some groups than in others. What *is* lacking is evidence that racial blending is biologically harmful, that the hereditary capacity of racially mixed persons is damaged by the fusion of racial traits, or that such persons are necessarily inferior or superior in potential learning ability.

There is, of course, abundant evidence that race, in its biological aspects, has important social, cultural, and psychological ramifications, not because of race per se but because of the positive or negative values placed on certain racial characteristics. These values so permeate many societies that minority peoples, racially distinct from the majority, often suffer serious handicaps as they become subjected to prejudice and discrimination and are objects of hostility or indifference. Often this is true of minority peoples of dual or multiple racial heritage.

The events and situations that have produced racial blending reach far back into the misty and unrecorded annals of history. Whenever and wherever peoples move about, coming into contact with others different in race and culture, amalgamation and acculturation are possibilities. In modern times the great movement of peoples has been made possible by technological developments, and contacts between groups diverse in

1

physical and cultural characteristics have generally increased. Many racially mixed minorities had their origin as recently as the last five centuries, the by-products of colonialism, imperialism, military conquest, and political-economic domination by a powerful racial group.

Colonialism and Race Mixing

Large-scale colonialism and military conquest were for centuries a feature of Western imperialist expansion in which European powers sent troops and civil personnel to the "backward" countries whose people usually differed racially and culturally from the Western conquerors. As the Europeans became entrenched militarily, politically, and economically, it was almost inevitable that contacts with local people would lead to sexual unions, either in conventional marriage or in unconventional relations. These unions were mainly between European males and darker women of the subjugated lands. Their progeny thus exhibited visible genetic traits, including color, inherited from both ancestral lines. Usually the offspring of such unions, or their own descendants, were distinguishable racially from either line of ancestors.

It is these people of dual or multiple racial heritage who are the subject of the essays in this volume. As racial minorities, they may be found in countries widely separated geographically and culturally. Of particular interest in this symposium are the Coloureds of South Africa, the Eurasians of Indonesia and Holland, the Anglo-Indians of India, the Burghers of Ceylon, the Metis of Canada, the Aborigines of Australia, the racial hybrids of Brazil, the "mestizos" of the United States, the Mexican-Americans, the racially mixed minorities of Hawaii, the mixed-bloods of Guyana, and the islanders of Tristan da Cunha. Each of these groups is unique in various respects: in the historical circumstances of its origin and development, in the status accorded it by the society of which it is a part, and in its relations with other peoples, but one thing they have in common is an awareness of their own racial heritage and the way in which racial blending has affected them individually and collectively.

By the middle of the present century European empire building and colonization in the classical style were more or less at an end. In the face of massive independence movements most of the colonial powers withdrew from the occupied countries and were superseded by new nationalist governments which represented indigenous peoples or Europeans who had settled permanently in the region. Since the people of mixed racial heritage were generally a numerical minority, facing in two racial and cultural directions, they often encountered difficulties in readjusting to situations created by the new regimes.

In the situation just described the Europeans journeyed overseas and as colonizers, traders, missionaries, or military forces established social contacts with the people in regions brought under military and civil control. These contacts were usually on the basis of inequality, in a hierarchically structured relationship in which the Europeans were in positions of superior power and prestige. This was the pattern that developed when the British became established in India, China, Burma, the Middle East, the Americas, and parts of Africa; the Dutch in Indonesia and Ceylon; the French in Africa and Southeast Asia; the Italians and Germans in Northeast Africa; the Spanish and Portuguese in Africa and Latin America; the Belgians in Central Africa; and the Americans in the Philippines.

In some cases this pattern was reversed. The intermingling of Negroes and people of European stock occurred when vast numbers of African blacks were transported as slaves from Africa and sold in the United States and Latin America. In most cases social contacts were selective, according to the accepted status system, and sexual cohabitation between white males and nonwhite females was almost entirely outside the bounds of formal marriage. Most of the "black" people in these countries today have a dual or multiple racial heritage, with physical traits inherited from both their European and African ancestors as a result of cross-racial breeding. Racial amalgamation also occurred between the blacks and Amerindians. Indeed, some of the racially blended people in the United States and Brazil today represent a three-way mixture of whites, blacks, and Indians.

Variable Patterns of Race Contact

A variation of this pattern may be observed in the movement to the Americas of people diverse in race or culture. Many came voluntarily as immigrants, others as contract laborers to work in the fields and factories. Whatever the circumstances of their journey to the United States, and of their experiences after arrival, their convergence resulted in extensive blending of bloods and cultures. Some were of mixed racial ancestry before they arrived, but cross-racial or cross-cultural sexual unions commonly occurred after arrival. The position of such mixed-bloods in American society varies considerably, according to the racial and cultural characteristics of the persons involved and the prevailing values in the region.

A unique situation developed in Hawaii when Caucasians, Asians of varied cultural and racial heritages, and Polynesians converged on the islands. The Polynesians were the original occupants of the region; other peoples arrived much later. Most of the Caucasians who settled there in the nineteenth century went as fortune seekers or as missionaries bent on converting the "heathen." In due course they came to exercise a dominant role in economic and political matters. As the economy expanded, large numbers from other lands were attracted to the region as contract laborers, to work in the developing agricultural economy, or as servants in the homes and establishments of the well-to-do. Most of them remained— Japanese, Chinese, Koreans, Filipinos, Portuguese, and Puerto Ricans. This convergence led to extensive genetic amalgamation and cultural assimilation. Many, racially mixed and "unmixed," moved upward in the social structure, some achieving positions of power and affluence or distinction in cultural or intellectual spheres. But the circumstances in Hawaii were different from those created by European colonization and domination in Asia, Africa, or Latin America or from the interracial convergence in mainland United States or Brazil when Africans were transported there involuntarily, as slaves, or when immigrants arrived from other lands.

Variable Statuses of Racial Hybrids

In some societies in which racial blending occurred mixed-blood peoples were judged to be of an inferior order, unacceptable socially by their European progenitors or native kinsmen. These attitudes can be accounted for in various ways, but especially by sheer racial or class prejudice or in the belief that racial hybrids are less capable and less moral than their kinsmen of "pure" racial stock. Sometimes the people of mixed racial ancestry were seen as a threat to the power and privileged positions of a dominant group; in other instances they were viewed by their indigenous kinsmen as traitors to the country of their birth if they identified with, and supported, an outside imperialist power. This, for example, was the lot of the Anglo-Indians in India, who were culturally and racially akin to the British and tended to identify with them; Europeans often rejected them as "half-castes," although making use of their occupational skills in consolidating the Empire in southern Asia. At the same time they were distrusted by their Indian kinsmen, not so much because of racial differences but for political and social reasons.

In some situations racially mixed peoples are not seriously disadvantaged because of racial miscegenation. The Portuguese, as an aspiring imperialist power in southern Asia or Latin America, did not exhibit the racial prejudices that characterized the British hegemony in the colonies. Indeed, intermarriage between the Portuguese civil and military personnel and natives was even encouraged, partly for political reasons. The Burghers of Ceylon also were advantaged in certain respects, but with the rise of Ceylonese nationalism after independence people of dual racial ancestry have experienced considerable social and economic disadvantages. A somewhat comparable situation developed in Guyana after independence. Often the hostilities directed toward those of mixed blood by ardent nationalists who came to occupy seats of political power were not based so much on racial or cultural differences as on considerations of national loyalty. A racially mixed people in some countries thus became a symbol of the discredited regime whose racial and cultural attributes they shared.

If the dominants were representative of a colonial power, the termination of colonialism often created a series of problems for the mixed-blood minority. With the end of colonialism, these minorities usually faced a serious crisis if they had identified with the colonial rulers and were viewed with suspicion or hostility by the indigenous population. Uncertainties concerning their present and future status invariably engendered anxieties and feelings of insecurity or produced hostilities toward the people who in their eyes were symbols of oppression, discrimination, and exploitation or were considered to be socially or culturally inferior to themselves.

Within the confines of a racially mixed people there may be cleavages and levels of status. In some societies a child born of an indigenous mother and, say, a European father is socially and legally, if not biologically, distinct from a child whose father is a native and whose mother is a European. This was the situation in India, Indonesia, and Ceylon, but the distinction within such groups, or between racially mixed peoples and those of "pure" racial stock in the same society, is not solely a matter of biological inheritance; it may also be a reflection of differences in social class, style of life, and power. A "Dutch Burgher" in Ceylon, for example, generally enjoyed a status superior to that of a "Portuguese Burgher." A similar social distinction is made between high status Mexican-Americans who claim to be "Hispanos" and the lower status "Chicanos." Even among certain racially blended minorities persons are sometimes evaluated socially in terms of color gradations and other physical characteristics, those with fair skins and "good" hair being rated somewhat above those having dark complexions.

At one time fair Negroes in the United States were generally favored by whites and even by dark Negroes. Lightness of skin color was a social asset because it established their kinship to Caucasians. Fair Negroes seldom became organized as a distinct community; their advantage was in terms of status and better job opportunities. But the prestige associated with fair skin is undoubtedly less important now than formerly: blackness has been redefined as beautiful by the black community. In Brazil the light-complexioned person of Caucasian-African descent also has a status advantage over the black individual, although color may be no more important than social-class position in the ascription of status roles. The Brazilian saying that "money lightens" dramatically depicts the imperfect correlation between color and status.

Peoples of dual or multiple racial ancestry may (or may not) develop a sense of community identity in which they view their own group as a people apart from other groups with whom they may share a racial or cultural heritage. Whether or not a community consciousness develops appears to depend in considerable measure on the nature of their relations with other groups as well as the relative size of the mixed-race population. If they are oppressed or exploited, subjected to discrimination, or labeled as inferior or immoral, a sense of community may emerge as a means of collective survival in an unfriendly milieu, provided that they are numerous enough to survive. Ethnocentrism and community pride may in turn generate forms of organization that are designed to maintain group unity and *esprit de corps,* to reinforce political or economic activities, or to support programs of welfare and education. In most of the peoples considered in this book a considerable variety of formal organizations has appeared, usually intended to meet the needs of members within the community. Some have achieved their goals; many have been short-lived and of limited value to the group.

Variable Reactions of Racial Hybrids

The reactions of mixed-blood peoples have varied according to the specific situation at a particular time in history. Some have identified with, and supported, the dominant group in the power structure and prestige system, even when the dominants were of foreign origin. By such identification they sought to elevate their own status and obtain a degree of security in the social and economic system. Generally they were assimilated, at least to a considerable degree, into the culture of the dominant group, accepting the major values and modus vivendi of that group even if they chafed under discrimination by their political and social superiors. But social and political integration into the prevailing system of the dominants did not always follow. In some instances the racial hybrids had no interest in becoming assimilated into the culture of the indigenous population or of being integrated into that social system. As might be expected in such cases, the reactions of the *indigenes* were generally unfavorable, often resentful of what they considered snobbish behavior by their "half brothers."

Whatever social position the racially blended minorities were accorded in the various societies, they were generally marginal, socially, culturally, or politically, in their relations with other groups, notably the dominants in the seats of power, but also with other people in the same society who represented different racial or cultural strains. If they were subjected to discrimination in the labor market, prevented from participation in the processes of political life, or excluded from intimate association in the social affairs of other groups, the reaction was usually a heightened collective consciousness commonly manifest in some form of organized community life.

The reactions have, as noted, varied according to the particular circumstances. Ways and means, for example, have been attempted by racially mixed groups to achieve a more satisfactory position in the social order—organization for increased political and economic power, emphasis on education and the support of educational facilities in the interest of the minority, and increased participation in the affairs of the larger society. With the termination of foreign rule and the emergence of independent nations, some groups assessed the situation and strove to demonstrate their loyalty to the "motherland" and to identify with the new social order.

But the reactions of many have indicated disenchantment, not hope or optimism. Some have migrated to other lands in search of opportunities denied them in the country of their birth. This has been especially true of the Eurasians of Indonesia, the Burghers of Ceylon, the Anglo-Indians of India, and the Guyanese colored minority. For economic or political reasons, however, the number of migrants usually represented only a small proportion of the racially mixed minority in any country; many who aspired to migrate could not afford the financial costs of migration or were unable to obtain entrance into the nation of their choice. In some countries with mixed-blood minorities the prospect of outward migration was remote for most of the people, even if they desired to leave. Most Mexican-Americans have elected to remain in the United States for economic reasons and because in Mexico, for some if they settled there, they would also be culturally and socially marginal. Other racially mixed peoples in the United States literally have no place to go even if they wished or were able to leave. This is certainly true of any who claim an Indian tribe as part of their heritage. It may also be true of many black Americans who, because their skin is too light or their skills are too limited, cannot return to their heritage in Africa.

Individual reactions to the situation undoubtedly vary widely, according to such factors as the treatment accorded by other groups, the socio-economic position in the larger society, and imagined prospects for the future. Some, unable to achieve social, economic, or political parity, have expressed their frustrations in cynicism and hostility toward those held responsible for their real or imagined plight. Others, manifesting the syndromes of hopelessness and entrapment, have withdrawn in disillusionment. Still others have resigned themselves to an unpromising situation in an effort to make the best of things. But any or all of these reactions may change as situations become more or less favorable to their needs and interests.

In some countries public opinion has registered considerable concern about the problems of minorities, and in most instances no distinction has been made, at least officially or publicly, between those of mixed ancestry and others assigned to the same group. Most of these minorities have been disadvantaged, economically, educationally, and politically, and efforts that have been made to alleviate the conditions have not achieved the stated objectives. Ameliorative or reform efforts have commonly been a response to protests by the underprivileged minority and often by minority leaders who have achieved distinction in political, cultural, economic, or intellectual affairs.

The problem of identity invariably arose in those societies in which either the masses or those in positions of power and privilege were negatively disposed toward their racially mixed kinsmen. Who am I, what rights and privileges have I or my people, or what are the prospects for the future are perplexing questions that have been troublesome indeed for many of dual or multiple racial ancestry. As might be expected, they were often oriented toward the group possessing power and prestige, viewing the dominants both as protector and reference group, whether or not they were accepted as social equals. One thing is certain: the moving hand of time in every country with mixed-blood minorities brings about changes in form and content of human relationships so that the position of such groups and their relations with other peoples may be different from one period to another. The essays in this volume point clearly to that fact. It is central to the quest for identity and concern about the future.

MARGINAL MEN AND A PARADIGM

So far we have argued that when people of distinct racial and cultural heritages meet and establish sexual unions the products of such unions often find themselves in a social situation laden with unique social strains and even hostilities. The consequences to individuals of mixed racial or mixed-ethnic backgrounds have been the topic of much speculation and theorizing during the present century. The rubric under which such individuals have been classified has sometimes been "the marginal man."

Issues in Marginality

Within the sociological literature is a tradition, first conceived by Simmel,[1] first labeled marginality by Park,[2] and first codified by Stonequist,[3] of concern for the characteristics of people who are somehow different, somehow unique, somehow strangers because of the exigencies and consequences of human migration. Park designated such people as marginal men. Because of the often obvious physical differences between the mestizo or mulatto and his own parents, the person of mixed racial heritage has been the prime candidate to test hypotheses regarding marginality.

According to Park's formulation in 1928, the marginal man is a product of human migration and culture conflict. Park suggested that the marginal man is a cultural hybrid. Such individuals as the Jew in Europe or the person of mixed race such as the mulatto of the United States or the Eurasian of Asia "is one who lives in two worlds, in both of which he is more or less of a stranger." Park adds in his discussion of the Jew after the destruction of the ghetto walls in Europe,

. . . there appeared a new type of personality, namely, a cultural hybrid, a man living and sharing intimately in the cultural life and traditions of two distinct peoples; never quite willing to break, even if he were permitted to do so, with his past and his traditions, and not quite accepted, because of racial prejudice, in the new society in which he sought to find a place. He was a man on the

---

[1] The turn-of-the-century German social scientist Georg Simmel proposed in his paper that "The Stranger" is one who is not of the group in which he participates but "imports qualities into it which do not and cannot stem from the group itself." Because he is not of the group, he brings to it a unique objectivity. He is marginal, and in an existentialist school he is alone. See *The Sociology of Georg Simmel* (Kurt H. Wolff, translation). New York: The Free Press, 1950.

[2] Robert E. Park's original formulation of the concept of the marginal man first appeared under the title "Human Migration and the Marginal Man," *Amer. J. Sociol.* 33, 881–893 (May 1928). Additional writings by Park on the topic appear in the collection of his essays compiled by Everett C. Hughes. This collection appears as Robert Ezra Park, *Race and Culture*. New York: The Free Press of Glencoe, 1950.

[3] Although Stonequist has made several reformulations of his thesis, the most detailed presentation is still his 1937 reworking of his 1930 University of Chicago doctoral dissertation. The reader is referred to Everett V. Stonequist, *The Marginal Man: A Study in Personality and Culture Conflict*. New York: Charles Scribner's Sons, 1937.

margin of two cultures and two societies, which never completely interpenetrated and fused.[4]

Park applied the concept of marginality to peoples of mixed race, but it was Stonequist who added precision to the model. Stonequist also attempted to specify the characteristics of marginal peoples. He suggested that they had double consciousness and that they were ambivalent, moody, temperamental, hypersensitive, and hypercritical. They may, because of their felt ambiguity and rejection, be more objective in their view of both cultures through which they could trace their heritage. Stonequist suggested that marginality was a dissonance-producing situation for both the individual and the society; hence pressures existed for the resolution of the tension. He proposed the following:

> In general, the marginal individual may evolve in one of three major directions: (1) assimilation into the dominant group; (2) assimilation into the subordinate group; or (3) some form of accommodation between the two societies.[5]

Critiques of the Marginal-Man Theory

A decade after the initial formulations by Park and Stonequist, Goldberg,[6] relying on substantially better data, proposed that the previous authors had overestimated the universality of the psychological impact of marginal situations on personality; that is, both Park and Stonequist assumed that individuals subjected to marginal situations would manifest the symptoms of ambiguity, double consciousness, moodiness, instability, and anxiety which represent the syndrome of anomie and marginality. Although Stonequist acknowledged that psychopathologies might not result from all situations of marginality, he felt that at least minimal symptoms similar to a malaise were characteristic of marginals.

Goldberg created the concept of the "marginal culture" to deal with cases in which marginal individuals were insulated from the effects of such marginality. The marginal culture was in essence a subculture or a hybrid culture and served to provide meaning, continuity, and normative order to the lives and interactions of individuals who might not otherwise

---

[4] Park, 892 (1928).
[5] Everett V. Stonequist, "The Marginal Man: A Study in Personality and Culture Conflict," in Ernest W. Burgess and Donald J. Bogue, Eds., *Contributions to Urban Sociology*, Chicago: University of Chicago Press, 1964, pp. 337–345 (see especially p. 337).
[6] Milton M. Goldberg, "A Qualification of the Marginal Man Theory," *Amer. Sociol. Rev.*, 6, 52–58 (February 1941).

fit into the dominant culture, the subordinate culture of one or the other of their ancestors, or other minority cultures in the same society.

Soon after Goldberg, Green[7] specified the necessary and sufficient requisite conditions for the emergence of the psychological condition of marginality. As summarized succinctly by Dickie-Clark,[8] the elements were as follows:

Psychological marginality occurs when (a) there are major cultural (we may also add racial) differences between the populations involved, (b) the person in the marginal situation attempts to identify with both his own and the dominant group (and any minority group in his heritage); (c) the individual strives to leave or "pass" from the marginal to the dominant population; and (d) when such passage is blocked by any number of social barriers.

Some investigators have debated whether the concept of marginality is too restrictive or too inclusive. Lewin[9] and Hughes[10] each argue that the concept should be expanded beyond the boundaries of mixed race or mixed ethnicity. Hughes's conception of status dilemmas represents one attempt to expand the concept. In such instances the configurations of a person's defining status characteristics are inconsistent with one another and with the normally acceptable prerequisites for his social role. Since race or ethnicity is an ascribed status characteristic, Hughes reasoned that certain status characteristics could, if dissonant with other status characteristics possessed by the individual, produce marginal situations. Thus the black doctor, the career woman, or the adolescent might be expected to be as much of a misfit as the individual of mixed race. Although there are universally prescribed prerequisites for certain careers, such as educational training, there are also prerequisites generally agreed on but rarely specified formally—"doctors ought to be men," "airline pilots should be white males," etc. When individuals meet the formal requirements, but not the unspecified ones, their legitimate claim to a status is often questioned. Black doctors are sometimes prohibited from practicing in certain hospitals; women professors are not always promoted and paid according to their academic merits. Such individuals, Hughes argues, suffer the effects of marginality.

Since marginal situations may reflect and produce imbalances, there

---

[7] Arnold W. Green, "A Reexamination of the Marginal Man Concept," *Social Forces,* **26,** 167–171 (October 1947).
[8] H. F. Dickie-Clark, *The Marginal Situation.* London: Routledge, Kegan Paul, 1966.
[9] Kurt Lewin, *Resolving Social Conflicts.* Harper: New York, 1948.
[10] Everett C. Hughes, "Dilemmas and Contradictions of Status," *Amer. J. Sociol.,* **50,** 353–359 (March 1945). Cf. E. C. Hughes and H. M. Hughes, *Where Peoples Meet: Racial and Ethnic Frontiers.* Glencoe, Illinois: The Free Press, 1952, pp. 188–200.

are drives toward equilibrium, as suggested by Stonequist. In the case of persons with status dilemmas the psychological resolution in the United States has often been in political radicalism. Since this society stresses achievement themes, resolution of the imbalance by denial of the higher achieved status is unacceptable; that is, it is not satisfactory for the professional woman to deny that she holds a college degree or the black doctor to deny his medical training. The alternative is to change the societal definition of the ascribed status. Civil rights protests, women's liberation participation, and similar activities attempt to effect changes in the societal definition of the ascribed status, thereby reducing imbalances and marginality. The body of literature on status consistency since Lenski deals with the particular status dimensions that produce particular marginal reactions.

In contradistinction to the attempts to expand the dimension of psychological marginality to status dilemmas, Golovensky[11] restricted the Park and Stonequist formulation to inter-racial or interethnic situations involving attempts to "pass." Thus he accepts Green's requirement that the marginal individual must strive to leave the marginal group. He does contend that the United States is a nation of many minority groups and that it is not possible to speak of a homogeneous dominant culture and a homogeneous but different minority culture. True psychological marginality, in this view, is not a group phenomenon but rather an individual experience of being torn between fragmented groups, often because of conflicting familial loyalties to them.

In a study conducted in 1953 of Jews in New Haven Antonovsky[12] proposed that individual adaptations to the marginal situation are not uniform. Thus Antonovsky and Golovensky support one another. Antonovsky suggests that the traditional conceptions of persons in marginal situations are those of people who demonstrate instability, conflict, and uncertainty. In contradistinction, his own subjects demonstrated a variable range of responses, not all of which differed from individuals not exposed to marginal situations.

Finally, investigators, including Mann[13] and Kerckhoff,[14] have at-

---

11 David I. Golovensky, "The Marginal Man Concept: An Analysis and Critique," *Social Forces*, **30**, 333–339 (March 1952).

12 Aaron Antonovsky, "Toward a Refinement of the 'Marginal Man' Concept," *Social Forces*, **35**, 57–62 (October 1956).

13 J. W. Mann, "The Problem of Marginality," in P. Watson, Ed., *The Psychology of Race Relations*. London: Penguin Books, 1969. See also Dickie-Clark, *op. cit.*, for the use of Mann's M Scale.

14 Alan C. Kerckhoff, "Marginal Status and Marginal Personality," *Social Forces*, **34**, 48–55 (October 1955).

tempted to measure the psychological dimension of marginality. The major conclusion to be drawn from their work is that until the social psychological perspective is quantifiable we can do little but speculate, as Park and Stonequist essentially did, about the effects of the marginal situation on some individuals as opposed to others.

Marginality as Temporal and Relative

Antonovsky is correct in stating that the responses to marginal situations are variable. In addition, the emergence of a marginal culture or of psychological marginality is always problematic. At one time a group may be marginal and manifest psychological marginality, at another it may evolve a marginal culture to insulate the individuals from such psychological conditions, and at still another be nonmarginal. The mestizos in Mexico and the American Southwest have, at different times in their history, experienced each of three states. Under Spanish rule they evolved a marginal culture. After the defeat of the Spanish this culture became the dominant form in Mexico. Under Anglo domination in the Southwest they developed many of the psychological symptoms of marginality described by Stonequist. Today, under the Chicano movement, we are seeing the re-emergence of a mestizo culture—a marginal culture. Mestizos living today in Mexico continue to be members of the dominant and hybrid culture. Thus, although marginal situations call for adaptations, these adaptations are dynamic and temporally specific.

Another example of the temporal aspects of marginality may be seen in the changing or changed positions of such peoples as the Eurasians, Burghers, Anglo-Indians, the Coloreds of Guyana, and perhaps in the future the Durban Coloureds. Each of these peoples has been stationed in terms of status and privilege between the indigenous and subjugated native population, on the one hand, and the colonial European population on the other. Because they were part white, they were given better jobs; because they shared the European culture, they were afforded greater freedom. They generally identified with the white imperialists and frequently did their "dirty work." They often served as petty bureaucrats with whom the natives had to deal.

When independence came, or even before, such people often found themselves in a unique position of double marginality in that they were not accepted by the native population. In fact, as they symbolized the former colonial condition, they often became scapegoats for the colonials who could no longer be held responsible for imperial domination and exploitation. When they tried to emigrate to the former colonial power, they often discovered that they were not welcome in the imperial country and society they had embraced. Some returned to their native lands to suffer at the hands of the natives. Others went to white societies culturally similar to the colonial society, hoping some day to find a country in which they would be acceptable. They best typify the strangers described by Simmel, Park, and Stonequist.

Marginality is also reciprocal and relative; that is, if we assume that marginality (perhaps not the psychological dimension seen as pathological) implies an absence of a coterminous identification and culture for peoples living in close association and interaction, we may need also to speak of dominant group marginality, for although the mixed-race individual is certainly marginal to his two "pure blood" relatives they are at once marginal to both one another and to him. In this sense marginality is counterposed against assimilation. To an extent we now experience this form of dominant group marginality, or reciprocal marginality, in WASP (White Anglo-Saxon Protestant) society today. Henshel[15] speaks of white college students and white liberals who feel guilty about the generations of prejudice toward blacks in the United States. The adaptation of the "Afro" hairdo by such whites reflects some of the anomia characteristic of marginality. Desiring to be black, but denied this opportunity by genetics, members of the dominant society may attempt to pass and to adopt the minority culture. Some have even attempted to change their skin color with hormone treatments.

A PARADIGM OF MARGINALITY

Throughout this symposium a common theme emerges: marginal situations are variable. The manifestations of marginality are varied. Thus to speak of marginality as a unitary concept is probably as inaccurate as the inaccuracy observed by Antonovsky: the failure to acknowledge individuality in the responses to varied marginal situations. Some marginal peoples, or at least those of mixed race, experience social rejection, negative stereotypy, prejudice, and discrimination in interpersonal relations. Others do not. Certainly the Metis, the Mexican-Americans, the mixed Aborigines of Australia, and the Durban Coloureds have experienced prejudice and discrimination. Others such as the Burghers and the Coloreds of Guyana have experienced less discrimination than the native population before the independence of their countries, but more recently they have been the objects of discriminatory acts and attitudes.

---

15 Richard Henshel, "The Ability to Alter Skin Color: Some Implications for American Society," *Amer. J. Sociol.*, **76**, 734–742 (January 1971).

Most of the people of mixed race discovered that their culture was different in some way from either the dominant or the subordinate culture. Although the Anglo-Indians, the Coloureds of Durban and of Guyana, and the Burghers were decidedly European-oriented, they were also viewed by some as "non-native." Others, such as the Mexican in Mexico were of a hybrid culture, not exactly equal to the sum of the cultures of the Spanish or the Indians.

Finally, for some people of mixed race laws were enacted to guarantee their equality with the dominant population, although in *de facto* practices these laws might be ignored. The Mexican-American is so protected *de jure*, if not *de facto*. Other people of mixed race are prohibited by law from full participation. The Coloureds of Durban are affected by apartheid, and similar restrictions are placed on the Ceylonese Burghers (historically the non-Dutch Burghers, in particular).

A consequence of these variations is that at least three separate and sometimes orthogonal dimensions of marginality emerge. One is cultural marginality, or the situations in which individuals or groups find themselves sharing cultural values and behavior patterns both of the dominant and one or more other groups; or in situations in which hybrid or marginal cultures arise to insulate such individuals from psychological strains. Another form of marginality is social, in which the individual is refused full participation in the groups and institutions of the dominant culture and is rejected, stereotyped, or discriminated against by the *indigenes*. Finally, there is political marginality, in which discrimination and prejudice are sanctioned not only by informal group pressures but by laws preventing the minority people from participating as full citizens of the society.

We may hypothesize that individuals or groups subject to all three forms of marginality are likely to experience greater effects of marginal status than those experiencing only one form of marginality. The type of social and personal disorganization and psychopathology described by Stonequist is more often observed in peoples who are rejected socially, who differ culturally, and who are legally inhibited than among people who differ only culturally. Further, marginality is not an absolute concept. Differing degrees of marginality are commonly manifest; for example, some social marginals may be subjected only to negative stereotyping and exclusion from certain clubs; other social marginals may experience overt hostility, physical attack, and even outright extermination.

Another variable that insulates marginality effects and often facilitates marginal cultures is the demographic aspect of numbers. The extent to which the mixed-race population represents a substantial percentage of the total population affects the probability of that group's ability to survive as an intact entity. The greater the number of individuals of mixed race, the greater the probability that they will develop a viable self-supporting community and culture. Further, in their numbers evolves their power to make demands on the dominant society. It is the political power wielded by the Guyanese Coloreds as buffers between the African and East Indian populations that is a measure of privilege. It is the sheer numbers of Mexican-Americans in the American Southwest that make the Chicano movement a potent force and make Mexican-Americans a group to be wooed by American presidental aspirants since the "Viva Kennedy Movement" of the 1960's. The most extreme example is, of course, that in which the hybrid or marginal culture evolves into the dominant culture. This is the case in modern Mexico, where the mestizo represents more than 80 percent of the total population and where the religion and language are synthesized versions of the Spanish and Indian heritages.

Still another psychologically insulating variable that facilitates the emergence of a marginal culture is physical isolation. The remoteness of some groups of American mestizos and of the islanders of Tristan da Cunha no doubt forced these people to generate their own norms, institutions, and value systems, despite their racial linkage to other dominant and subordinate groups. Their societies are not unique and unrelated to their respective larger cultures, since isolation is rarely ever total and complete. Nonetheless, when peoples are isolated long enough, new patterns of social life, institutions, norms, values, and, in fact, cultures emerge. When such peoples are isolated for eons, new races emerge. With the widespread breakdown of social barriers and the expansion of intercultural and intersocietal relations, we ought not, however, to expect this last phenomenon to occur.

Some Operationalizations

At this point let us attempt to establish a set of operationalizations of the three dimensions of marginality we have posited. Paraphrasing Tylor's classic definition of culture, we might construct a description of cultural marginality: *cultural* marginality exists when a people who are in interaction with a dominant (and sometimes a subordinate indigenous people) population of a society and who are members of that society do not fully share the "complex whole which includes knowledge, belief, art, morals, law, custom, and any other capabilities and habits acquired" (including the language and religion) of that dominant society. It should be noted that one need not be estranged from all these components in order to be culturally marginal but that the more elements not shared, the greater the psychological intensity of cultural marginality. Further, it should be realized that not all cultural elements bear the same valence. Not sharing an art form may be less marginal, for example, than not sharing a religion or a language.

Social marginality is the differential treatment of a group of people by members of a dominant or a native population. Social marginality applies only to interpersonal relations, including rejection from occupational, friendship, and marital groups. Enforcement of such rejection is usually supported by informal rather than formal sanctions against violators. Displays of prejudice, discrimination, hostility, avoidance, or sheer indifference characterize the rejection that signifies social marginality. Still another form of social marginality occurs when a people voluntarily decline to participate in the social institutions of the dominant group.

Political marginality is the formalization in terms of law of social marginality. It involves restrictions on suffrage, the right to hold public office, and the right to equal representation and judgment under law. Political marginality, in essence, suggests the absence of citizenship for the group so restricted.

The accompanying schematic summary is intended to serve as a paradigmatic presentation of the marginal conditions of the peoples discussed in the symposium. Because, as we argued earlier, marginality is temporarily specific, we have concentrated on more than one time period in which to discuss the mixed racial groups. One is the present; the other is a significant period in the past. Our selection of a particular period is dictated by events deemed significant by the chapter authors. Often the past is the time before the granting of independence to the society; sometimes it is the point at which the present dominant population made its entry or somewhat before that point. The term "dominant" refers to relative power rather than numbers. We have also noted all three forms of marginality: cultural, social, and political.

As the reader can observe, some people such as the Mexican-Americans were historically nonmarginal, but presently marginal. Others such as the people of Tristan da Cunha and the mixed Aborigines of Australia have undergone successive "demarginalization." Still others, such as the Durban Coloureds, have experienced no abrupt change in their marginality across time.

We must never forget, however, that the experience of any form of marginality is relative. Not only are some groups marginal in more dimensions than others (the Metis versus Tristan da Cuhna's mixed races), but the extremeness of the marginal situations on each dimension shows

Table 1 Marginality to the Dominant Society: A Schematic Presentation of the Peoples in the Symposium at Two Time Periods

	Past			Present		
	Cultural	Social	Political	Cultural	Social	Political
Durban Coloureds	No	Yes	Yes[a]	No	Yes	Yes[a]
Anglo-Indians	No	Yes	Yes[a]	Yes	Yes	No
Burghers	No	Yes	Yes[a]	Yes	Yes	Yes
Eurasians[b]	No	Yes	Yes[a]	No	Yes	No
Guyanese Coloreds	No	Yes	Yes[a]	Yes	Yes	Yes
Mixed Aborigines	No	Yes	Yes	No	Yes	No
Metis	Yes	Yes	Yes	Yes	Yes	No
Mexican-Americans[c]	No	No	No	Yes	Yes	No
American mestizos	Yes	Yes	Yes	Yes	Yes	No
Mixed Hawaiians	Yes	Yes	No	Yes	Yes[d]	No
Brazil's mixed	Yes	Yes	Yes	Yes	Yes	No
Tristan da Cunhans	No	Yes	No	No	No	No

[a] Although not afforded full political and civil rights under colonial rule, these peoples had privileges not granted to the unmixed native population.
[b] Eurasian comparisons are between Indonesia under colonial Dutch rule and their present life in Holland.
[c] Mexican-Americans, as noted earlier, have shifted from marginals to nonmarginals more than once. Although they were marginal during Spanish rule, the time period represented as "past" is in the 1830's when the mestizos were dominant. The present period is post-World War II, when political marginality was removed by various Supreme Court rulings and Civil Rights legislation.
[d] Hawaii's mixed-racial groups may be becoming more marginal socially as the proportion of whites from the mainland increases in the Islands.

variation (e.g., the social marginality of the Hawaiians is less severe than for the Durban Coloureds or the mixed Aborigines).

INTERPRETATION OF THE SCHEMATIC DESIGN

With these considerations in mind, let us expand by describing the marginality of each group in the two time periods:

Durban Coloureds. Because the white minority of South Africa still dominates the vast black population, the conditions of the racially hybrid Durban Coloureds have not undergone sufficient change to alter their marginality. Culturally they are British and thus similar to the political elites during colonial rule, but socially and politically they are excluded and subject to discrimination, increasingly so since the rise to political power of the Afrikaner element in South Africa. Yet they have more privileges than the vast native black population. Perhaps like the Burghers, the Anglo-Indians, the Eurasians, and the Coloreds of Guyana, the marginality of the Durban Coloureds will increase once the blacks of South Africa are successful in replacing their white rulers.

Anglo-Indians. The marginal condition of the Anglo-Indians before Indian independence in 1947 is not unlike the present stated condition of the Eurasians, the Guyanese Coloreds, the Durban Coloureds, and the Ceylonese Burghers in their respective colonial times. Their language and religion more closely resembles that of the British colonials. They were socially marginal in that social distance was maintained between them and the British, and they were politically restricted by law, although somewhat less so than the unmixed Indian population. After independence constitutional guarantees ensured them participation and representation in the political sphere; hence their political nonmarginality.

Burghers of Ceylon. Like the Durban Coloureds, the Eurasians, and the Anglo-Indians, the Burghers (Dutch, Portuguese, and other) were culturally similar to the dominant power group, the white Europeans, sharing their language, norms, and religion. They were marginal in the social and political dimension, however, but less so than the "pure" Ceylonese population. With independence, the fortunes of the Burghers declined. Their language and religion occupied minority positions, their European orientation became a symbol of the discredited colonial regime, and they were often excluded politically because they did not speak the indigenous Sinhalese language.

Eurasians of Indonesia. When the Dutch ruled Indonesia, the Eurasians, being Dutch in cultural heritage, were nonmarginal in this dimension. Because they were not "pure-bloods," however, they were subject to social exclusion by the dominant whites. They were also limited in their political participation, although not so much as the "pure" native stock. With the coming of independence to Indonesia they became culturally, socially, and politically more marginal than before. Like the Coloreds of Guyana, the Burghers, the Durban Coloureds, and the Anglo-Indians, they have become the symbols of a defunct colonial system. The Eurasians who emigrated to Holland, and who are discussed in the chapter by Professor Wittermans, remained culturally nonmarginal, and because of their equalitarian political rights in Holland they were nonmarginal on this dimension as well. Generally, however, they were not fully accepted socially and were (and still are) only partly integrated into the fabric of existing institutions.

Guyanese Coloreds. Before independence in 1967 Guyana's people of mixed race shared the British cultural heritage with the ruling whites. They, unlike the numerically dominant black population, were not marginal culturally, but like the Eurasians, the Durban Coloureds, the Anglo-Indians, and the Burghers, social distances were maintained between them and the British whites. Politically they were less marginal than the blacks, the East Indians, and the native Amerindians, but they were still restricted in their rights to full citizenship. After independence and the ascendency of the black population to a position of political dominance the Coloureds found themselves triple marginals. Their cultural, social, and political marginality is evidenced by their large-scale exodus to England and Canada in recent years.

Australia's Part-Aborigines. Unlike the native population, the racial hybrids have shared the same religion and language as the dominant white Europeans. Today, as in the past, they remain culturally nonmarginal, but socially they are marginal; in interpersonal relationships a wide social distance still exists between them and the white population. They were also politically marginal to the whites until the most recent laws were passed in 1967 to protect Aborigines. Like their Aboriginal relatives, they are gradually gaining citizenship and full political rights.

The Metis. Like others identified as North American Indians and especially as "half-breeds," the Metis were rejected socially, excluded politically, and marginal culturally from the British and French European populations of Canada. Today their civil rights are guaranteed, and so at least *de jure* they are nonmarginal. They may become socially nonmarginal as a more open Canadian society evolves in the district. As Professor Slobodin observes, there is a growing convergence between those who are Metis and those who, like other regional proletarians, are "getting to be Metis."

The Mexican-Americans. Marginality and nonmarginality for the Mexican-Americans have been nearly a cyclical phenomenon. During the postconquest era in the sixteenth century the mixed-race minority shared the Spaniard's religion, language, and total culture. Socially, they were somewhat restricted and politically they were denied full civic participation. After the defeat of the Spanish, however, the mestizos became the politically dominant population. Anglo rule of the Southwest since the middle of the nineteenth century converted the Mexican-Americans into cultural (in terms of language and religion), social (in terms of prejudicial patterns), and political (segregationist laws) marginals. Since World War II, political marginality has declined, as Mexican-Americans have been extended *de jure*, if not *de facto*, civil rights.

American Mestizos. Like other American minorities, we must differentiate between the period before and after the Supreme Court rulings on segregation since 1938 and the civil rights legislation of the 1960's. Before this time social marginality with its *de facto* discrimination was conjoined with political marginality with its *de jure* discrimination in certain regions. To claim to be Indian and to search for an Indian cultural heritage make these people culturally marginal to the American white middle class. To be rejected by white friendship groups and cliques suggests that they are socially marginal, and to have been forbidden to attend white schools suggests that once they were politically marginal.

The Mixed Races of Hawaii. Like Brazilians, Hawaiians are more liberal concerning race relationships. The various mixtures, established before white American control, were culturally marginal to the then numerically dominant Polynesians. They were socially marginal, too, but there is no evidence that they were politically so. After the imposition of white control they became increasingly more socially and culturally marginal. Political nonmarginality is ensured, however, by the various civil rights acts in the United States. Nonetheless, it is probably true that as more and more white American mainlanders settle in Hawaii the state of race relations will more closely resemble that of the mainland. As such, we suggest that social marginality may increase in comparison with conditions a little more than a decade ago—before Hawaii's statehood.

Mixed-Racial Brazilians. Because of the relatively large numbers of the mixed-race population and an enlightened attitude toward race, marginality among Brazil's hybrid peoples is less extreme and severe than in certain other societies. Thus some hybrids have achieved high social and political positions. Although the African and Indian cultural heritages pervade much of Brazilian society, the exclusion of most people of mixed race from high public office and the practice of discrimination by the white majority suggest a historical condition of cultural, social, and political marginality. Greater entry into public office for the mixed population in the last few decades also suggests that political marginality has decreased.

Tristan da Cunhans. The isolation and small numbers of these people have prevented cultural and political marginality. Nonetheless, before their sojourn in England in 1962 lighter complexioned islanders were kept some social distance from those who were darker in color. The realization that the British did not distinguish among them has reduced even the social marginality, and as such we may speak of the nonmarginal population of Tristan da Cunha.

The reader at some point in reading this symposium may ask what rationale can be given for the exclusion of a chapter on black Americans.

The history of slavery in the United States and of forced miscegenation has ensured that nearly every black individual in America is a mulatto. The black person in America is thus a member of the largest mixed-race group in modern history. The magnitude of the black population, however, and the immense social, cultural, and political dimensions to their role in American history literally prevented us from covering this group in a single chapter. Besides, there have been so many texts written on black Americans in the last decade that the task of presenting the story of these people would not only be monumental but an inadequate duplication. The many social and political factions in this massive population also militate against a satisfactory presentation and make any schematic model such as we have presented in the introduction hopelessly confounded. The editors had at one time sought to include the black Americans but later decided that such a brief inclusion would do an injustice to the 22 million blacks in the United States.

CONCLUSION

The 12 racially mixed peoples presented in this book vary considerably in geographic location, historical circumstances of their origin, position in the social order, relations with others in the same society, and the social structure of their groups. It is not assumed, therefore, that they are necessarily representative of hybrid peoples the world over; indeed, there are many other peoples whose genetic blending make them highly visible and who occupy a marginal position in the society to which they belong. If they were enumerated, the list would be quite long, but our knowledge of most of them is limited because of the paucity of relevant empirical information.

In a sense, however, the groups considered in this book *are* representative of peoples of mixed racial ancestry. It seems reasonable to believe that other peoples whose racial mixture results in high visibility, like the groups included in this volume, are also aware of their dual or multiple racial heritage and of their unique position in the social order.

SELECTED BIBLIOGRAPHY

American Academy of Arts and Sciences, "Color and Race," *Daedalus*, **96** (Spring 1967): whole issue.

Antonovsky, Aaron, "Toward a Refinement of the 'Marginal Man' Concept," *Social Forces*, **35**, 57–62 (October 1956).

Ashley-Montague, M. F., *Man's Most Dangerous Myth: The Fallacy of Race*, 3rd ed. New York: Harper, 1953.

Barzun, Jaques, *Race: A Study of Superstition*. New York: Harper, 1965.

Cheng, C. K., and Douglas S. Yamamura, "Interracial Marriage and Divorce in Hawaii," *Social Forces*, **36**, 77–84 (October 1957).

Dickie-Clark, H. F., *The Marginal Situation*. London: Routledge, Kegan Paul, 1966.

Gillin, John, "Race Relations without Conflict: A Guatemalan Town." *Amer. J. Sociol.*, **53**, 337–343 (March 1948).

Goldberg, Milton M., "A Qualification of the Marginal Man Theory," *Amer. Sociol. Rev.*, **6**, 52–58 (February 1941).

Golden, Joseph, "Characteristics of Negro-White Marriage in Philadelphia," *Amer. Social. Rev.*, **18**, 177–183 (April 1953).

Golden, Joseph, "Patterns of Negro-White Intermarriage," *Amer. Sociol. Rev.*, **19**, 144–147 (April 1954).

Golovensky, David I., "The Marginal Man Concept: An Analysis and Critique," *Social Forces*, **30**, 333–339 (March 1952).

Gossett, Thomas F., *Race: The History of an Idea in America*. Dallas: Southern Methodist University Press, 1963.

Green, Arnold W., "A Reexamination of the Marginal Man Concept," *Social Forces*, **26**, 167–171 (October 1947).

Hughes, Everett C., "Dilemmas and Contradictions of Status," *Amer. J. Sociol.*, **50**, 353–359 (March 1945).

Hughes, Everett C., and Helen M. Hughes, *Where Peoples Meet: Racial and Ethnic Frontiers*. Glencoe, Illinois: The Free Press, 1952.

Kerckhoff, Alan C., "Marginal Status and Marginal Personality," *Social Forces*, **34**, 48–55 (October 1955).

Lewin, Kurt, *Resolving Social Conflicts*. Harper: New York, 1948.

Lieberson, Stanley, "A Societal Theory of Race and Ethnic Relations," *Amer. Sociol. Rev.*, **26**, 902–910 (December 1961).

Mann, J. W., "The Problems of Marginality," in P. Watson, Ed. *The Psychology of Race Relations*. London: Penguin Books, 1969.

Park, Robert E., "Human Migration and the Marginal Man," *Amer. J. Sociol.*, **33**, 881–893 (May 1928).

Park, Robert E., *Race and Culture*. New York: The Free Press of Glencoe, 1950.

Simmel, Georg, *The Sociology of Georg Simmel* (Kurt H. Wolff, translation). New York: The Free Press, 1950.

Stonequist, Everett V., *The Marginal Man: A Study in Personality and Culture Conflict*. New York: Charles Scribner's Sons, 1937.

Stonequist, Everett V., "The Marginal Man: A Study in Personality and Culture Conflict," in Ernest W. Burgess and Donald J. Bogue, Eds. *Contributions to Urban Sociology*, Chicago: University of Chicago Press, 1964, pp. 327–345.

Tumin, Melvin M., *Caste in a Peasant Society: A Case Study in the Dynamics of Caste*. Princeton: Princeton University Press, 1952.

UNESCO, *The Race Question in Modern Science*. Paris: Morrow, 1956.

van den Berge, Pierre L., *Race and Racism*. New York: Wiley, 1967.

Wirth, Louis, and Herbert Goldhamer, "The Hybrid and the Problem of Miscegenation," in Otto Klineberg, Ed., *Characteristics of the American Negro*. New York: Harper and Row, 1944.

H. F. Dickie-Clark

The New University of Ulster

CHAPTER TWO

THE COLOURED MINORITY OF DURBAN

Third in size of the cities of the Republic of South Africa, Durban is situated on the east coast in the province of Natal. In 1966 it had an estimated population of

Africans	350,024
Indians	302,642
Whites	250,390
Coloureds	32,636[1]

That these four groups of people have been legally so classified and that they live, to an unprecedented extent, within the parallel institutions established by law for each of them is due to the peculiar nature of South African society or what has come to be known as *apartheid*. The South African social system of racial segregation has since the 1950's come increasingly under the scrutiny of scholars and others and has been variously described and analyzed.

This system of racial segregation, as it has evolved in South Africa, is the larger social framework in which the Durban Coloureds along with all other South Africans live and which very largely determines for them, as a subordinate "black" group, what their life chances are to be. Their marginal situation within this larger framework is peculiar to them and probably to other urban Coloureds as well and, although of secondary

---

[1] See H. L. Watts, R. J. Davies, and G. W. Waters, *The Spatial Distribution of the Present and Future Residential Population of Metropolitan Durban*. Durban: University of Natal, 1967.

importance, is an additional factor that may explain differences between them and the Indians and Africans who share their subordinate status.

This chapter, after briefly distinguishing the Durban Coloureds from other South African Coloureds, attempts a sociological definition of marginality and then suggests what effect this kind of marginal situation may have had on the Durban Coloureds' political behavior, on their formal associations, on their relations with members of the other racial groups, and on their attitudes toward themselves.[2]

THE COLOUREDS OF DURBAN

In earlier times the Coloureds of Durban and other urban parts of Natal were more clearly distinct from people of color elsewhere than they are now. Broadly, the change has been relentlessly away from a position of near equality with whites toward a subordinate status only very slightly above that of Indians and Africans.

Until the outbreak of World War II the majority of Coloureds in Durban were of Mauritian or St. Helenan stock whose forebears had come to Natal around the middle of the nineteenth century. The Mauritians came in an organized way to work as skilled artisans on the Natal railways and in the sugar mills. The St. Helenans were fewer in number and came independently, either directly from the island or via the Cape. It seems likely that at first they were employed as superior domestic servants in wealthier households. The most important thing about both groups was that they were completely Western in culture. This, at a time when few Indians and Africans had adopted Western dress and mannerisms, when skills were in short supply, and the colony still under British rule, led to the Mauritians and St. Helenans being accorded the legal status of white persons. As long as the Coloured population was small, and until the intensification of segregation after 1948, the "privileges" of the Mauritians and St. Helenans were enjoyed to a considerable extent by all Coloureds in Natal. In this way skilled trades and other better paid occupations were open to them, and they became, and have remained, rather better off than Coloureds elsewhere in South Africa. On this firmer economic base they have been able to maintain "white" standards and preserve their cultural parity with the whites. The small size of the Coloured group in Durban probably has also contributed to their being

---

[2] This chapter is based on parts of the study reported in my *The Marginal Situation* (1966), which should be consulted for the detailed evidence of many of the statements made here.

accorded a slightly higher status. The presence of large numbers of Africans and Indians enables them to pass almost unnoticed.

Other differences between the Durban Coloureds and of most of those elsewhere are of lesser importance but have nonetheless some effect on their marginal situation. Thus more than 80 percent of the Durban Coloureds speak English at home, whereas in South Africa as a whole more than 90 percent speak Afrikaans at home. Nearly half the Durban Coloureds are Roman Catholics, whereas in South Africa as a whole fewer than 10 percent belong to the Roman Catholic Church. There is no large Muslim subgroup among the Durban Coloureds such as the Cape Malays among the Cape Coloureds.

Although continuing migration of Coloureds from elsewhere into Natal has tended to swamp the original Mauritian and St. Helenan stocks and legislation has deprived the Coloureds of the remnants of their near equality with whites, the bulk of the Durban Coloureds may be fairly described as being, apart from their appearance, indistinguishable from whites of the same economic and educational status. Among those who resemble the whites in looks also the only difference between them and the whites whose culture they share is the discrimination exercised against those who have been classified as Coloureds.

The Sociology of Marginality

The theoretical matrix out of which this discussion developed is the body of ideas that has taken shape over the 40 or more years since Park and Stonequist first spoke of "the marginal man." By the end of the 1950's the many criticisms and reformulations made of the Park-Stonequist theory had done little to remove its main difficulties. There still remained a lack of clarity in the basic concepts of "marginal man," "marginal person- ality," and "marginal situation," the resulting inability to determine precisely who was and who was not "marginal," and whether being mar- ginal brought about a fundamentally different personality type or in- volved merely superficial attitude changes.[3]

Psychological and sociological studies of marginality made at the University of Natal and reported on by J. W. Mann and me were directed at these difficulties. A brief statement of the scope and findings of the

---

[3] These earlier criticisms and reformulations have been detailed by a number of writers. For a review of the literature on marginality see J. W. Mann, "The Problem of Marginality," in P. Watson, Ed., *The Psychology of Race Relations,* London: Penguin Books, 1969.

Natal studies will show how complex and elusive "marginality" proves to be when an attempt is made to investigate it empirically.

A community survey of a Coloured housing development of 1260 persons in Durban had been carried out in mid-1955 by the Institute for Social Research of the University of Natal, and from this community a sample of 50 people was drawn. The sample consisted of 25 individuals who were like whites in appearance and 25 others who could not in the judgment of the investigators pass as whites. These two groups were matched on the variables of age, sex, education, income, vocational training, and knowledge of Zulu (the language spoken by the Africans in Natal). Using scaling techniques and factor analysis, Mann developed a definition of psychological marginality as consisting of feelings of insecurity, self-pity, and sensitivity (in the sense of being "thin-skinned" and "vulnerable") and a "marginality" scale with which psychological marginality could be measured. With this and other measures an attempt was made to test some of the existing assumptions about marginal men. The results were almost entirely negative.

A comparison of white and Coloured schoolchildren made by Mann, who used a marginality scale, showed that the Coloureds were no more psychologically marginal than the whites. This suggested that there was no simple relation between the different situations in which the Coloured and white schoolchildren found themselves and psychological marginality. Moreover, when those with high scores on the psychological marginality scale were compared with low scores, no difference was found between these groups in matters such as their political attitudes and actions, their attitudes toward and contacts with other racial groups, their attitudes toward the Coloured group itself and toward "passing" as white for a variety of purposes. These results seem to indicate that psychological marginality (or, at least, what the marginality scale measured) makes little difference in people's attitudes and behavior in matters of some considerable importance to them. All this would seem to make psychological marginality a very mild malaise indeed. Certainly, the overall subjective impression that I have gained from nearly 15 years of contact with Durban Coloureds is that they are a sensible, balanced people and far from being the unstable, moody, irrational "marginal men" of the popular notion.

In both the earlier and the later writings on marginality the marginal situation is seen as a hierarchical one with barriers that are in some way or other "permeable" or "incomplete" and thus create the uncertainty and confusion that in turn produces psychological marginality, for when the barriers and distinctions are complete and clear, marginal phenomena cannot occur. The concept of a "permeable" barrier is logically rather dubious and there are many difficulties in pinning down the exact nature of a barrier. Hence it may be better to conceive of the decisively marginal element in hierarchical situations in some other way.

The hierarchical situations actually found in society can be thought of as made up of a number of rankings in respect of the various matters regulated by the hierarchy; for example, the color-caste hierarchical situation in South Africa embraces many of an individual's crucial rankings, including legal status, economic position, political rights, social acceptability, standard of education, and the extent to which he has access to health, welfare, and recreational facilities.

In such "hierarchies" marginal situations develop with any departure from complete consistence or congruence among the rankings of an individual or stratum in the various matters regulated by the hierarchy. Perfect equivalence of all the rankings serves as an ideal yardstick, even though it is never attained and regardless of whether inconsistencies are perceived as such by the people concerned. The notion is well established in sociological writings and has been used in the analysis of a wide variety of rankings by a number of writers.[4] Its application to marginal situations makes possible a clear-cut definition based on observed rankings. In this way marginal situations can be defined as those hierarchical situations in which there is any inconsistency in the rankings in any of the matters falling within the scope of the hierarchy.

This sociological definition, based on observable rankings, precludes any confusion about the meaning of "being in a marginal situation." Neither biological factors such as racial mixture and appearance nor psychological factors such as "double consciousness" and divided loyalty have any place in a definition that rests entirely on the inconsistencies of ranking. Marginal situations of this kind have important consequences for the people in them, quite apart from any personality traits that they may develop as a result of such situations.

Because situations in which there is complete consistency in rankings must be rare, this definition is a wide one. In the argument about whether to restrict or extend the application of the concept of marginality this definition comes down heavily on the side of extension.

Although the inconsistencies in rankings impart a marginal character to hierarchical situations, the other features of the hierarchy, that is to say, its composition, duration, scope, and the criteria of member-

---

[4] A list of the earlier writings is given in H. F. Dickie-Clark, "The Marginal Situation," *Social Forces*, **44**, 367 (March 1966). More recently the concept of "status inconsistency" has become firmly established in sociological literature, whereas the term "marginality" has not been so generally used.

ship, can be used to identify the different types of marginal situation that vary in these respects. The distinction between the cultural and the social dimensions of the situation yields a further, and especially useful, basis of classification, for a common and important social situation is that in which individuals or groups possess some or all of the learned cultural traits of a society but are nonetheless still not admitted to full membership and equality of status. At one theoretical extreme would be complete cultural similarity accompanied by absolute social rejection. At the other extreme would be the opposite, or the total absence of acculturation or socialization along with complete social acceptance. In between these unlikely cases would fall those marginal situations of varying degrees of cultural similarity accompanied by differing and inconsistent degrees of social status and participation. These are the situations found in concrete societies and most often discussed in the literature on marginality.

Such a marginal situation is the one in which the Durban Coloureds find themselves. Using the framework sketched above, they are a marginal stratum in a hierarchy that contains two other subordinate strata (the Africans and Indians) in addition to the dominant white stratum. This hierarchy is a composite one embracing the whole society and affecting almost every aspect of people's lives. Short of the destruction of the hierarchy, membership of the strata (for all but the few who are reclassified differently) is lifelong and based on criteria that are biological and hereditary. The barrier between the whites and Coloureds has not, however, prevented the Coloureds from being the cultural equals of the whites, but it has very largely excluded them from the white system of social relations. Thus the Coloureds have formal equality with whites in civil rights relating to movement, residence, property rights, summary arrest or detention, and freedom of thought, religion and public expression and association. (In considering the Coloureds' ranking in the matter of civil rights, other than the franchise, an important qualification to be kept in mind is that the question here is the extent to which they have *the same civil rights as the whites* and not whether the civil rights that exist in South Africa are those recognized in any absolute sense as being the essential ones.)

There are also the remnants of earlier equality in employment chances, use of municipal transport, and informal contacts in their still, not completely segregated condition. For the rest the Durban Coloureds are excluded from the social relationships of the white stratum. Their situation is therefore a marginal one in a double sense. They are in a marginal situation because there is inconsistency between their cultural equality with the whites and their social inequality with them. Furthermore, if the social dimension is considered alone, there is inconsistency between their ranking of equality in the matter of certain civil rights, for instance, and their lower, unequal ranking in other matters such as the franchise or entry into the armed services. In brief, the Durban Coloureds' "marginal situation" is made up of cultural equality with the whites, a very small measure of social equality with them, and a very large amount of social inequality which they share with the Africans and Indians.

Effects of a Marginal Situation on the Coloureds

On Political Behavior. In order to be able to say with any real certainty what the consequences are for a particular group of being in a marginal situation, we should make comparative studies of nonmarginal groups. Short of this, we can only try to determine what constitutes the marginal situation in specific fields (e.g., politics or intergroup relations) and then suggest possible concomitants in the attitudes and actions of the individuals considered to be in such situations. There would seem to be at least two ways in which the suggested links might become more plausible. First, when it can be argued that factors not included in the marginal situation as defined could be expected to influence the Coloureds in one direction, whereas the features of the marginal situation could be expected to have the opposite effect; second, when the Coloureds show a response that is different in kind or degree from that displayed by either Africans or Indians who are subjected to the same overall conditions.

In politics the marginal situation of the Durban Coloureds means that political actions and even attitudes are closely regulated by the dominant white stratum; that the Coloureds are threatened by the existence of two other even "lower" subordinate strata in that they are constantly in fear of being reduced in status (i.e., of being treated like Indians and Africans); that their cultural "whiteness" makes them share the whites' political values and on this basis to claim equality for themselves while denying it to the Africans and Indians; and finally, their marginal situation means that Coloureds have a slightly better legal position and a significantly better economic position than the other subordinate groups.

Essentially, their marginal situation in politics consists of a complex of cross-pressures. Pushing them in one direction is the combination of their cultural "whiteness," the remnants of social equality with the whites, and their intermediate status as Coloureds. Counter to all this goes the large measure of social exclusion they share with the other subordinate strata.

However, before trying to suggest what effects this situation has on their political behavior, we must recognize that the close political control exercised over *all* population groups in South Africa obviously affects the Coloureds also, and therefore the marginal situation begins to operate only *after* these crucial factors have had their effect. Nevertheless, as suggested above, the cross-pressures of their marginal situation do seem to provide a feasible explanation of the Coloureds' political behavior when it runs counter to what the overall, nonmarginal factors would lead one to expect or when the behavior of the Coloureds is markedly different from that of other subordinate groups also subject to the same overall factors; for example, when compared with Africans and Indians, Coloureds seem to have been especially slow and reluctant to form purely political organizations. Thus the Indian National Congress was founded by Gandhi in 1894 and the African National Congress was formed in 1912. Until they were banned in the early 1960's, these two organizations were avowedly political in aim and were conducted on a national scale.

In contrast, and until the formation of Coloured political parties for the special purpose of elections of members of the Coloured Persons' Representative Council, Coloured organizations in Durban have never been solely political, and any attempt to make them so or to involve them in national politics has so far always led to their losing popular support. Further evidence of the Coloureds' reluctance to engage in politics may be found in the fact that, unlike the Indians and Africans, Coloureds in Durban and Natal have not developed *two* opposing but complementary political organizations, one of which plays along with the dominant stratum in order to get whatever the whites are prepared to offer in the way of education, welfare services, etc., whereas the other is left free to oppose the status quo unreservedly and without the hindrance of having to compromise for the sake of the benefits they can wring from the whites.

A second aspect of Coloured political behavior which seems to be due to their marginal situation is their inability to support any clear-cut political policy. This is most easily seen in their ambivalent attitude toward the whole policy of *apartheid*. As excluded blacks, one would expect them to reject the *apartheid* policy entirely, and some of them do. Depending on the phrasing of the questions on this topic, 42 to 60 percent of the sample of Durban Coloureds could see advantages as well as disadvantages in *apartheid*. This is surely a realistic assessment of the alternatives facing them in their marginal situation at the present time.

Stated in an oversimplified form, the Coloureds have lost by *apartheid* their earlier legal equality with the whites, but they have gained by it their separation from, and slightly more advantageous position as compared with, the Indians and Africans.

However, we need to be very cautious in thus attributing the Coloureds' ambivalence altogether to their marginal situation, for if white dominance were not seemingly so unyielding and had not lasted so long their attitudes toward *apartheid* might well be different. Certainly the opening up of some realistic alternative would have a marked effect on the political morale and policies of all the "opposition" groups in South Africa.

Until such an event takes place, it would seem that the Durban Coloureds, because of their marginal situation, are faced with a political choice so finely balanced that no clear choice decisively outweighs any other. As long as their situation remains marginal the cross-pressures so created will keep the Coloureds helpless and politically immobilized. For the time being they seem to be settling without enthusiasm into the separate status and institutions designed for them by the government.

On Formal Organizations. From the sample studied it would seem that the Durban Coloureds are ready enough to join formal associations and to participate regularly in their meetings. The very existence of a Coloured group probably explains the major part of this willingness to be active in formal organizations, for if a single stratum, even when larger than that of the Durban Coloureds, is to have parallel associations for its members only it would need to draw on a high proportion of them and to make the fullest use of the inevitably small reservoir of leaders and those with organizing ability.

Despite this readiness to belong to, and participate in, associations of many kinds, observation has revealed that the organizations were not correspondingly effective in gaining their manifest aims. A large number of the organizations reported were short-lived or had long "dormant" periods. A majority of the sample questioned felt that their organizations did not really get much done and that they were often the source of trouble and quarrels among the people. The proceedings of the local ratepayers' association, which were closely followed over a period of eighteen months, were marked inefficiently beyond what might be expected from an organizations that drew its membership from groups of similar education and socioeconomic status.

It is difficult to say how much of this inefficacy could be laid fairly at the door of the marginal situation of the Coloureds rather than the disabilities they share with other subordinate groups; for example, being without real power and able to exert only small influence over their fate denies to both leaders and their followers the satisfaction and support they might derive from the knowledge that the policies they propound and the decisions they make really matter. Without this sustaining factor people must soon become disheartened and, in time, stop even expecting to achieve their avowed goals. Then only the latent functions of self-expression, display, and enjoyable social contacts retain their appeal.

As proposed above, one way of getting at the influence of the Coloureds' marginal situation, as distinct from that of such factors as the above which are common to all subordinate groups, would be to compare the Coloureds' overall situation with that of the Africans and Indians. Summarily stated, the choices placed before the two latter groups are such as to make for comparatively decisive and unified action by them. For the Africans, although their cultural difference from whites and, for some, a vested interest in tribalism may lead to a measure of acceptance of subordinate separation, complete and disadvantageous exclusion from the white social system and their numerical preponderance suggests that the perpetuation of white dominance is unacceptable to the majority and that this provides a solid basis for clear policy making and decisive action.

The Indians are like the Coloureds in that numerically they are neither dominant now nor can they hope to be in the future. Their selective blend of Indian and Western culture and their wider range of social and economic status set them off from the other groups and produce some tendency toward separation. This is overshadowed by the intensity of their exclusion and rejection by the whites. In the absence of anything like the Coloureds' remnants of social equality one would expect a greater readiness among the majority of Indians to decide on equality for all as the political goal.

In contrast, the marginal situation of the Coloureds presents them with at least three very different broad possibilities: to strive after full equality with whites for themselves alone; to accept the separate and distinctive status the whites offer them; or to make common cause with the other subordinate groups and strive for equality for all. The Coloureds' marginal situation consists of elements that back up, to some extent, each of these three choices and all are sufficiently weighty to prevent any one choice from overwhelming the others and from leading to decisive action. Thus it could be argued that their marginal situation complicates the difficulties faced by the Coloureds and contributes to the inefficacy of their formal organizations.

A specific example of this may be seen in the way in which their "white culture," bolstered by their remaining meager "privileges," requires them in their publicly expressed sentiments and demands to set goals that are unrealistic and unattainable in the face of their social exclusion. On their own and in the spurious shelter of segregated associations they do not have to face the realities of their situation so immediately and thus are able to think and speak as their cultural parity with the whites leads them to do. Indeed, not to do so would be a betrayal of deeply felt convictions and unseemly in public utterances.

The actual status afforded to Coloureds falls far below the level dictated by their cultural equality and makes nonsense of the conventional public fiction. So behind the pretense lies the wry recognition of their exclusion and of the need to be careful not to endanger the scraps of social equality that remain; for instance, they sometimes talk of their rights as taxpayers who pay the same rates as anyone else and of the need to register as voters, just as if they could indeed bring adequate pressure to bear on the city council in the same way as fully enfranchised white taxpayers. In fact, few of them have the franchise and fewer actually vote, so that they have to rely on personal representations to well-disposed white city councilmen. Again, in the actual running of the association, the members know how such enterprises ought to be run and are to the point in their criticisms of the organizations' shortcomings, but poverty, too little leisure, and a dearth of educated and experienced personnel along with other effects of exclusion, frustrate their attempts to make the ratepayers (taxpayers) association more efficient. Similarly, they rightly, in terms of their "white culture," complain of inadequacies like unplastered, roughcast walls, the absence of internal doors, and small plots, but economic discrimination against them prevents many from being able to afford the quality they desire.

The discrepancy between the requirements of their "white culture" and the actual treatment accorded the Coloureds has more general and diffused consequences than directly hindering the detailed working of the association, for the divergence imparts to the organization a characteristic quality of unreality which in turn brings the latent functions into prominence. Because the members know they cannot get what they really want, the serious purposes of the association lose much of their importance and the conduct of the organization becomes something of a game. Thus, although their avowed purposes are systematically frustrated, the associations perform certain unintended functions well. Apart from the satisfactions gained by individuals, they also, and this is more important, provide a platform for the public reiteration, both verbally and by participation in a typically "white" activity, of the Coloureds' white bias and deepest hopes.

Perhaps this is why, despite the tremendous handicaps of social exclusion and the grave doubts about the efficacy of Coloured organizations the exclusion engenders, the associations persist and a comparatively high level of participation is maintained in them. Thus their marginal situation creates a need, that of acting out their "cultural whiteness," which is partly satisfied in associations of this type, even though their manifest purposes are sacrificed in the process.

On Relations with Whites, Africans, and Indians. The Durban Coloureds' marginal situation means that in the area of intergroup relations the contacts are with a culturally similar superordinate group and with two culturally distinct "lower" groups. Moreover, the remnants of social equality with whites along with the separate but slightly more advantageous status of Coloureds, compared with Africans and Indians, makes the Coloureds especially vulnerable to the threat of losing what little they have.

Under these circumstances it is not surprising that they display a marked bias in favor of the whites and a widespread tendency to be prejudiced against Africans and Indians and a reluctance to have much to do with them. Thus the marginal situation would appear to operate in a way opposite to that one might expect. The Coloureds' cultural parity with whites could be expected to lead to considerable contact between these two groups but does not because of the social exclusion of the Coloureds. On the other hand, the large amount of social exclusion the Coloureds have in common with Africans and Indians does not have the effect of bringing them together in frequent and harmonious contact. In short, the Coloureds' marginal situation, by hindering and so keeping at a minimum their relations with the other groups, serves to reinforce their isolation as a separate group.

On Their View of the Coloured Group from Within. How its members view the Coloured group and how they feel about being Coloured persons may fairly be considered an outcome of the marginal situation in which they are placed. Summarily stated, the Durban Coloureds see themselves as a group of people who possess "some white blood" and who also maintain a "decent, white" style of life. The majority see their group as some kind of "appendage" of the whites which ought nevertheless to have a separate existence. For some 20 percent the hope of ultimate inclusion in the white group is not yet dead, even if, as a few believe, the Coloureds would have to "breed white" first during a period of separation!

Being a Coloured means, above all, being discriminated against by exclusion from the advantages of the whites. It would seem that only those who are able to pass as whites do not feel this discrimination to at least some extent. That this state of affairs is not more disruptive of both personality and the social order may be partly explained by the fact that, for many, direct personal experience of discrimination is avoided by "keeping out of trouble" and "by not going where I know I am not wanted."

This kind of avoidance does not blind Coloureds to their disadvantageous position nor to the fact that a number of their fellows try to escape from their situation by passing as whites either temporarily or permanently. This knowledge is a part of being a Coloured and the majority approves of passing in all its forms. Under these circumstances it is not surprising that, although most of the sample studied *said* that they were proud of being Coloureds, they had great difficulty in explaining why they felt so, and the reasons they gave were not the good qualities they (and others) say they possess but things like their white blood and their slightly better status compared with Indians and Africans.

These feelings about being a Coloured tell us something of what the group looks like from within. They also reveal what kind of group it is. In a world that makes much of the believed advantages of racial, national, and other group affiliations the Coloureds find membership in "their" group unrewarding and unsatisfactory and "belong" to it without enthusiasm and sometimes considerable reluctance. Many would be happy to see it simply absorbed socially into the white group to which culturally it has always belonged.

The fact that the Coloureds, although excluded from the white social order, are "culturally white" has important consequences also for their position within the rest of South African society; for instance, it frustrates the goal of a separate Coloured group, even if this could be achieved without discrimination, for as long as they are culturally the same as the whites social separation will always remain less than wholly satisfying because the Coloureds would find it harder than ever to retain and practice the white cultural values which are also their own. Thus they are more harmed by social separation from the whites than are acculturated Africans and Indians who are supported by cultures of their own onto which they have grafted selected elements of white culture.

Moreover, the Coloureds' "cultural whiteness" and consequent dependence on the whites renders them less able to defend themselves consistently and effectively against the discrimination they suffer. Not only does it hinder the Coloureds from making common political cause with Africans and Indians but their white culture is a ready source of confusion and prejudice in their thinking about race and color. The cross-pressures developing from the combination of cultural parity with whites and exclusion from the white social order have in this, as in other aspects of the lives of Durban Coloureds, the effect of stultifying consistent, decisive action and of keeping them almost immobilized in the separate category in which they find themselves.

SELECTED BIBLIOGRAPHY

Debeer, Z. J., *Multi-Racial South Africa*. London: Oxford, 1961.

Dickie-Clark, H. F., *The Marginal Situation*. London: Routledge and Kegan Paul, 1966.

Dickie-Clark, H. F., "The Marginal Situation," *Social Forces*, **44**, 363–370 (March 1966).

Hellman, Ellen, Ed., *Handbook of Race Relations in South Africa*. London: Oxford, 1949.

Kuper, Leo, et al., *Durban: A Study in Racial Ecology*. Pietermaritzburg, South Africa: Natal University Press, 1960.

Marquard, Lee, *Peoples and Policies of South Africa*. London: Oxford, 1962.

Marquard, Lee, *South Africa's Colonial Policy*. Johannesburg: S.A. Institute, 1957.

Patterson, Sheila, *Colour and Culture in South Africa*. London: Routledge and Kegan Paul, 1953.

Simons, H. J., and R. E. Simons, *Class and Colour in South Africa*. Harmondsworth: Penguin Books, 1969.

van den Berghe, Pierre L., *South Africa: A Study in Conflict*. Berkeley: University of California Press, 1967.

van den Berghe, Pierre L., *Race and Racism: A Comparative Perspective*. New York: Wiley, 1967.

Noel P. Gist

University of Missouri

CHAPTER THREE

THE ANGLO-INDIANS OF INDIA

Wherever intermingling has occurred among peoples of diverse cultural and racial backgrounds, the consequences have often been acculturation and amalgamation—the blending of cultures and blood. Probably such intermingling has occurred throughout most of man's history. Contacts between diverse peoples were multiplied and intensified as developments in transportation and communication, in political and economic organization, brought peoples together from afar. The colonial and imperialist expansion of Europe was unprecedented. For the first time, and on a mass scale, Europeans as conquerors or colonizers (or both) confronted the indigenous peoples of Asia, Africa, the Middle East, Oceania, and the Americas. The forms, frequency, and consequences of these contacts varied according to the specific situations and circumstances. In some situations there was acculturation without amalgamation; in others there was amalgamation without acculturation; commonly both occurred with far-reaching social, cultural, and psychological effects.

This chapter is concerned with the Anglo-Indians, a minority "community" in India representing a racial blending of Europeans and indigenous peoples. The initial sexual contacts were mainly between European men and Indian women. Some of the relationships were unconventional and doubtless casual; others culminated in marriage. The

---

This study was initiated by the author in 1963–1964 when he was a Fulbright visiting professor at the University of Calcutta. Additional field work was done in South India in 1967.

progeny of these unions, whether licit or illicit, represented a genetic merger in which physical traits were inherited from both racial stocks. As the numbers of racial hybrids increased, it was virtually inevitable that their associations and intimate relations would be mainly with others of similar genetic composition and social position. For the last two centuries or so the vast majority of marriages have occurred between Anglo-Indian men and women.

It seems probable that numbers of hybrid children, especially those born out of wedlock, were reared by their mothers and socialized into Indian society without close or continuous contacts with European cultures or people. To the extent that this occurred, these children, or subsequently their own offspring, were enveloped by the culture and social system of their mothers and thus disappeared as identifiable racial hybrids. However this may be, the majority of Anglo-Indians now constitute a self-conscious community whose members are socialized into a system and way of life characteristically European. Their mother tongue is English, their religion Christianity; their family organization and home life are patterned after that of Europeans, mainly British, and their schools resemble the British model.

The Anglo-Indian Minority in Historical Perspective

The origins of the Anglo-Indian minority go back to the early arrivals of the Europeans in India—first the Portuguese and later the British, Dutch, and French. The Portuguese settled mainly in southern India, and from that colonial beachhead became active in spreading the Portuguese language and culture and converting the local people to Catholicism. They viewed intermarriage with a tolerant eye, and the offspring of such unions were generally treated with generosity.

It was a different story in the regions of India dominated by the British as a colonial power. In the early years of British control the East India Company did not discriminate against persons of mixed racial heritage; in fact, intermarriage was tolerated, even encouraged, because many administrators believed that the racially mixed people would represent a "bridge" between Britain and India and would probably support the British in their imperial ambitions.

By the end of the eighteenth century the official policies of the East India Company had changed; the people of dual racial ancestry came to be regarded with distrust as a potential threat to the Empire. Job discrimination practiced against them worked severe hardships on many of the families. Although members of the minority were culturally oriented to the Europeans, and most of them probably felt a loyalty to their kinsmen the British, they continued to be objects of social and occupational discrimination until the middle of the nineteenth century.

It then became apparent to the British Crown, which had replaced the East India Company in colonial governance, that the people of dual racial ancestry could be used as an ally in the event of an uprising by the Indian population against the British. An abortive revolution, the Sepoy Mutiny of 1857, in which many Anglo-Indians supported the British, appeared to be the turning point in the discriminatory policies of the colonial overlords. In the second half of the century an increasing number of the minority were provided employment in transportation and communications, sectors of the economy regarded by the British as vital to their colonial strategy.

Minority Group Labels. Persons of Portuguese-Indian ancestry were initially referred to as Luso-Indians, Mesticos, Topasses, or Feringhees (or Feringis), terms generally used descriptively rather than opprobriously. These terms have fallen into disuse, or at least are rarely used. Many persons of Portuguese-Indian racial heritage prefer to be identified as Goans (from the erstwhile district of Goa, until recently a Portuguese possession), and most of them have Portuguese family names such as d'Souza, d'Cruz, or d'Costa, although their Christian names are commonly English. Many of the Goans tend to identify socially and culturally with the Anglo-Indian community, even though they may not apply that term to their own group.

Over the years various terms have been applied to those of North European-Indian kinship ties. Eurasian, Anglo-Briton, Indo-European, country-born, and East Indian were widely used terms in the nineteenth and early twentieth centuries. The most widely accepted term was Eurasian, used throughout most of the nineteenth century, but at the request of members of this community "Anglo-Indian" was adopted by the Indian government and officially used for the first time in the 1911 census.[1] Even this change created some confusion since it was applied to the racially mixed minority and to Europeans permanently residing in India, although the latter were often designated as Domiciled Europeans. Certain opprobrious terms, reflecting the prejudices of Europeans and Indians toward the Anglo-Indian community, were often used, privately if not publicly. These included such terms as "half-caste" and "chee-chee."

---

[1] Throughout this chapter the term Anglo-Indian will be used, even when referring to the community at an early date when other labels were in vogue.

Since the definition of Anglo-Indians as a minority people was never precise throughout most of the community's history, the Government of India Act of 1935, well before the British withdrew from the country, undertook to specify the meaning of the term: this act applied the term to all persons in India who were of European descent in the male line, whether of mixed or unmixed racial ancestry. The new constitution adopted in 1950 was somewhat more specific: "An Anglo-Indian means a person whose father or any of whose other male progenitors in the male line is or was of European descent but who is domiciled within the territory of India and is or was born within such territory of parents habitually resident therein and not established there for temporary purposes only." (Article 366). The term Domiciled European thus fell into disuse, at least officially, although the social distinction between those of so-called "pure" European ancestry and the Anglo-Indians of mixed racial heritage was often observed. Indeed, Domiciled Europeans were commonly accorded social or occupational preference to the Anglo-Indians when the British were in power.

Demographic Trends. The number of Anglo-Indians in India at present is unknown, since no census enumeration of the community's members has been taken for several decades. Estimates, which vary considerably, range from 100,000 to 300,000. Probably a realistic estimate would be 200,000. Heavy out-migrations to England and other countries have reduced the population below what it otherwise would be. On the other hand, a fairly high birth rate has tended to compensate for the losses through migration. The community is located almost entirely in cities, with heavy concentrations in Calcutta, Madras, Bangalore, and Bombay. Many are also located in smaller cities, especially railway transportation centers such as Secunderabad, a suburb of Hyderabad, and Kharagpur, near Calcutta.

The Transition: Its Political and Economic Consequences

The long struggle of the Indians to gain independence from Britain placed the Anglo-Indians in a difficult position. Political events clearly indicated that the days of British rule were numbered. Knowing full well that many other Indians regarded them with suspicion, and at times with hostility, the Anglo-Indians feared that the new government, once independence was achieved, would take retaliatory action against them because of their pro-British sympathies. Their anxieties were unfounded. Instead of adopting a punitive policy toward the Anglo-Indians, or any other ethnic or religious minority, the new secular regime asserted the right of all minorities to equal treatment under the law.

In the case of the Anglo-Indians it sought to ease the strains occasioned by the transition from a Crown colony to an independent nation by providing certain preferential employment advantages for 10 years, beginning with 1950. After 1960 the Anglo-Indian community would be accorded no special consideration in the allocation of jobs in the public sector. Furthermore, the community was given special representation in Parliament (*Lok Sabha*) and in several state legislative assemblies. Since independence the community has been represented by two members in the Parliament and one or two in each of several state legislative bodies, depending on the number of Anglo-Indians in the state.

The transition of India from a Crown colony to an independent nation eased certain social strains for the Anglo-Indians and intensified others. The new constitution spelled out specifically the rights of the community, declaring that all minority peoples would have equal protection under the law. At least the official policy of the new government helped to allay the anxieties of Anglo-Indians whose status and rights had been uncertain, but termination of the policy of preferential employment during the British regime, and for a decade after the new constitution went into effect, created serious problems for a people who had enjoyed special protection in the labor market. It was not so much that discrimination was practiced against the community but that Anglo-Indians were forced to compete with other Indians for jobs at a time of increasing unemployment and inflation in the entire country. This situation was made all the more frustrating with the blasting of hopes that the British would assist all who wished to go to England after independence.

Community Consciousness and Social Organization

The many difficulties encountered by the Anglo-Indian minority, particularly discrimination by the British or even other Indians, had the effect of arousing a sense of "community" among its members. This community consciousness, based on ties of blood and culture, emerged in the eighteenth century and has continued to this day, fluctuating in intensity with the rise and fall of Anglo-Indian fortunes, the presence or absence of effective leadership in the group, and discriminatory acts against its members. Community solidarity was also enhanced by the wide cultural gap between the Anglo-Indians and the vast Indian majority, mainly Hindus and Muslims.

This self-awareness has been manifest in various forms of organization which have strengthened community bonds and made possible collective action. One such indication of community is the All-India Anglo-Indian Association, organized as a federation of local chapters, or branches, in all the states and many cities of the Indian union. The association and its 70 or more affiliated branches serve such functions as maintenance of educational scholarships, welfare programs, and recreational activities. In assembling the members in local, state, and national meetings an effort is made to foster *esprit de corps* in the group. Still, many Anglo-Indians do not hold membership in the association, and even if they do their participation is often limited. The association publishes *The Review*, the official organ of the organization, and at each annual meeting elects (or re-elects) the "president in chief." Frank Anthony, representing the community in Parliament, has been the president for more than a quarter of a century.

Although a number of social clubs have been "integrated," most Anglo-Indian club members belong to organizations maintained by and for the community. Perhaps the best known social organization is the Rangers Club of Calcutta, which contributes sizable sums in support of educational and welfare programs and sponsors various social activities. The Catholic churches commonly have auxiliary clubs whose members are exclusively Anglo-Indian. The Bowring Institute of Bangalore was at one time predominantly Anglo-Indian, but it now has an open membership and most of its members represent other communities.

Anglo-Indians as a "Marginal" Minority. A clear perspective of the status of the community and the relations of its members to other peoples in India, either the British when they were a dominant power or other Indians representing different "communities," is obtained by viewing them as a marginal group. This concept in no sense implies an invidious comparison but rather indicates the nature and extent of their relations with other peoples and their integration into the social fabric of India.

When viewed in their relation to the British, the community may be considered socially *but not* culturally marginal to the Europeans in India. It is (and was) socially marginal because the social life of the Anglo-Indians did not involve extensive and intimate interpersonal or intergroup contacts with the British, except in institutional situations for work or worship. This was true mainly because they were socially rejected by the British, at least in the higher echelons of conventional society. They were certainly not culturally marginal, because Anglo-Indians and Britons alike were products of European culture. They had a common language; most of them embraced the Christian religion; their general style of life, including dietary practices, attire, and cultural interests, were similar. About the only distinguishing difference was color or physiognomy, and even these traits were not always readily apparent. In color the Anglo-Indians ranged from fair to black.

In their relation to the majority of other Indians the Anglos are (and were) *both* socially and culturally marginal. They are socially marginal because they do not participate intimately and extensively in the social life of Hindus, Muslims, Sikhs, Parsees, or other indigenous communities. There are, of course, numerous situations in which intermingling does occur. School children commonly interact informally; intimate neighborhood interaction may occur between Anglo-Indians and others; some of the clubs now have a mixed membership, and Indian-Christians and Anglo-Indians do participate in religious services in Christian churches, but more often than not intimate interaction is restricted to the in-group. Marginality on the social level may be the result of a cultural gap that separates Anglo-Indians from most other Indians—a gap that involves religion, language, dietary habits, family organization, caste, belief systems, and often attire.

A third level of marginality is in the realm of political and civic activity. As long as Anglo-Indians occupied a relatively secure position under the protective imperialist umbrella of John Bull, political involvement was minimal. This habit of noninvolvement in broad political issues has persisted. When Indian independence became imminent, and even before, Anglo-Indian leaders made representations to the ruling powers in behalf of the community, but although Anglo-Indians exhibited great concern about their future after independence, they seldom became involved in mass political action. Except for appointed representatives in state and national legislative bodies, who do function as champions of the community in various aspects of life, particularly education, Anglo-Indians for the most part are not politically oriented. Doubtless their political inactivity is influenced somewhat by the realization that they are a microscopic minority in a society overwhelmingly dominated by Hindus, although they are not denied the right to vote and hold office. Their noninvolvement in civic or political activities on the local or national level, except for issues directly affecting the community, places them in a relatively powerless position in the political system. As one knowledgeable member of the community remarked in an interview, "The average Anglo-Indian is not a political animal." He remains on the political sidelines. Politically, he is a marginal man.

One criterion of marginality is intermarriage. Although there were

times and situations in which many Anglo-Indians did frequently intermarry with the British and Portuguese, in recent decades such marital
unions have been relatively rare. Even more infrequent have been marriages between Anglo-Indians and other Indians, with the possible exception of Indian-Christians. Whenever intermarriages have occurred,
they were usually between Anglo-Indian women and males from other
communities. Since independence there has apparently been some increase
in the number of marital unions between Anglo-Indians and other
Indians, but the actual number of such marriages is still very small.
Because many Anglo-Indian men have had serious economic problems
in recent years, Anglo-Indian females are sometimes reluctant to assume
the heavy obligations of marriage, knowing that part or all of the financial
responsibilities of family support may fall on their shoulders. A knowledgeable Anglo-Indian in Calcutta remarked to the writer that some
Anglo-Indian women would prefer to marry a well-to-do Indian man
than an impoverished Anglo-Indian with little prospect of a comfortable
life in the future.

Degrees and Forms of Marginality. Social and cultural differences
contribute to marginality, but at certain points the Anglo-Indian community is becoming increasingly integrated into the main stream of
Indian life. Few Anglo-Indian children now attend schools maintained
exclusively by and for members of the community, and even the so-called
Anglo-Indian schools seldom have a majority of Anglo-Indian children.

These schools provide a common ground for formal and informal
reciprocity between students of different cultural and religious backgrounds. Anglo-Indian children, along with children of Hindu, Muslim,
Sikh, Parsee, Jewish, Indian-Christian, or tribal parents, are required to
study at least one indigenous language and learn something of the art,
literature, and history of the Indian people, about which the community
was indifferent throughout much of its own history. The military establishment also provides another institutional situation in which distinctions are reputedly prohibited on the basis of religion or ethnicity. An
effort is thus being made to narrow the cultural gap between the Anglo-
Indians and the other Indians.

But even in these equalitarian situations ethnic cohesion does not
disappear altogether. In the schools, for example, Anglo-Indian children
tend mainly to find intimate friends within their own community, and
these fraternal relations are likely to be continued after school hours and
on completion of academic studies. Yet caution should be exercised about
broad generalizations. The social climate of the present youthful genera-

tion certainly involves more friendly relationships between Anglo-Indians and others than in the past. An Anglo-Indian parent commented: "When I was a child my parents did not permit me to play with children from other Indian families; today my own children have many friends among their age-mates in other communities."

Attitudes, Images, and Stereotypes

After the middle of the nineteenth century the British, especially in view of the support the Anglo-Indians gave them during and after the Sepoy Mutiny of 1857, came to regard the Anglo-Indian minority as an asset to their imperial plans in India, but they did not generally accept them socially. Rather, they regarded them as pariahs of a lower social and moral order. There were, of course, many exceptions; missionaries or other humanitarians did attempt to apply their own ethical principles to a community that had been generally excluded from the precincts of Europeans.

Stereotypical images, often inherently contradictory, were applied to the Anglo-Indians. They were recognized as competent workers and disciplined soldiers, evidenced by their contributions to building and operating the railway and telegraph systems or their work in hospitals and offices. Alongside these favorable conceptions were negative stereotypes that held the Anglo-Indians to be irresponsible, immoral, shiftless, and inferior in intelligence. Doubtless these negative stereotypes found support in the widespread myth that peoples of mixed racial ancestry were somehow inferior to the "pure" racial strains, particularly those of Anglo-Saxon heritage.

The Anglo-Indians certainly were aware of these stereotypes and chafed under the discriminatory restrictions imposed on them by the British. Nevertheless, they tended to identify culturally with the Europeans and to regard England as their spiritual home which they hoped to reach at some future time. Socially they "looked up" to the British, even though they were excluded from intimate social groups maintained primarily by and for the British in India. This paradoxical combination of attitudes, admiration-resentment, directed toward the British may be understood partly in terms of the distribution of political and economic power. As long as the British were firmly located in the seats of power, it might be expected that the Anglo-Indians, who had both cultural and kinship ties to the Europeans, would be resentful of them for the arrogant treatment accorded their own countrymen but at the same time admiring them for certain attributes and achievements seen as character traits of the British people.

Since the Indians were not in positions of great economic or political power, except for a few wealthy princes or landholders, they did not become objects of admiration as far as the Anglo-Indians were concerned. Furthermore, the cultural gap separating the people of European and oriental heritages was so wide that a mutual cultural appreciation was difficult to achieve. To the Anglo-Indians the other Indians were less civilized, less clean, and less industrious than they themselves were, the products of a culture that was alien to their own Western way of life and thought. British arrogance toward the Anglo-Indians was matched by Anglo-Indian arrogance toward other Indians.

The prevalence of these attitudes, clearly manifest in their behavior, did not endear them to Indians with Asian backgrounds. It was almost inevitable, therefore, that negative stereotypes would emerge. To the other Indians the Anglos were unpatriotic interlopers, lacking in a sense of responsibility, and committed to forms of behavior that ran counter to the traditional mode of life of Hindus, Muslims, and other Indian peoples. Anglo-Indian women, whose behavior was unconventional, as judged by traditional Indian standards, were often regarded as immoral. If they smoked, drank, or dated men with no supervision, this was evidence of unacceptable moral behavior which would not be tolerated among their own womenfolk. Such conflicting cultural values often gave rise to mutual hostilities. Although their attitudes have been softened by the flow of events in recent decades, their persistence has blocked complete understanding and reciprocity between the vast Hindu majority and the miniscule Anglo-Indian minority.

How Other Indians View the Anglo-Indians. A survey of student attitudes was conducted by me in 1964 among 67 sociology students in Calcutta and Jadavpur universities and St. Xavier College, all in Calcutta. Most of the participating students were Bengal Hindus. On a Bogardus-type scale one of the questions asked was concerned with intermarriage: "I would _____, or would not _____, be willing to marry a person from this group, or approve a member of my community or family marrying such a person; or I have no opinion _____." Six national or ethnic groups were selected. Probably few, if any, of the students were personally familiar with Egyptians and African Negroes, but doubtless most of them had had contacts with Parsees, Jews, Anglo-Indians, and British. The following percentages indicate those favorable to intermarriage with these groups:

		Percent
1.	British	56
2.	Parsee	44
3.	Egyptian	35
4.	Anglo-Indian	26
5.	Jew	25
6.	African Negro	12

The students were then asked to take an overall view of these groups and rank each in terms of the group's acceptability, using whatever criteria seemed to them most applicable. An acceptability score was obtained by recording the number of expressed preferences on each level from 1 to 6, multiplying the number of preferences by the numerical value of that level, adding the results to obtain the gross sum, and then dividing by the total number of student respondents. If, for example, *all* the students had ranked the Egyptians first, the acceptability score would have been 1; if they had been ranked last by all the students, their score would have been 6. From the scores obtained by this method it was clear there was no unanimity of preference for any of the six groups. The British ranked first, well above any of the other groups, with the Anglo-Indians ranking at the bottom, slightly below the Jews.

1.	British	1.7
2.	Parsees	3.5
3.	Egyptians	3.5
4.	African Negroes	3.6
5.	Jews	4.2
6.	Anglo-Indians	4.3

Stereotypes of Anglo-Indians. The students were then asked to indicate three terms that, for them, most appropriately applied to each of the six groups. We were, of course, primarily interested in their assessment of the Anglo-Indians. In designating the qualities or attributes of Anglo-Indians, 34 different attributes mentioned were judged to be "likable" or favorable, compared with 68 unfavorable characteristics. Many of the expressions, although worded somewhat differently, referred to essentially similar attributes. Among the stereotypical qualities of the Anglo-Indians most admired by the students were their industriousness, their sportsmanship, their capacity to enjoy life, and their friendliness. On the negative side were their allegedly uncertain loyalty to India and their questionable morality, snobbishness, and imitation of the British. Most of the students listed both positive and negative stereotypes, which would suggest an ambivalent stance toward the community. In attitudes toward the British the favorable stereotypes outnumbered the unfavorable by a ratio of two to one.

It should be emphasized that the sample of university students did not necessarily reflect the attitudes of all or even most Indians toward the Anglo-Indian community. Numerous interviews with many Indians did, however, confirm in a general way the attitudes expressed by the students and tended to be distributed on a continuum ranging from admiration at one extreme to hostility and contempt at the other. It is quite clear that there is no clear-cut attitude of the Indian people toward the Anglo-Indians.

How Anglo-Indians View Other Indians. How do the Anglo-Indians view the other Indians and assess their interpersonal and intergroup relations? As in the case of the students, Anglo-Indians tended to vary widely in their own attitudes toward Indian nationals in other communities. Whatever may have been their feelings concerning other Indians, most of those interviewed expressed considerable concern about the unfavorable economic situation as it adversely affected the community; they were particularly concerned about prospects for the future of their children. Some of them tended to place part of the blame on members of the community for their misfortunes; more often there was a tendency for much of the blame to be directed toward others, either the British or Indians.

This diversity of attitudes was brought out in a survey of 52 employed Anglo-Indians in Bangalore in 1967 and in numerous personal interviews with members of the community in Bangalore and Hyderabad as well as earlier in Calcutta, Kharagpur, and Patna. About half of the respondents in Bangalore stated that they had received special advantages from persons representing other communities, which would suggest that at least some of them regarded the actions of non-Anglo-Indians as expressions of good will. "We Anglo-Indians are treated by other communities as one of their own, and they have a lot of respect, especially for a well-behaved Anglo-Indian," remarked a mechanic. A service officer said, "Muslims accept us more readily, first because they are a minority like us, and second because of religious reasons."

Not all Anglo-Indians are satisfied with the situation. Many feel threatened by the prospect of an overpowering Hindu *raj,* and some believe they are discriminated against in the job market. "I have felt very discriminated against, especially by Brahmins. They have called me 'khaki,' 'eight anna,' and 'legacy of the British,' " remarked a male teacher. A service officer commented: "Other communities 'accept' us formally, but hate our guts for various reasons. Not obviously, of course, but one has to admit it exists."

How Anglo-Indians View the British. Among most Anglo-Indians there is a feeling of cultural kinship with the British, but most of them are resentful of official British policies. They assert that the Anglo-Indians worked, fought, and died for England, yet when the crisis of independence came they were ruthlessly abandoned by the British government. This was ingratitude of the worst sort in the opinion of many Anglo-Indians. "When the British were in power," said an official of the Anglo-Indian Association, "I could not get a job at a decent salary." A clerk in a British firm in Calcutta said, "I hate their guts, but I have to keep my job because other posts are difficult to get." He berated himself for not obtaining a British passport and migrating to England when this could have been done easily, exhibiting the reactions of a "trapped" individual whose future is not very bright. A young Calcutta factory manager, preparing to migrate to Australia, asserted that he could never have attained his administrative post when the British were in India, but because of the uncertain future of the country, especially as it might affect his own children, he had decided to leave.

Seepage and Infiltration

There is considerable "seepage" out of the community and "infiltration" into it from the outside. Numerous Anglo-Indians—the actual number is of course not known—have chosen to conceal their ethnic identity by "passing," either temporarily in the work situation or permanently. While on the job they may not mention their ethnic affiliation, but after work hours they usually resume their social life with family and Anglo-Indian friends. In the case of intercultural marriage, especially if the Anglo-Indian is a female, ties with the community may be weakened or even severed altogether. Among Anglo-Indians who have migrated to England this kind of seepage often occurs as a result of frequent marriages to English men or women.

Infiltration occurs when persons from other groups seek to identify with the community for particular advantages such as qualifying for welfare or educational benefits. Local Anglo-Indian associations have sometimes required appropriate ethnic certification for membership, and there has been some effort to limit such membership to persons whose ancestry and culture are British-Indian. Such efforts would exclude Goanese or Portuguese-Indian ancestry, some of whom identify socially with the Anglo-Indian community, especially if they reside in northern cities beyond the region historically dominated by Portugal. There are many Goanese of Portuguese-Indian ancestry who "more or less" identify with the Anglo-Indian community, and this relationship is also true of some Europeans who are not racially mixed.

Occupation and Status

The community has never achieved conspicuous affluence or power, but during the latter part of the nineteenth century and even the early years of the twentieth Anglo-Indians had the special benefit of stable jobs controlled by the British. Incomes of persons employed as manual or clerical workers in such sectors of the economy as transportation and communications (railway workers, telegraph operators, minor customs officials, and the like) were generally sufficient to enable most of them to maintain a reasonably adequate standard of living. Many Anglo-Indian women qualified as nurses or as clerical workers in situations in which proficiency in English was a requirement.

Even before independence, however, jobs became increasingly competitive as other Indians sought employment in these fields. Large numbers of Anglo-Indians became unemployed and were thus forced to live under degrading conditions in the slums. Lacking the education and skills that might have permitted them to enjoy a reasonably adequate standard of living, their pauperization often produced feelings of despair, hopelessness, and even hostility.

There is, of course, a small elite and a fairly sizable middle class who are professionals, mainly teachers, officers in the military, minor government officials, skilled mechanical personnel, and clerical workers in both the private and public sectors, but the status gap is wide between the "haves" and the "have nots" within the community.

Vertical Mobility. The dynamics of social and economic change in Indian cities makes possible a considerable amount of vertical mobility for Anglo-Indians as well as other Indians. Available evidence, obtained mainly from interviews with Anglo-Indians in 1964 and 1967, suggests that the trend in general has been downward for several decades and that declining incomes and increasing inflation have made paupers out of many who at one time lived comfortably. A survey of 1207 persons in Calcutta in 1957–1958 reveals that one-third of the respondents (male and female) over 14 years of age were "in need of employment."[2]

Nevertheless, some have moved upward on the occupational ladder

---

[2] *Pilot Survey of Socio-Economic Conditions of the Anglo-Indian Community, 1957–58.* Calcutta: Baptist Mission Press, 1958, p. 20.

or have at least retained their jobs and possibly increased their incomes. For the most part these are persons with considerable education or marketable skills that qualify them for professional careers, government service, or commissions in the armed forces. Anglo-Indian women, generally speaking, are more successful in obtaining acceptable employment than are men. At the end of the work day in such cities as Calcutta or Bombay the downtown streets are full of Anglo-Indian women emerging from the offices and shops.

Anglo-Indian Education

The educational history of the Anglo-Indian community has varied from one period to another. During the initial period of colonialism in India the education of Anglo-Indian and European children was mainly in missionary schools, except that well-to-do British parents usually sent their children to boarding schools in England. A few European fathers of mixed-blood children sent or accompanied their children to England, but most of them either could not afford to do so or were reluctant to face the social ostracism they anticipated at home. Undoubtedly many European fathers abandoned their racially hybrid children, either leaving them in care of their Indian mothers or arranging for them to be placed in orphanages maintained by the community or church.

The East India Company did little to provide educational facilities for Anglo-Indian children or youth. When the British government superseded the East India Company, efforts were made to send to England a limited number of young Indian men to be trained for the Indian civil services, but Anglo-Indians were not included in this arrangement. During the nineteenth century a number of schools were established for children of Anglo-Indian and Domiciled European parents, most of them maintained by Catholic or Protestant churches or with funds contributed by individuals. Among the well-known institutions are the LaMartiniere schools, located in Calcutta and Lucknow and financed initially by a Frenchman who gave his name to them; others are the Bishop Cotton schools in Bangalore and Simla and the Christ Church school in Bombay. By the middle of the nineteenth century the British government had established three universities at Bombay, Calcutta, and Madras. Theoretically these were open to Anglo-Indian students, but few were considered qualified to attend or were interested or able financially to meet the costs of such an education.

The Anglo-Indian School System in Transition. After the turn of the century a number of changes occurred in the Anglo-Indian school system. For one thing, the term "Anglo-Indian school" replaced "European" as a broad classification, but even these schools, with a few exceptions, were not designed exclusively for Anglo-Indian children or youth. The essential features of Anglo-Indian schools were (and still are) the use of English as the principal medium of instruction and a curriculum similar to the educational program in British schools. The staffs were made up mainly of European or Anglo-Indian teachers, but most of the teachers of indigenous languages were Indians.

With independence came a resurgence of interest in English-medium schools open to all Indian residents regardless of race, religion, or nationality. This meant that Anglo-Indian students would have an opportunity to associate with their age-mates from various communities in the locality. At present there are some 250 Anglo-Indian schools in the country. One notable development in Anglo-Indian education has been the establishment of the Frank Anthony "public" schools, named in honor of the long-time president of the All-Indian Anglo-Indian Association. Twenty of these schools are planned to supplement the three that are presently located in Calcutta, Delhi, and Bangalore.

Curricular changes in Anglo-Indian schools since World War II have redefined their objectives as the appreciation and understanding of Indian history, culture, language, and art and some familiarity with the problems of Indian life. This is in contrast to the early Anglo-Indian schools which were strongly oriented to European society and which offered instruction only in the English language. Although most Anglo-Indian children or youth attend these schools, the tuition fees in the "quality" institutions, including the Frank Anthony schools, arbitrarily limit the enrollment of Anglo-Indians to a small proportion of the total student body, and even the students who do attend are generally supported by scholarships or other forms of assistance. Thus about 20 percent of the students in prestigious LaMartiniere in Lucknow, 10 percent in St. John's in Bangalore, 15 percent in Christ Church in Bombay, and about 4 percent in the Bishop Cotton School for Boys and the Frank Anthony school, both in Bangalore, are Anglo-Indian. For Anglo-Indian schools as a whole the percentage estimates of Anglo-Indian students enrolled generally range from 10 to 30, although actually some have as few as 2 or 3 percent and some at least half of the student body. Schools situated in the slum areas of cities generally have a higher proportion of Anglo-Indian students than more expensive schools located elsewhere. Doubtless some of the so-called Anglo-Indian schools have no Anglo students enrolled.

Learning and Scholarship. The academic performance of Anglo-

Indian children in general is less impressive than that of other children attending the same school. Their academic marks tend to be lower, there are more dropouts, and relatively few attend college after high school. Their spotty scholastic record seems to be mainly a matter of motivation, which in turn reflects the cultural and social experiences of the community. Students perform well in courses involving manual dexterity, physical prowess, or dramatic talents—manual arts, housekeeping skills, office training, and athletics—but in strictly academic subjects such as languages (other than English), mathematics, or science they do not usually muster the necessary effort or interest for a superior performance. Always, of course, there are exceptions.

In a survey that involved several hundred students in West Bengal in 1964 two-thirds of the Hindu males preferred regular academic subjects, compared with one-third of the Anglo-Indian students. Only 4 percent of the Hindus preferred nonacademic subjects such as handwork, but one-fourth of the Anglos liked these subjects best.

Some of the explanation seems fairly clear. As long as Anglo-Indians had preferential treatment in certain kinds of employment, mainly clerical or skilled manual work or in the police or military forces, an elementary or secondary education was almost mandatory, but in few instances was training on the college level required or even needed. A reasonably good job could be obtained without such training, sometimes at a better wage or salary than earned by well-educated Indians with college degrees. Furthermore, most of the functionaries in the best jobs were Europeans—the British retained an almost complete monopoly of positions of power and prestige.

The expense and effort to obtain a university degree could hardly be justified, in their opinion, especially when the prospect of a professional or administrative job was slim. Consequently there was little serious interest in university or college study, hence no tradition of higher education in most Anglo-Indian families.

After the preferential system of job selection was terminated and Anglo-Indians were compelled to compete with other Indians in an open job market, they were at a distinct disadvantage in obtaining lucrative or prestigious positions. The long tradition of learning among Hindus, Parsees, Jews, and Indian-Christians placed the Anglo-Indians at a competitive disadvantage, except perhaps in military service. Furthermore, economic destitution of many Anglo-Indian families after independence made it impossible, or at least difficult, for parents to send their children to college or even high school. Today a considerable number of fellowships or scholarships are available to Anglo-Indians interested in a college education, but even with the increase in college attendance by members of this community they represent only a microscopic portion of Anglo-Indian youth.

The Problem of Identity

One of the problems the community has always faced is identity, by others as well as by themselves. Even in the early days the community was differentially defined: to many Indian nationals the Anglo-Indians were really Europeans with some Indian blood; to many British they were really Indians with some European blood. The fact that the Anglo-Indians were Indian nationals by birth but culturally oriented to Britain often made their status confusing to themselves and to others. It has not been easy for them to provide a satisfactory answer to the question, Who am I? Because of their alienation from both the British and the Indians they were almost literally forced to think of themselves as a people apart and this self-image has persisted to this day.

This self-image cannot obviate the fact that they are also Indian nationals and as such are a part of Indian society. Yet many feel that other Indians often regard them as unwanted interlopers who do not qualify as authentic and loyal Indian citizens. As one Indian woman in Bombay remarked, with reference to the matter of Anglo-Indian identity: "Go into any Anglo-Indian home and what do you see? Almost invariably a picture of the British royal family." This is undoubtedly a half-truth but it does reinforce the image that many Indians have of the community.

The problem of identity in any society involves the presence or absence of cultural heroes who may serve as models. These models may become a source of inspiration for children and adults and thus leave an imprint on the character of thought and action in the group. The Anglo-Indians have cultural heroes, but for the most part they are not distinguished in the realms of philosophical, artistic, scientific, or literary achievement. Except for a gifted poet, Henry Louis Derozio (1809–1832), who is eulogized as the first national bard of modern India, there are few who are nationally recognized for their major intellectual contributions. But there are other cultural heroes. There are warriors renowned for their military achievement in the defense of India or of England; there are famous athletes noted for their physical prowess; and there are numerous persons, notable Sir Henry Gidney and Frank Anthony, who have provided outstanding political leadership for the community. These men are revered as models by the Anglo-Indians and thus figure importantly as symbols of community identity.

Thoughtful Anglo-Indians are acutely aware of this problem of identity and of the attitudes held by many Indians toward the community. They realize that it is incumbent on them to demonstrate their loyalty to India and their willingness to work for the motherland. They insist that as Indian nationals they accept all the responsibilities of citizenship and in turn expect to be treated as authentic and responsible citizens. They point to their records of achievement in the interests of India and especially to the sacrifices made by Anglo-Indians in the military services. Some leaders of the community decry the migrations of their members to other countries, asserting that it is their duty to remain in India and work for equal rights and opportunities for all peoples.

Outward Bound

In spite of these admonitions, many Anglo-Indians have elected to leave the country and settle in the West. During the first three decades of the twentieth century the movement outward was a mere trickle, and most of the outmigrants went "home" to England. At the end of World War II it became increasingly evident that the days of the British in India were numbered and that a new all-Indian government would replace the British *raj*. Because of widespread anxiety that the new government would enforce discriminatory policies against the community, a wave of migrations to England occurred. These fears turned out to be groundless. The new government assumed a conciliatory stance, even continuing, for a decade, a policy of preferential treatment favorable to Anglo-Indians in the allocation of government jobs. With assurances from the national government that the Anglo-Indians would have the same protection under the Indian Constitution as other communities, the fears of retaliation subsided.

During the 1950's it appeared likely that England would adopt an exclusionist policy against Indians and other Commonwealth peoples. A second wave of Anglo-Indian migration occurred as many individuals rushed to England before the doors were closed to them. When in the early 1960's restrictive immigration policies were actually adopted in Great Britain, Anglo-Indians looked elsewhere, mainly to Australia, Canada, and New Zealand as possible homelands. England still admits a limited number of Indian nationals, but the main flow in recent years has been to the Commonwealth countries, whose immigration policies have been considerably liberalized.

Whatever may be the private hopes and intentions of Anglo-Indians concerning migration to other countries, any realistic assessment of their economic situation clearly indicates that the majority will be unable to leave India. Most of them cannot afford the cost of transportation to overseas countries or lack the occupational skills that would gain them admittance even if they could travel. This is particularly true of the indigent and others who are barely able to eke out a mere existence, with little prospect that their financial situation will improve significantly in the foreseeable future. Many of these persons have experienced a feeling of being trapped in a situation not of their own making and have often become embittered and frustrated to the point of desperation.

Prospects

The problem of identification is closely tied to other situations and relationships concerning the status of Anglo-Indians in India. If they are self-identified as members of the Anglo-Indian community, they must also be self-identified as Indian nationals, unless they reject or are indifferent to Indian identity and hope to migrate to another country. Self-identification as an Indian national involves, on the one hand, a genuine willingness to be integrated more fully into the fabric of Indian society and to be assimilated into Indian culture; on the other hand, it involves a willingness of other Indians to accept the Anglo-Indians as authentic fellow-citizens and accord them the same consideration in all affairs of social life as they extend to other communities.

This does not imply that the Anglo-Indians must abandon their own community or their own culture and institutions, but that by deed and thought they must demonstrate their loyalty to Mother India and their dedication to national ideals. Many thoughtful Anglo-Indians, recognizing this dilemma, have made a sincere effort to identify with their Indian compatriots in the common cause of working for a New India. Others, fearful of the future, have serious misgivings about the destiny of their community and the nation and have serious intentions of migrating to other lands. Indeed, the outflow to Western countries continues.

SELECTED BIBLIOGRAPHY

Anthony, Frank, *Britain's Betrayal in India*. New Delhi: Allied Publishers, 1969.

Cressey, Paul F., "The Anglo-Indians: A Disorganized Marginal Group." *Social Forces,* **14,** 263–268 (December 1935).

Dover, Cedric, *Half-Caste*. London: Martin Secher and Warburg, 1943.

Gaikwad, V. R., *The Anglo-Indians*. Asia Publishing House, New York, 1967.

Gist, Noel P., "Cultural Vs. Social Marginality: The Anglo-Indian Case." *Phylon* **28,** 261–275 (Winter 1967).

Gist, Noel P., "Conditions of Inter-Group Relations: The Anglo-Indians." *Intern. J. Comparative Sociol.*, **8**, 199–208 (September 1967).

Goodrich, Dorris L., *The Making of an Ethnic Group: The Eurasian Community in India*. Unpublished doctoral dissertation, University of California, Berkeley, 1952.

Grimshaw, Allen D., "The Anglo-Indian Community: The Integration of a Marginal Group." *J. Asian Studies*, **18**, 227–240 (February 1959).

Hedin, Elmer L., "The Anglo-Indian Community." *Amer. J. Sociol.*, **40**, 165–179 (September 1934).

Stark, Herbert A., *Hostages to India*. Calcutta: Calcutta Fine Arts Cottage, 1926.

Stark, Herbert A., *The Call of the Blood*, or *Anglo-Indians and the Sepoy Mutiny*. Rangoon: British Burma Press, 1932.

Wallace, Kenneth E., *The Eurasian Problem*. Calcutta: Spink, 1947.

Wright, Roy Dean, *Marginal Man in Transition: The Anglo-Indians of India*. Unpublished doctoral dissertation, University of Missouri, 1969.

Tissa Fernando

University of British Columbia

CHAPTER FOUR

THE BURGHERS OF CEYLON

Ceylon is a plural society consisting of many ethnic and religious communities. Ethnically the majority of Ceylonese are Sinhalese, but the
Tamils are an important minority both in numbers and influence. In
their religious affiliation the Sinhalese and the Tamils are predominantly
Buddhist and Hindu, respectively. They represent Ceylon's two major
language groups, in addition to which there are two important minority
communities: the Muslims who are "sometimes farmers, but more often
traders, businessmen, or the keepers of small shops,"[1] and followers of
Islam, and a small community of Burghers, Christians by faith, most of
whom are of mixed racial ancestry. The population of Ceylon by ethnic
groups follows:

Total Population	10,590,060
Sinhalese	7,517,750
Ceylon Tamils	1,170,310
Indian Tamils	1,122,850
Ceylon Moors (Muslims)	661,590
Indian Moors (Muslims)	27,290
Burghers and Eurasians	46,050
Malays (Muslims)	24,130
Others	20,090

SOURCE: Census of Population, Ceylon, 1963.

---

[1] W. H. Wriggins, *Ceylon: Dilemmas of a New Nation*. Princeton: Princeton University
Press, 1960.

The maritime provinces of Ceylon were under Portuguese rule from 1505 to 1656 and the Dutch East India Company from then until 1796, "when the Dutch Governor, Gerard van Angelbeek, surrendered Colombo, with the remaining Dutch territory in Ceylon and the dependencies in South India, to the superior British forces." The Burghers of Ceylon are, strictly speaking, the descendants of those European officials who worked in Ceylon for the Dutch East India Company and of the *Vryburghers* who were engaged in trade and other occupations in Dutch Ceylon. During Dutch rule of the maritime provinces[2] the term "Burgher" referred specifically to Dutch citizens who had emigrated to Ceylon of their own accord. The Dutch community was then divided into company servants and Burghers. After the British conquest of Dutch territory this distinction ceased to have significance and all persons of Dutch descent came to be called "Burghers." The tendency since has been to include those of Portuguese descent, as well as Eurasians (the descendants of mixed European and Asian parentage), in this category although this usage is repudiated by persons of "unbroken paternal Dutch descent."[3]

The Burghers have always been few in numbers. Early estimates of the size of the Burgher community are problematic because of inconsistencies in definition. The Reverend James Cordiner, the chaplain to the garrison of Colombo, estimated in 1804 that there were about 900 Dutch inhabitants in Ceylon. "They are chiefly composed of officers (prisoners of war) with their families, and widows and daughters of deceased civil and military servants of the Dutch East India Company." The descendants of the Portuguese, according to Cordiner, numbered about 5000. Although they "exhibit complexions of a blacker hue than any of the original natives," he noted that "they retain a considerable portion of the pride of their ancestors; wear the European dress; profess the religion of the Church of Rome; and think themselves far superior to the lower classes of the Sinhalese."[4]

Cordiner's estimate of the size of the Burgher population in the early decades of British rule is roughly corroborated by Bertolacci, a

---

[2] The maritime provinces of Ceylon were under Portuguese rule from 1505 to 1656 and under Dutch rule from then until 1796. The British took over the Dutch territories in 1796, but it was only in 1815 that the whole of Ceylon came under the British.

[3] For discussions on definition see, for example, Edmund Reimers, "The Burghers of Ceylon," *JDBU*, **17**, Pts. 1, 2 (1921); R. G. Anthonisz, "The Burghers of Ceylon," *ibid.*, **17**, Pt. 1 (1927); J. R. Toussaint, "The Dutch Burghers of Ceylon," *ibid.*, **29**, Pt. 1 (1939); and G. V. Grenier, "Burgher Etymology: Some Relevant Reflections," *ibid.*, **56**, Pts. 1–4 (1966). *JDBU* refers to *Journal of the Dutch Burgher Union*.

[4] Quoted in William Digby, *Forty Years of Official and Unofficial Life in an Oriental Colony: Being the Life of Sir Richard F. Morgan, Kt.*, Vol. 1. Madras: Higginbotham, 1897, p. 15.

Corsican who accompanied Frederick North, the British governor of the
Maritime Provinces of Ceylon from 1798 to 1805, to Ceylon as his secretary. Defining Burghers to include "those who are called Portuguese,"
Bertolacci estimated in 1816 that the Burghers "were not more than five
to six thousand of a total Ceylonese population of around a million and
a half."[5] *Ferguson's Directory* for 1863 gave the number of "European
descendants" as 4000, but this is clearly an underestimate, for at the time
of the 1871 Census there were more than 15,000 European descendants
who could be broadly classified as Burghers. Table 2 indicates the propor-

Table 2   Population of Burghers in Relation to Total Population of Ceylon

Census Year	Ceylon Population	Burghers	Burghers as a Percentage of Total
1871	2,400,380	15,335	0.6
1901	3,565,954	23,482	0.7
1921	4,498,605	29,439	0.7
1946	6,657,339	41,926	0.6
1953	8,097,895	45,950	0.6
1963	10,590,060	46,050	0.4

SOURCE: Ceylon Census Reports.

tion and growth of the Burgher population in relation to the total population. The drop in the rate of growth of the population of Burghers in
the last two decades is partly the result of large-scale emigration of
Burgher families, mainly to Australia.

The Burghers are predominantly an urban community. At the 1871
Census of Ceylon nearly half the Burgher population lived in the
Colombo municipality. In 1946 "more than 68 per cent of the Burghers
and Eurasians in the island were living in the Colombo District, and of
these Colombo City alone claimed 17,412 persons or over three-fifths of
the Dutch population."[6] To this day the large majority of Burghers are
residents of towns; that is, they live within municipal, urban, and town-
council areas. This residential pattern is related to employment preferences. There are not many Burgher "peasants," and few Burghers have
invested their money in landed property. As a community they have
depended almost exclusively on the professions and on urban white-
collar employment in government service and in the mercantile sector. In
recent years, however, with urban unemployment, there has been some
drift of Burghers to rural areas, but they remain to this day the urbanites
par excellence of Ceylon.

---

5 "A Burgher Census," *JDBU*, 6, Pts. 2, 3, 1913, 60–61 (1913).
6 *Census of Ceylon*, Colombo, 1946, Vol. 1, Pt. 1, p. 161.

The Status System and Problems of Identity

Despite an appearance of unity and homogeneity in the eyes of non-Burghers, the Burghers are in fact sharply divided. As mentioned earlier, the tendency in Ceylon for considerably more than a century has been to use the word "Burgher" as a generic term to include not only those of Dutch and Portuguese origin but also Eurasians, the offspring of mixed European and Asian unions. Thus, when a Sinhalese or Tamil identifies a fellow Ceylonese as a Burgher, he simply takes his cue from their fairer skin color and from certain names associated with this community; normally he would be oblivious to the subtle distinctions that prevail among the Burghers themselves, but just as caste behavior has persisted covertly among the Sinhalese and the Tamils similar niceties are observed by the Burghers in evaluating one another.

The most important distinction made within the Burgher community is between the "Dutch Burghers," who claim unbroken paternal Dutch descent, and all the rest that in Ceylonese usage are lumped together as Burghers. The Dutch Burghers have consistently rejected the suggestion that "the possession of Burgher blood, derived only through a man's mother,"[7] should make a person a Burgher.[8] They have objected to extending the term to those of Portuguese origin and to Eurasians who, according to one Dutch Burgher at least, were "arrogant nondescripts who are so stupidly impertinent as to think they have a right to call themselves Burghers."[9] The strength of this resentment is partly a matter of religion, for Dutch Burghers are largely Protestants, whereas those of Portuguese origin are mainly Catholics.

But it is more a matter of class attitudes. The Dutch Burghers who have always been a minority among the Burghers have also been the economically well-to-do as well as the "respectable" section of the community. The "Portuguese" Burghers, for example, have in general not

---

[7] *Ceylon Independent*, May 17, 1910, letter by "G.V.G."

[8] The definition of a Burgher is based mainly on geneology, but even then the classification of individuals is not always specific. Dutch Burghers trace their ancestry through male Dutch Burghers. If, however, the mother is a Dutch Burgher but the father is not, the children are considered "non-Dutch" Burghers. If a male Dutch Burgher married a "non-Dutch" Burgher, the child would be classified as Dutch Burgher. On the other hand, if a male Dutch Burgher married a non-Burgher, such as a Sinhalese or Tamil, the ethnic identity of the children would probably be "non-Dutch" Burgher, although in succeeding generations the descendants might regain Dutch Burgher status. If a Dutch Burgher married a person of European extraction, the children would probably be considered Dutch Burghers.

[9] *Ceylon Independent*, May 19, 1910: letter by "Dutch Burgher."

risen to positions of importance in public life in Ceylon, having been employed mainly as shoemakers, mechanics, and artisans. Class differences in life style divide all communities in Ceylon and the Burghers are no exception. The society of the affluent Burgher lawyer, doctor, or civil servant has always been strikingly different from that of lower class Burghers, most of whom are of Portuguese origin and have for generations intermarried with Sinhalese and Tamils.

The pride the Dutch Burgher has of his *Dutch* ancestry is not simply class feeling: it is something more, for it often borders on sentimentality. Even C. A. Lorenz, a distinguished lawyer, newspaper owner, and the Burgher member in the Legislative Council from 1855 to 1864, could not help feeling euphoric when he first sighted Holland.

Well now, really, am I in Amsterdam after all; and have I realized the dreams of my ambition, and are these the cousins of our old Dutch ancestors; and is this the veritable old Amsterdam to which our forefathers turned with fondness from their far homes in the East.[10]

Because of what they strongly felt were the "proud inheritance of their past and the sense of their oneness in origin and in feeling,"[11] the Dutch Burghers were resentful of the fact that not only the Sinhalese and the Tamils but even British government officials in Ceylon failed to distinguish them from "those who, although classed with them under one general term, were of different origin from, and had little or nothing in common with them."

Social Organization. As a result of such feeling a group of prominent Dutch Burghers met informally in 1907 and decided to form an association that would promote the special interests of the Dutch Burgher community. The inaugural meeting of this association—named the Dutch Burgher Union (DBU) was held in 1908. F. C. Loos, the Burgher member in the Legislative Council, was elected its first president. The bond which was to unite the members of the DBU was their common Dutch ancestry which was made a *sine qua non* for membership. To this day to be enrolled as a member of the DBU "the genealogical test must be passed."[12] The main purpose of the Union was to keep alive among Ceylon Burghers "the feeling of kinship with the people of Holland."[13] This was to be achieved by reviving Dutch customs and celebrations, by the study of the Dutch language, and especially by promoting research into the history

---

10 *Ceylon Examiner*, August 27, 1875.
11 *JDBU*, **3**, 1 (1910).
12 *JDBU*, **14**, Pt. 4 (1925).
13 *Ibid.*, **1**, Pt. 1, 4–5 (1908).

of the Dutch Burgher community itself. To encourage serious research a
periodical was founded, the *Journal of the Dutch Burgher Union of
Ceylon* (JBDU), the first number appearing in 1908. The high level of
motivation of the Burgher elite is reflected in the fact that this journal
has been published for more than 60 years, a rare achievement for a
Ceylonese publication.

   The Crisis of Identity. The identity crisis of the Dutch Burghers
affected not only their relations with the rest of the Burgher community
but even more so their relations with the Sinhalese and Tamils. Being
"Europeans" in an Asian society, the Dutch Burghers wished to preserve
their identity and resisted any action that could lead to their absorption
into the larger Ceylonese community. Thus marriages with Sinhalese and
Tamils, for example, were actively discouraged until recent years. For
purposes of administration, however, the claims of Dutch Burghers to
exclusiveness were usually ignored. A good example was the government's
attitude when the elective principle was first introduced into the Ceylon
Constitution in 1910. The Burghers (among others) were permitted to
elect a representative to the Legislative Council. The Dutch Burghers
lobbied the government in an effort to confine the definition of "Burgher"
for electoral purposes to those with unbroken paternal Dutch descent and
to exclude the larger body of persons of mixed European and Ceylonese
racial heritage. The Constitutional Commission, which inquired into
electoral matters, disregarded these objections and included in the electoral register "all persons having Burgher blood in their veins. . . ."
This definition was strongly opposed by the Dutch Burghers who ap-
pealed to the British Secretary of State for the Colonies, asking him to
confine the franchise to male descendants of the servants of the Dutch
East India Company who had settled in Ceylon after the British conquest.
The Colonial Office refused to give official recognition to this appeal.

   An important aspect of the Dutch Burgher identity crisis during
the British *raj* concerned their status in relation to the British "ruling
class" in Ceylon. Being "Europeans" like the British civil servants,
commercial executives, and tea planters, the Burghers—especially the
Dutch Burghers—felt a sense of affinity with the British community
in Ceylon and wanted these feelings reciprocated. As a British writer
observed, "at first the European may easily mistake the yellow complexion of the Burgher for a compatriot, but the native accent will soon dis-
illusion him."[14] This was the problem. Although the Burghers wanted
to be treated as social equals, the British treated them as just another

---

[14] P. R. Smythe, *A Ceylon Commentary*. London: Williams and Norgate, 1932, p. 30.

category of "natives." Certainly the British civil servants, planters, mercantile officials, and other residents in Ceylon had greater social contact with Burghers than they had with any other indigenous group, and they viewed the Burghers as a superior stratum of the local population. W. T. Stace, who had 22 years experience of life in British Ceylon, made the following observation:

> In British eyes the indigenous population could be divided into a series of social layers one below another . . . below the British themselves (in their view) came the "Burghers." They were the descendants of The Dutch who had been the earlier rulers of Ceylon. Most of them had Dutch names . . . . Some of them claimed to be, and perhaps were, of pure European origin, and were quite white-skinned . . . . The Burghers were treated as inferiors by the British, but enjoyed a certain degree of respect above what was accorded to lower layers.[15]

Rejection by the British. In Colombo, the capital, the British community was large enough to be socially self-sufficient and was thus able with impunity to exclude all non-Europeans from its social activities. Not so in the provinces. Outside Colombo social exclusiveness had to be modified if there was to be any social life at all. This was not easy, for, as Leonard Woolf said of his days in the Ceylon civil service, there was "the complete social exclusion from our social suburbia of all Sinhalese and Tamils."[16] In the provinces it was to the Burghers that the British turned for companionship, but this special relationship that the Burghers enjoyed with the "ruling race" proved to be tenuous. It was no unmixed blessing, either. It made the Burghers keep aloof on matters that were all-important to the Sinhalese and the Tamils, especially during the nationalist agitation of the early twentieth century. This had the unfortunate effect of isolating them from the mainstream of national politics. As for the British official or planter, his enjoyment of a game of tennis or a drink at the club with a local Burgher lawyer or doctor did not, of course, mean that there was acknowledgment of social equality. The Burghers were often painfully reminded that they were "natives" after all and that the British found them only a shade more tolerable than "those who had no admixture of European blood."

The British were completely uncompromising when it came to marriage with Ceylonese, Burghers notwithstanding. Stace refers to the fate of a Burgher doctor and his English wife.

---

15 W. T. Stace, "Notes on Life in Ceylon from 1910 to 1932," Mss. in Institute of Commonwealth Studies Library, London, p. 97.
16 Leonard Woolf, *Sowing: An Autobiography of the Years 1904–11*. London: Hogarth Press, 1961, p. 18.

But though she was English, the social ban on her husband because of his mixed blood was extended to her and their daughter. This was the principle universally applied to all English women who married either natives or Burghers.[17]

The Englishman who married a Burgher fared no better. Thus an English civil servant of Ceylon, B. Hill, who was heir-apparent in 1915 to the Government Agency of the Central Province, was passed over in favor of a junior in the service because (to quote the Governor of Ceylon) "Mr. Hill's wife is not of pure European descent—a fact which would have been a cause of much inconvenience in a province where the planting community is of the first importance."[18] Significant as revealing attitudes is the comment of a British civil servant of Ceylon on the marriage of a colleague to a Portuguese Burgher. Not only did he feel the marriage to be "a real misfortune" but he went on to call it "a union based solely on the lowest instincts of the human animal. . . ."[19]

The Burghers thus fell between two stools. They could not identify themselves with the Sinhalese and the Tamils because they thought of themselves as Europeans, and the British did not treat them as social equals because they were considered an Asian people. Despite these difficulties, the evidence is clear that the Burghers found the British *raj* moré palatable than did any other indigenous community.

The Burghers in Political Life

The role of the Burghers in the political life of Ceylon has been only marginal. Being numerically insignificant, they have on the whole been outflanked in the political scene by the Sinhalese and the Tamils. Their strong sense of identity has also meant that their political strategies, especially during British rule, have not always been the same or even compatible with those adopted by the larger communities. The Burghers had to be indifferent to nationalist campaigns if they were to gain the confidence of the British, and such an attitude was understandably unpopular with the Sinhalese and Tamil leaders.

Yet, paradoxically, it was the Burghers who pioneered political agitation against the *raj*. Together with English planters and merchants

---

17 W. T. Stace, *op. cit.*, p. 102.
18 Colonial Office Files, Public Record Office, London, 54/783, Chalmers to Bonar Law, Confidential, August 3, 1915.
19 Frederick Bowes, "Bows and Arrows—An Autobiographical Journal, 1867–1923" (Mss.), 2 vols., Rhodes House Library, Oxford University, pp. 109–110.

(who had their own grievances), the Burghers played a key role in founding the Ceylon League. This association, formed in 1865 to secure an unofficial majority in the Legislative Council, was the first major political organization in Ceylon to agitate for constitutional reform. Among Burghers in the political scene during this period the most prominent was C. A. Lorenz, who from 1855 to 1864 was the Burgher member in the Legislative Council. Apart from being the leading Burgher politician, he had "a great reputation for his skill as a writer and debater."[20] Also influential, though in a different way, was A. E. Buultjens, a Burgher-turned-Buddhist, who was a pioneer trade unionist.

By the turn of the century, as the Western-educated Sinhalese and Tamils gradually increased in numbers, we find the Burghers shifting from the center to the periphery of political life. The early decades of the twentieth century saw a growing movement for constitutional reforms, led mainly by the Sinhalese and to a lesser degree by the Tamil Western-educated elite. The Ceylon National Congress, founded in 1919 on the Indian model, was the rallying point for this movement. It is significant that the Burghers, as a community, kept aloof from the Congress and its activities. The only Burgher who was actively associated with the Congress was G. A. Wille, and he too resigned when he became the elected Burgher member of the Legislative Council in 1924.

The Crown Colony government established by the British in 1802 was authoritarian in the extreme; executive, legislative, and judicial powers were vested in the governor. He was assisted by an advisory council of British officials, but he was not obliged to accept their advice. This rule of the governor and advisory council was modified in 1833, with the introduction of an executive council of senior British officials and a legislative council composed of official and nonofficial members. Three of the six nonofficial members were to be Ceylonese, and it became customary for the governor to nominate one low-county Sinhalese, one Tamil, and one Burgher, although this procedure was never prescribed in the instructions from the Colonial Office.[21]

The first Burgher appointed was J. G. Hildebrand, who later became a judge of the Supreme Court. In 1910, when the elective principle was introduced to the Legislative Council, Burghers, too, were allowed to elect a representative. The controversy that surrounded the demarcation of the Burgher electorate highlighted the divisions within the com-

---

20 E. F. C. Ludowyk, *The Modern History of Ceylon*. London: Weidenfeld and Nicolson, 1966, p. 120.
21 W. J. F. LaBrooy, "Development of Legislative Councils in Ceylon," *Ceylon Economist*, **3**, Pt. 3 (1956).

munity. However, the right to elect a separate Burgher member to the Legislative Council—retained until the Donoughmore Reforms of 1931 —reinforced the widely prevalent idea among Burghers that they were different from the Asian people of Ceylon and must therefore preserve their identity at any cost. Thus, when the Sinhalese leaders were agitating for the superseding of communal electorates by territorial ones, the president of the Dutch Burgher Union told members:

> It is easy to conceive what it would be to have this representation taken away from us. It will be a loss of all social and political prestige and must lead eventually to our being blotted out as a separate community.[22]

Decline of Burgher Political Power. The Donoughmore Commissioners, however, recommended in their report, published in 1928, that all communal electorates be abolished, despite appeals by minorities, including the Burghers, for their retention. By one stroke they did away with the principle that had dominated local representation for a century and which the Commissioners found was "a canker on the body politic, eating deeper and deeper into the vital energies of the people, breeding self-interest, suspicion and animosity, poisoning the new growth of political consciousness, and effectively preventing the development of a national or corporate spirit."[23]

The Burghers were never an active force in twentieth-century post-Donoughmore mass politics of Ceylon. In independent Ceylon it even became necessary to give the Burghers nominated representation, since they were numerically too weak to elect members from territorial electorates. Indeed, the only prominent Burgher politician in contemporary Ceylon is Pieter Keuneman, the secretary of the Ceylon Communist Party and Minister of Housing and Construction in the present government.

Burghers and Employment

Although numerically a small community constituting less than 1 percent of the total population both in 1921 and 1963, the Burghers were conspicuously overrepresented in public service throughout British rule. A few examples would suffice to illustrate this fact. Thus in 1910, out of

---

[22] *JDBU*, 11, Pts. 3, 4 (1918). Proceedings of a Special General Meeting, January 18, 1919.
[23] *Ceylon: Report of the Special Commission on the Constitution*, Colombo: Ceylon Government Press, 1928, p. 39.

a total of 12 Ceylonese in the Ceylon civil service (the higher adminis-
tration), three were Burghers. In 1920, out of 24 Ceylonese, nine were
Burghers. Even as late as 1946 14 percent of the 116 Ceylonese in the
Ceylon civil service were Burghers.[24]

This pattern was also true of individual departments. Of the 33
Ceylonese in the Home Ministry in 1935, one-fourth were Burghers. The
only two Ceylonese in the Survey Department in 1910 and three out of
the five in 1920 were Burghers. Similarly, in the Public Works Department 15 out of 25 Civil List officers in 1910, 23 out of 41 in 1920, and 27
out of 64 in 1930 were Burghers. The medical profession was also dominated by Burghers. In the nineteenth century well-known Ceylonese
doctors were invariably Burghers; for instance, Dr. P. D. Anthonisz, "the
father of the medical profession in Ceylon," was the first president of
the Ceylon branch of the British Medical Association and the first Ceylonese to act for the Principal Civil Medical Officer. Similarly, Dr. James
Loos was the first principal of the Ceylon Medical College in 1875. Table 3 shows the ethnic distribution in the medical department in the
years 1910, 1920, and 1930.

Table 3   Ethnic Distribtuion of Ceylonese Government Medical Offices

	1910		1920		1930		Percentage of Total Population at 1921 Census
Burghers	34	(51%)	37	(32%)	65	(19%)	0.7
Sinhalese	14	(21%)	36	(31%)	163	(47%)	67
Tamils	19	(28%)	41	(36%)	117	(33%)	11
Others	—		1		4		

SOURCE: *Ceylon Civil Lists*, 1910, 1920, and 1930.

For further evidence we could look to the legal profession. Throughout the nineteenth century and in the early decades of the twentieth the
Burghers were overrepresented in the legal profession. At the 1921 Census, of a total of 816 lawyers in Ceylon, 129 were Burghers. This trend
is seen in legal and judicial appointments as well. In the latter half of
the nineteenth century, when the British government in Ceylon began
giving high office in the legal-judicial sphere to Ceylonese, it was the Burghers who benefited most. The preponderance of Burghers in high office
continued until the 1930's. Thus, of the six persons who held the office
of solicitor general in the first three decades of this century, two were

[24] S. J. Tambiah, "Ethnic Representation in Ceylon's Higher Administrative Services,
1870–1946," *University of Ceylon Review*, **13**, Pts. 2, 3, 133 (1955).

Burghers. Of the nine Ceylonese appointed to the Supreme Court in the same period, five were Burghers, as were most of the acting appointments to the Supreme Court. In 1910 three of the five Crown counsel were Burghers. This recruitment pattern was understandably resented by the Sinhalese and the Tamils.[25] How favorable employment prospects were for Burghers is clear if it is realized that they never exceeded 0.7 percent of the population after the first Census of 1871.

Why Were the Burghers Favored? How is it that such a small community came to get a major share of government jobs and to be distinctly preferred for high office? The answer to this reveals not only distinctive features of the Burgher community but also employment policies of the British *raj*.

When the British took over the Maritime Provinces of Ceylon from the Dutch, they were confronted with a genuine problem of administration, for there was only a small number of British officials in Ceylon; hence circumstances compelled them to depend heavily on the indigenous population for administration at different levels. The Burghers proved to be an invaluable asset in the circumstances. As Digby explained:

> As soon as British rule became consolidated, it was found that in the civilized, fairly educated European descendants the authorities had in their hand material which could be manipulated for a thousand and one inferior offices rendered necessary by modern systems of government. The natives were altogether unacquainted with the English tongue, and generally were not apt for the performance of the duties required. Their sympathies, too, were likely to be anti-European, while the Dutch and Dutch descendants would, naturally, be on the side of the European rulers who upheld the civilization which placed them in a position superior to the inhabitants of the country.[26]

Thus from the early days of British rule the Burghers sought employment under government, and the great majority of Dutch Burghers in the eighteenth century were government clerks. Sir Alexander Johnstone, Chief Justice and President of the Council in Ceylon, wrote in 1810 that on his recommendation Burghers were also appointed to "the office of registrar, keeper of records, advocates, proctors, notaries of the Supreme Court, members of the *landraads*, secretaries of the provincial courts, sitting magistrates, justices of the peace, and superintendents of

---

[25] Tissa Fernando, "The Legal Profession of Ceylon in the Early Twentieth Century: Official Attitudes to Ceylonese Aspirations," *The Ceylon Historical Journal*, **19**, Pts. 1–4, p. 13 (1969–1970).
[26] William Digby, *op. cit.*, p. 17.

police, to the office of proctor for paupers . . . to that of deputy advocate fiscal, and under certain circumstances, even to that of acting advocate fiscal. . . .[27]

There are many reasons why the Burghers were favored for government employment under the British. For one, the Burghers had little interest in landed property, trade, or agriculture and thus achieved social mobility almost exclusively via government service. By virtue of their European descent and westernized life style they were probably more acceptable to the British socially. When the British were compelled to have "colleagues" among Ceylonese, it was understandable that they would prefer the native community closest to them in attitudes, values, and style of life. Apart from this advantage of being themselves "European," the Burghers were also the most pro-British element in the colony. As mentioned earlier, the Burghers as a community kept aloof from the nationalist movement led by the Sinhalese and Tamils and refused to join the Ceylon National Congress. It is likely that their conspicuous loyalty to British rule worked to their advantage in obtaining good employment under government.

Education. It would be misleading to interpret the predominance of Burghers in public life as being merely a reflection of racial prejudice of the British community in Ceylon, for the fact was that the Burghers were indisputably superior to every other indigenous community in Ceylon in their command of the English language. English was in British Ceylon the language of government, commerce, and the courts of law. The origins of English education in Ceylon can be traced back to the beginnings of English rule itself, to the ambitious educational schemes of the first governor, Frederick North. The Colebrooke-Cameron reforms of 1832 made explicit the position of English in Ceylon. Since English was the language of administration, the commissioners recommended that the government establish English schools to qualify Ceylonese for government employment. Consequently, in 1832 five English schools were established in Colombo, Galle, Kandy, Chilaw, and Jaffna. The number of English schools increased gradually and by 1848 there were 60, attended by 2714 pupils.[28]

The Burghers—with their European background—made use of these early facilities for an English education far more than any other community in Ceylon. When the Colombo Academy (renamed Royal College

---

27 *Ibid.,* p. 21.
28 G. C. Mendis, *Ceylon Under the British.* Colombo: The Colombo Apothecarien, 1952, p. 76.

in 1881) was established to provide a "classical" secondary education, it
was more largely attended by Burghers than by Sinhalese or Tamils.[29]
It was easy for Burghers to take to English education because from the
early days they had adopted English as their home language. Here they
had a clear advantage over the Sinhalese and the Tamils, to whom English was essentially a foreign language. Table 4 shows how much more
familiar the Burghers were as a community with the English language
compared with the two major ethnic groups in Ceylon.

Table 4 *Percentage of English Literates Among Burghers, Sinhalese, and Tamils
in 1911 and 1921*

	1911		1921	
	Males	*Females*	*Males*	*Females*
Burghers	77.7	74.1	82.6	81.4
Low-country Sinhalese	4.1	1.2	5.9	2.0
Kandyan Sinhalese	0.8	0.2	1.3	0.3
Ceylon Tamils	5.7	1.3	8.5	2.1

SOURCE: *Reports of the Census of Ceylon, 1911 and 1921.*

There is no doubt that other reasons, apart from their greater proficiency in the English language (by its use as the home language), gave
the Burghers a clear advantage in the professions and in employment in
a context in which all administration was conducted in English. It was
a popular complaint of British government officials in Ceylon that their
Sinhalese and Tamil subordinates were not adequately fluent in the English language.[30] It seems likely, therefore, that, other factors being
equal, they would have preferred to recruit Burghers with whom they
could communicate more easily. The Burghers had the same advantage
in the professions. If we take the legal profession as an example, it would
be obvious what greater fluency in English implied. As a distinguished
Sinhalese lawyer and writer of the nineteenth century pointed out, "Burgher boys spoke English from their infancy; we did not. They were not
embarrassed with the study of Sinhalese at an early age; we were."[31]
The work of the courts being conducted in English was clearly to the
benefit of the Burghers. The striking achievements of the Burghers in

[29] William Digby, *op. cit.*, p. 22.
[30] See, for example, the evidence given before the Education Committee of 1911–1912.
Session Paper, Ceylon Legislative Council, XX (1912), *Education Committee*, 1911–1912.
[31] A. C. Seneviratne, *Memoirs and Desultory Writing of the Late James D'Alwis.*
Colombo: Ceylon Observer Press, 1939, p. 73.

the legal and judicial spheres are a reflection of the correlation between competence in English and employment opportunities in Ceylon until recent years.

The Burghers in Independent Ceylon

When Ceylon gained her freedom from British rule in 1948, changes occurred that dramatically altered the position of the Burghers in relation to other ethnic groups in Ceylon. This was seen in many spheres.

In the political scene Burghers, whose influence had declined progressively since the turn of this century, were now entirely dependent on the Sinhalese and Tamils. As a political force they had ceased to exist by the 1940's and had to be given special nominated members in the House of Representatives. In employment, likewise, Burghers had to give way to increasing proportions of Sinhalese and Tamils in almost every branch of government service. A few illustrations at random would suffice to show this trend. Whereas 37 percent of the Ceylonese civil servants were Burghers in 1920, there were only nine Burghers out of a total of 168 in 1962. In the Attorney-General's department in the same year there were only four Burghers out of 38 legal officers.[32]

The preponderance of Burghers in government service gradually diminished when Sinhalese and Tamils began to clamor for employment commensurate with their numerical strength. The introduction of universal franchise in 1931 meant that these demands had to be acted on by politicians. The Burghers suffered most by the influx into the labor market of Sinhalese and Tamil talent. This was the beginning of a reversal of fortunes from which the Burghers have not recovered. By 1934 the problem of poverty among "certain classes of the community" was serious enough for many to adopt "genteel begging as their occupation,"[33] and the situation has worsened. A sample survey of the rural sector conducted by the Central Bank of Ceylon in 1969–1970 revealed that 10.4 percent of the work force in the Burgher community were unemployed. The percentage of unemployed among the low-country Sinhalese alone was even higher.

The campaign for the replacement of English by Sinhala as the "official" language, initiated by S.W.R.D. Bandaranaike's *Sinhala Maha Sabha* in the 1930's and becoming official during his tenure as prime minister in 1956, sealed the fate of the Burghers in Ceylon. Just as much

---

[32] *The Ceylon Civil List Supplement*, Colombo: Ceylon Government Press, 1962.
[33] *JDBU*, **23**, 4 (1934), Presidential address to DBU by H. V. Leenbruggan.

as English, the language of administration, had worked to the advantage of the Burghers in the nineteenth and early twentieth centuries, this "changeover" helped Sinhalese and Tamil students from rural areas, for their upward mobility was no longer stifled by their poor command of English. By the dethronement of English, Burghers were automatically deprived of all the advantages they had enjoyed for more than a century. Preoccupied with and obsessed by their European origins, a great many Burghers found the adjustment to a situation in which Sinhala was the official language for administration and education far too traumatic. They felt alienated and preferred to emigrate to countries in which they could feel more at home. As the president of the Dutch Burgher Union explained,

We are being gradually out-numbered by non-Burghers who find it more easy than we do to attain proficiency in Sinhala, and in Tamil too, so that in competition with them the scales are heavily weighted against us. The desire to emigrate, therefore, to lands where we can still freely use the English language and thereby perhaps find suitable employment, is a natural one.[34]

The "Sinhala Only Bill," which made Sinhalese the official language of the country, placed the Burghers in a dilemma, for it compelled them to choose between English and Sinhalese, "either to relegate the former to the background and adopt Sinhalese as their first language, or to quit Ceylon for a country where English had the first place." A large number chose the latter.

The older members of the community disliked the idea of leaving a country endeared to them by various associations. . . . But those who had youthful sons and daughters felt that the interests of their children would be endangered if they remained. . . . A way of escape offered itself; Australia was willing to accept them as suitable emigrants, and they thankfully seized the opportunity to make new homes "down under."[35]

These developments in recent decades have resulted in important changes in the attitude of the Burgher community toward other ethnic groups in Ceylon. Conversely, the manner in which Sinhalese and Tamils perceive the Burgher community is today significantly different to what it was in the early decades of this century.

In the days of the *raj* the Dutch Burghers, in particular, found the company of Sinhalese and Tamils socially embarrassing. In pursuing social equality with fellow "Europeans"—British officials, planters, and merchants—the Burghers wished little contact with other local commu-

---

[34] *JDBU*, **51**, Pts. 1–2 (1961), Presidential address to DBU by E. S. Brohier.
[35] R. A. Kriekenbeek, "Emigration and the Burghers," *JDBU*, **52**, Pts. 3–4, 1962.

nities. There was, as a result, little social intercourse between the Burghers as a community and non-Burgher Ceylonese. Based on notions of racial superiority, they also looked down on Burgher marriages with Sinhalese and Tamils. This aloofness became dysfunctional after independence, and in the last two decades marked changes have become evident in Burgher attitudes. Social intermixing is now commonplace and uninhibited. Marriage with non-Burghers is now condoned by the Burgher community as a realistic strategy for social acceptance. Indeed, hypergamous unions by Burgher working girls of the city with affluent and educated Sinhalese and Tamils have become a popular mobility device for a community now stripped of many of its early avenues of upward social mobility. These changes reflect an awareness—albeit a late one—that the old order is no more and that the future of the Burgher community lies in its capacity to adapt to new demands. This involves primarily a shift away from the obsessive pursuing of a European identity and toward becoming a Ceylonese community in every sense of the word.

This change in Burgher attitudes is paralleled by the new way in which the Sinhalese and Tamils perceive the Burgher community. Under British rule the Burghers were looked up to and emulated by other communities in Ceylon. After all, they were "Europeans" like the ruling race and were closer to the British people than any other local group. Their conspicuous facility with the English language, apart from giving them better jobs, made the Burghers seem different and superior in the eyes of Sinhalese and Tamils. Not so today. The increasing reaction against Western influence in Ceylon has meant that there is no longer any special advantage in being a Burgher, either for social status or employment. On the contrary, their fair skin color and Westernized life style are now a hindrance, for they enable other communities to see the Burghers as an alien people with an alien subculture. Thus, although 50 years ago it would have been prestigious for a Sinhalese or Tamil to be married to a Burgher—for it was, in a sense, a means of getting closer to the ruling race—such unions are disapproved of today by the larger communities. Partly as a result of recent middle class Buddhist revivalism, marriage with Burghers is looked down on by the Sinhalese; the Burghers are considered a Christian people with a life style incompatible with a Buddhist ethos.

Fortunately, attitudes have still not hardened enough to be irreversible, and there is still hope that the Burghers will get back to more active participation in national life. The Sinhalese and the Tamils are sufficiently divided among themselves to offer no physical threat to the Burghers in the foreseeable future. Their numerical insignificance at least means that the Burghers are not an economic threat to these larger communities. Besides, there is a long tradition of religious tolerance in Ceylon which I feel will permit the Burghers to remain Christians in a largely Buddhist and Hindu nation. If, however, they wish to preserve their ethnic identity—and the evidence is that they do, despite frequent violations of endogamy—they can no longer succeed along the old lines of keeping themselves aloof from the *hoi polloi*. They will have to make concessions to the larger community, notably by acquiring a high degree of proficiency in the official language, *Sinhala*. By this means they could also remove that linguistic barrier that still to some extent separates the Burgher community from the rest of Ceylon. They will also have to join other communities and actively participate in efforts at economic development of the nation, for in the last analysis economic development is a *sine qua non* for racial harmony.

CONCLUSION

Although small in numbers, the contribution of the Burghers to public life in Ceylon has been considerable. Among the great Ceylonese lawyers, judges, engineers, doctors, and civil servants many Burgher names stand out, and in the educational and cultural spheres their contribution has been equally great. Their achievements, however, have been facilitated by the Westernized ethos characteristic of Ceylon. Changes that have taken place in Ceylon over the last two decades have made the future of the Burgher—with his Western orientations—uncertain. It is this that has led to a mass exodus of Burghers to Australia. But only a minority can hope to have this escape from the stresses and strains of unwelcome social change. The majority have no choice but to go on living in Ceylon. They are now at the crossroads. It is clear that if the Burghers are to cease being a marginal group and are to re-enter the mainstream of public life in Ceylon they need to make a deliberate adjustment to the changes that are taking place around them. They will have to achieve a sense of community with other ethnic groups in Ceylon.

SELECTED BIBLIOGRAPHY

Arasaratnam, S., *Ceylon*. Englewood Cliffs, New Jersey: Prentice-Hall, 1964.

Ludowyk, E. F. C., *The Modern History of Ceylon*. London: Weidenfeld and Nicolson, 1966.

Mendis, G. C., *Ceylon Under the British*. Colombo: The Colombo Apothecarien, 1952.

Smythe, P. R., *A Ceylon Commentary*. London: Williams and Norgate, 1932.

Wriggins, W. H., *Ceylon: Dilemmas of a New Nation*. Princeton, New Jersey: Princeton University Press, 1960.

Elizabeth P. Wittermans
University of Hawaii

CHAPTER FIVE

THE EURASIANS OF INDONESIA

The racially mixed minority discussed here had its origin in colonial
and precolonial times in the Indonesian archipelago which, at the time
of the first contact, had no collective name. Even in the seventeenth and
eighteenth centuries, when the feet of the Dutch East India Company
were firmly embedded in Indonesian soil, there was no political entity
of that name. There was only an aggregate of thousands of islands, some
economically and culturally more important than others.

In 1800 the United East India Company expired and the Indonesian
archipelago became a Dutch possession, named *Nederlands Indie* (Netherlands India). It remained a Dutch colony—with the exception of a
brief period of British rule between 1811 and 1816—until December
1949, when the Dutch surrendered their colonial power to the Indonesians.

Physical and Social Variety

One problem that confronts all students of mixed-descent groups is how
to compress the many variations into a workable category without re-
sorting to empty stereotypes. Among the Eurasians, too, the combination
of numerous racial and social variables has produced a nearly endless
number of types. On the Indonesian side the physical characteristics may
range from the light skin and straight hair of the Sundanese of West
Java or the Menadonese of northern Celebes to the dark skin and curly

or kinky hair of Melanesians and Polynesians inhabiting the eastern islands of the Indonesian archipelago. The European component shows an equally wide variety between the dark Mediterranean type and the blue-eyed blonds of northern Europe. The following mixed unions occurred: European-Indonesian; European-Eurasian; Eurasian-Eurasian; and Eurasian-Indonesian. In addition, the Europeans, Eurasians, and Indonesians had sexual relations with the Chinese, Arabs, and other ethnic groups. The cosmopolitan population of Indonesian port cities also included freed slaves and former Portuguese servants of Indian and Philippine racial backgrounds as well as a number of Japanese soldiers in the service of the East India Company.

The racial mixture, as such, was of less importance to the status, role, power, and life style of the individual Eurasian than the status of both his parents, and particularly his father, within the structure of the colonial society in which he lived; for example, the legal offspring of a Dutch father and a non-Dutch mother, whatever her racial or national category, was socially and legally considered Dutch. This was specifically stated in the 1842 law on Dutch nationality. The offspring of an Indonesian or Chinese father and a Dutch mother, a rare phenomenon in the colonies, likewise assumed the father's nationality. Although the children, in both cases, were Eurasians, their legal status and social position were vastly different. Much depended on the climate of opinion both in the mother country and in the colony at a given time, but the degree of broadmindedness of the individual Eurasian's immediate environment also played an important role. These spatial-temporal elements can best be described sequentially.

Initial Stage of Racial and Cultural Encounter

Although little is known about this first phase of a continuing intercultural meeting, it is certain that sexual unions between Europeans and Indonesians began with the arrival of western merchant ships in the archipelago. In 1596, four ships of the first Dutch trading company in the East sailed into the port of Bantam, a century after the Portuguese had reached the Orient.

This first stage, when white merchants and adventurers came into contact with the native population, was one of casual encounter. Whatever children the sexual unions of this period may have produced were unintentional and incidental. They were, however, the beginning of a steadily growing category of people of mixed European and Oriental descent. Another characteristic of this first encounter was that both sexual partners belonged to the lower fringes of their respective societies.

Eurasians During the Tenure of the Dutch East India Company

Although casual encounters between visiting sailors, soldiers, and adventurers, on the one hand, and indigenous women of easy morals, on the other, continued from the sixteenth century on, at the same time a steadily growing community of Eurasians of accepted social standing had been forming. Together with the Dutch merchants and the few Dutch women who had accompanied their husbands or fathers to the East, these Eurasians were the first of a colonial elite. At that time, however, Dutch influence in the archipelago was still unofficial.

The growth and nature of these colonial communities may be seen as a response to the needs of a struggling group of Dutchmen abroad. Far removed from the warm, but often stifling, ties of kinship and local community and surrounded by foreigners, many of whom they did not trust, there was a pressing need for women and relaxation and also for friends and trusted personnel. This was true not only of the Dutch in Indonesia but also in Ceylon, India, Malacca, and other places where the East-India Company conformed to local custom rather than to the patterns of their home environment.

The difference between these two modes of behavior drew the attention, and sometimes indignation, of visiting Dutchmen. A Dutch physician in the service of the Company, who made five trips to the Indies during the seventeenth century, was representative of those who found the people of mixed blood offensive:

> East-Indian women are the ones that were born in East-India of Dutch parents. These are commonly called *liblabs* children because there is something wrong with most of them. *Kastiesen* are the ones born of a Dutch father and a *Misties* mother, and these come closest to the Dutch women. *Mistiesen* are the children born of a Dutch father and a black mother.[1]

Liblab, or more frequently *liplap,* is even today used as a derogatory term for Eurasian or local-born Dutch. The term *lipper* is also sometimes used. The origin of these terms is unknown. Various stereotypes of the Eurasians are mentioned in the literature. The same writer describes the Eurasians as follows:

---

[1] Nicolaus de Graaff, *De Oost-Indise Spiegel,* 1703, as quoted in E. du Perron, *De Muze van Jan Companjie.* Bandoeng: A. C. Nix, 1948, pp. 111–117.

These women, particularly the *Kastiesen* and *Mistiesen*, are generally . . . so drunk with wealth, pride, pleasure, and luxury that they do not know how to behave themselves. . . . Particularly those born in the Indies are unable, or better yet too lazy, to raise their own children. Almost as soon as they are born they are ordered into the care of a wetnurse, a slave prostitute or someone among her own slave women who nurse them and raise them.[2]

In later centuries the difference in life styles between the colonies and the mother country became increasingly evident, often with dismay and criticism. The alleged laziness of Eurasians, their dependence on servants, their speech, and the display of wealth, all continued to color the Dutch image of Eurasians.

From de Graaff's account there was already at that time a "colonial Dutch" community which constituted not only Dutch men and women but also Eurasians. The values and customs of this community were almost diametrically opposed to those of the middle-class Dutch in Holland. Colonial society, also highly stratified, ranged from Dutch high functionaries to various ethnic and socioeconomic levels down to the slaves and former slaves. Most of the latter came originally from India and the Philippines.

The Eurasians as an Ethnic Community

During the first century of the Dutch presence in Indonesia personal contacts were largely limited to those between merchants, traders, middlemen, and suppliers of various needs in a few port towns. It did not take long, however, for the Dutch merchants to realize that in order to maintain a steady flow of commercial products of marketable quality it was necessary to control the production. This resulted in further penetration by the Dutch into the interior of Java and the Spice Islands and contacts with a greater variety of people were made possible. On one level they dealt with members of the Javanese nobility; on another the casual encounters typical of port cities continued. Some young Dutch men, however, were not interested in casual encounters with prostitutes but wanted more stable unions. The East-India Company discouraged, and at times forbade, her officers and merchants to marry natives or "mestizos." In the seventeenth century Europeans married to non-Europeans were denied repatriation,[3] although in the Moluccas (adjacent

---

2 The delegation of childrearing to servants remained a frowned-upon feature of colonial family life.

3 For this section I have freely used A. van Marle's carefully documented article: "De

islands) the rules on interethnic marriage were more liberal. There the Company's servants were explicitly allowed to marry non-Europeans provided they were Christians.

In spite of the obstacles to inter-racial marriages, such unions occurred in steadily growing numbers. One reason was the surplus of European men. In 1880 there were only 471.6 European women per thousand men; in 1890 the ratio was 635 European women per thousand males; in 1945 the proportions were about equal.

In the census of 1905, which did not include members of the armed services (who as a rule were not permitted to marry local women anyway), 11 mixed marriages were listed per 1000 men of marriageable age, with regional differences ranging from six in East Java to 100 in the Moluccas. The percentages rose sharply after 1905 until in 1925 an overall average of 27.5 percent was reached. This is the more significant if we take into account the rising number of European women who arrived in the colony in the twentieth century. Probably as a result of this influx the percentage of European men concluding mixed marriages decreased by 1940 to 20 percent, more than 4 percent of which were with Chinese women.

Who were these European men who married non-European women? In 1930 about two-fifths of them were "import Dutch." This trend was even more pronounced on the outer islands. In 1929 almost half of all Europeans on the islands outside Java and Sumatra married non-European women. Most mixed marriages occurred between representatives of the working class, which was particularly true for the non-European women. Some Dutch men, however, married women of the Javanese nobility, and a few European aristocrats married non-European women.

Although in most cases the mixed marriages took place between European men and non-European women, the reverse also occurred, especially in the latter part of the nineteenth century and in the twentieth century, when more and more Indonesian men were educated in the Netherlands.

Concubinage. Much more numerous than the legal forms of marriage were the casual sexual unions and quasi-conventional concubinage. The restrictions on marriage in the Indies for members of the armed forces and other servants of the Company were factors in the rise of concubinage. It is important to note that in Southeast Asia customs regarding marriage and other sexual unions have always been liberal.

Groep der Europeanen in Nederlands-Indie, iets over ontstaan en groei" (The Group of Europeans in Netherlands India, some data about its origin and growth), *Indonesie*, **V**, 97–121; 314–341; 481–507 (1951–1952).

This often created clashes between the religious and social norms of the Dutch, on the one hand, and more pressing social forces, on the other, or between the ideal and the real. In spite of official disapproval, however, the conditions in the early days of the East-India Company facilitated the growth of concubinage as an institution. By the middle of the nineteenth century the military authorities faced the situation realistically and allowed concubinage in the barracks. In 1888 almost one-fourth of the European members of the Dutch East Indies Army lived in concubinage. Even in 1915 the proportion remained the same, whereas only one-tenth were legally married. The first attempts at curtailment of concubinage in the barracks were made in 1913 as a result of social pressures. Later the concubines disappeared from the barracks, although not from the scene.

Another locus of generally accepted concubinage was the plantation. Far away from the urban centers were the tea, sugar, and rubber plantations where lonely young Europeans frequently lived in concubinage with girls from the surrounding native villages. According to one source, in 1902 about 90 percent of all unmarried men over 18 lived with concubines.[4] Most of the children born of these unions were not legitimized. According to popular belief, they "disappeared into the kampong (native village)." In quantitative studies of the Eurasian group these descendants of the Dutch are usually ignored.

These developments resulted in a hierarchically structured Eurasian community with a variety of social norms and attitudes. Although the Dutch merchants and officials still occupied the top, more and more Eurasians achieved positions in the civil administration, especially in the second half of the nineteenth century. The establishment of a colonial administrative system entailed the creation of a large number of civil servants in middle positions. At first these positions were not open to local-born Dutch or Eurasians because the training for such posts was available only in The Netherlands. After a protest action in 1848,[5] however, the local-born Europeans were given better opportunities. The number of primary schools rose sharply. Plans for the establishment of schools for girls and of vocational schools were also made.

The number of better educated, socially more prominent Dutch men who married Eurasian women grew. Their children, Eurasians too, usually received a good education. Many were sent to Holland for higher education and returned as civil administrators, officers in the Netherlands Indies Army, or as doctors, engineers, teachers, and the like.

---

4 Quoted in van Marle, *op. cit.*, 486.
5 Dr. I. J. Brugmans, *Geschiedenis van het Onderwijs in Nederlandsch-Indië* (History of Education in Netherlands India). Groningen: J. B. Wolters, 1938, 83, 147.

Although growth of the Eurasian community made its position more secure, it was also through better education and closer ties with The Netherlands that the Eurasians achieved a greater awareness of the hierarchy in a colonial society and their own ambivalent position within this particular one. This inevitably led to dissatisfaction. The differential rate of pay and the greater privileges of the Holland-educated were factors contributing to their discontent. Newly acquired notions of equality and democracy began to fan a protest movement, unusual for a people brought up to respect authority.

A first attempt at organization of Eurasian forces for a general nationalistic movement was made in 1912 by E. F. E. Douwes Dekker,[6] when he established the *Indische Partij* (Party of the Indies). The goal of this party was the abolishment of Indonesia's colonial status and the creation of an independent state under combined Eurasian and Indonesian leadership. As could be expected, the Dutch colonial government took a negative view of these aspirations and terminated the activities of the *Indische Partij*.

The growth of Indonesian political awareness and economic competition gave a second effort to organize Eurasians an entirely different character. In 1919, one year after the *Volksraad* (People's Council), a semirepresentative body, had been set up, the *Indo-Europees Verbond* (Indo-European League), abbreviated IEV, was established as a political organization, specifically aimed at the representation and protection of the Eurasian community. This focus became a controversial issue. Many Dutch people, local-born as well as *totoks*,[7] were unpleasantly affected by the separation of the racially mixed Eurasians from the general category of Dutch or Europeans generally.

The upper layer of the Eurasians in particular were against this turning away from the Dutch with whom they had always identified.[8] For that top group there was no reason for a separate identity. Many of their members had full-blooded Dutch spouses, and they themselves or their children had received an education in The Netherlands or local training comparable to a Dutch education. Their incomes and life style were usually on a par with those of the "import" Dutch. Even if they did experience some form of discrimination, it would be of a minor de-

---

[6] For a discussion of this interesting personality, see Paul E. van der Veur, "E.F.E. Douwes Dekker: Evangelist for Indonesian Political Nationalism," *J. Asian Studies*, 17, 551–566 (August 1958).

[7] *Totok* is the generic term for the white "import" Dutch, comparable to *haole* in Hawaii and *pakeha* in New Zealand.

[8] Several Eurasians in this category were members of the *Vaderlandsche Club* (Fatherland Club), a conservative, strongly Holland-oriented political party whose members were predominantly "import" Dutch.

gree that could conveniently be ignored. Moreover, they did not wish to be identified with the "little Indos," marginal Eurasians of high racial visibility, low education, and small resources, whose life style resembled that of Indonesian villagers more than of the Dutch in Holland.

In spite of the lack of support from those Eurasians qualified for leadership but unwilling to identify with the Eurasians' struggle, the IEV was successful in bringing about better salaries for their group, although still lower than those of "import" Dutch.

The peculiar position of the Eurasian community in Indonesia is illustrated by the changing policies emanating from IEV leaders. Poised as they were between the more prominent Holland-born Dutch, and the far more numerous and culturally more deeply rooted Indonesians, their insecurity resulted in fluctuating aims. During the 1930's the IEV emphasized better living conditions not only for Eurasians but for all Europeans who regarded the Indies as their permanent home. Indeed, among the IEV members were a small number of Holland-born Dutch, many of them married to Eurasians, who regarded the Dutch East Indies as their new home country. Several Eurasian men, moreover, had Dutch-born wives who were no less active in committees and social work within the framework of the IEV.

On the other hand, being Dutch citizens entailed one great disadvantage: the exclusion from land ownership in Indonesia. The Eurasians living outside the cities in particular felt this as a curtailment of their rights in their land of birth. Indeed, before the agrarian law of 1870 declared Indonesian land inalienable several Dutch and Eurasians, as well as some Chinese, British, and other non-Indonesians, already owned land. The agrarian laws and regulations were meant to protect the Indonesians against rapacious foreign businessmen. For the Eurasians, however, owning land did not mean the chance to establish plantations and other commercial enterprises, although several of them did have small agricultural holdings. It meant living the good life of a landed gentleman, hunting and fishing and having a spacious home with gardens and orchards. It meant the kind of rural life that can be lived with dignity even if there is little cash available. For the "little Indo" the alternative was scurrying around for a living in the city slums.

The Eurasians During the War Years[9]

Dutch citizenship entails Dutch military service. Therefore Eurasians fought together with their Holland-born colleagues against the Japa-

---

[9] Some details in this section derive from my own observations during World War II.

nese. They filled the prison camps and died in a war which the Dutch in the colonies had brought on themselves by declaring war on the Japanese immediately after the attack on Pearl Harbor.

It took the Japanese only three months to occupy all of the Indonesian archipelago. Much of their success was due to good organization and decisive action. Instant death in cases of resistance and disobedience, severe punishment for illegal acts, and constant vigilance enabled the Japanese to assert their power in spite of their relatively small numbers. Probably most effective, however, was their immediate division of the population on a racial basis. Japan's role of the "liberator" of colonies instantly brought about a dividing line between the Dutch and all others.

Soon another distinction was emphasized, the racial one between full-blooded Dutch and Eurasians. In 1942 the Japanese ordered a country-wide alien registration, at which time the "pure" Dutch were carefully separated from their mixed-blood descendants. Those who bore the physical characteristics of non-Western descent were issued identity cards that proclaimed them Eurasians. By the end of 1942 the women whose identification cards bore the label "Dutch" were required to register for the "protective camps," whereas those that bore the label of Eurasian could stay outside. Thus another rift in the presumed unity of the Dutch group was created. Women who had been friends or colleagues for years now found themselves at opposite sides of the barbed wire.

The Dutch citizens outside the camps did not starve to death, as did many inmates of the prisons and internment camps. Their problems were of a different kind. Although women in the camps suffered collectively and tried to cope with their problems collectively, those outside were more exposed and lonely. They were usually deprived of their husbands and other male relatives as well as sources of money. Many were forced to move out of their houses, and such evictions occurred more and more frequently. The ministers and priests they once turned to for help were replaced or the churches were closed. Schools were also closed. Many good friends were imprisoned either at the beginning of the occupation or at various times between 1941 and 1945. Hence the normal sources of moral and social support were cut off at a time when they were needed most.

The Eurasians had been set apart from the "pure" Dutch because it was hoped that they could be won over to the Japanese cause.[10] There

---

[10] D. van Velden, in her *De Japanse Interneringskampen voor Burgers gedurende de tweede wereldoorlog* (The Japanese internment camps for civilians during World War II), Groningen: J. B. Wolters, 1963, has a separate chapter on the noninterned citizens from which many data in this section have been derived.

was abundant propaganda toward that end, coming not only from the Japanese in official statements and exhortations but also from Indonesian leaders as well as Eurasians willing to cooperate with the Japanese. There had always been a small minority of Eurasians who felt discriminated against under the Dutch colonial system, many of whom had been sympathetic toward Indonesian nationalism long before the Japanese occupation.[11] This category of Eurasians was sometimes called "belanda haters" [a part-Indonesian, part-Dutch term meaning those who hate the (import) Dutch].

In 1943 a Japanese statement by Major-General Yamamoto was directed specifically to the Eurasians. They were told that in the future they were to be considered part of the Indonesian population. They could now work, send their children to Indonesian schools, and join the Co-Prosperity Sphere of Greater East Asia. Since they wanted young male Eurasians out of the way, many of them were pressed into service in agricultural settlements established in several areas. Some of these were penal institutes for youths who were suspected of having worked in underground movements. Others had the character of pauper settlements.[12]

Added to all these pressures was the Eurasians' fear of the Indonesians. Individually, many Eurasians had Indonesian friends, relatives, and trusted servants, but as a group they saw the Indonesians as an outgroup. This implied that they could never be sure that the Indonesians would not make use of the Eurasians' helpless situation to harm them in a variety of ways. Actually, few cases of abuse were recorded during the period of Japanese control. There had been bands of terrorists and robbers in Bantam and the outskirts of Djakarta in the early days of the occupation, but the decisive way in which the Japanese dealt with such actions soon ended them. When the war was over and the Japanese had been disarmed, acts of terrorism flared up against the Dutch and Eurasians alike during the *bersiap* (Indonesian: prepare—i.e., for bloody revolt) period, which preceded and later merged with the actual Indonesian struggle for independence.

One problem was what to do with the children at a time when all values seemed to be reversed or diluted. Although Eurasian children could go to Indonesian schools, many mothers hesitated to send them,

---

11 See especially J. Th.Koks, *De Indo*. Amsterdam: Dissertation, Univ. of Amsterdam, 1931, *passim*.

12 For more details see D. van Velden, *De Japanse Interneringskampen voor Burgers gedurende de tweede wereldoorlog* (The Japanese internment camps for civilians during World War II), 448–449.

not merely because few Eurasian children knew enough Indonesian to benefit from the instruction but because of the pro-Japanese, anti-Dutch propaganda that came with it. Some Japanese innovations were improvements, such as the daily morning exercises, gardening, and language teaching. New children's songs might emphasize the value of neighborhood groups, such as the widely known *ton, ton, ton, tonarigumi*,[13] but another popular song with a catchy refrain went, "*Hapuskanlah musuh kita, itulah Inggeris Amerika—Blanda djuga* (Let us wipe out our enemies, namely England and America—the Dutch too).

In 1944, faced with the choice between swearing a loyalty oath or going to prison, many Eurasian youths were locked up in the notorious *Glodok* prison in downtown Djakarta, where many of them died. For the mothers who had taught their sons loyalty to the Dutch cause these were crushing experiences. Even many of those who had signed the loyalty oath, feeling that a forced oath could not be considered binding, were captured and sent to prison. The constant decision making and the many conflicts of loyalty were perhaps most characteristic of the Eurasian problems outside the camps.

What made the general situation even more difficult to understand were the glaring differences in treatment of Eurasians in various places. In Djakarta Eurasian wives of interned Dutch men could remain outside the women's camps. In a city approximately 40 miles away, however, all wives of prisoners, whether Dutch, Eurasian, or Indonesian, were sent to the camp. At Surabaya, a port city, the attitude toward Europeans and Eurasians was initially much more lenient than in the rest of Java, but even there the situation changed as time went on.

For those fortunate enough not to be imprisoned, nor picked up by the *kenpeitai*,[14] the war years were a period of reinterpretation of many values and a discovery of creative talents. It was no longer degrading to do manual work nor to deal with Indonesians on an equal basis. Many women proved themselves to be expert cooks, seamstresses, painters, and slipper and toy makers. Before the war few Eurasian women could knit or crochet because the climate did not favor knitwear. However, a Japanese demand for knitted socks and a supply of cotton yarn suddenly brought out knitting talents. Soon knitting and crocheting became a necessary skill, because women now had to manufacture their own under-

---

[13] Patterned after the system in Japan, the occupied cities had been subdivided into (*tonari*) *kumi* or neighborhood groups of approximately 20 families headed by a *kumicho*, who had numerous duties such as distributing food.

[14] *Kenpeitai*, military police, a body feared because of its severe methods of investigation which included torture. Several Eurasian men and women died as a result of the *kenpeitai's* actions.

wear. This continued until some time after the war when machine-made clothing reappeared.

There is no doubt that the fears and problems of the war years produced closer ties among the Eurasians and others outside the camps. Most of these ties, however, dissolved when, after the war, husbands, relatives, and friends were released. Unlike the ex-prisoners and internees, those outside never organized themselves into associations that kept alive the shared experiences of the war years.

The Eurasians After the War

For the Eurasians insecurity and decision making did not end with the outcome of the war, although the early postwar years meant a reestablishment of their Dutch identity. Many Eurasian ex-P.O.W.'s—and many Ambonese who had served in the Netherlands Indies Army—had no time for recuperation because they were needed to guard and help the women and children, to rebuild transportation, and fight Indonesian terrorists. Most Eurasians visualized the postwar years as a continuation of what had occurred before, and they were ready to resume their prewar positions as buffers between the colonial powers and the Indonesian masses. However, there was no longer a colony after 1949, nor a dominion, nor any other form of politically dependent territory envisioned by many Dutch people. The Holland-born Dutch had a home country, however ravaged and impoverished, to which they could go after the war. The Indonesians, too, had their own country, now an independent Indonesia. Where did this leave the Eurasians?

When Indonesian revolutionary activities and pressure by the big powers resulted in the termination of Dutch colonial rule, it was the Eurasians who felt the full impact of this change. For them there was the choice between retaining Dutch citizenship and migrating to The Netherlands or opting for Indonesian citizenship and staying in Indonesia, neither of which could replace the loss of their true home, the Dutch East Indies. The former choice implied moving to a country most of them knew only from schoolbooks and films but whose attractive image had been widely diffused in the colonies for generations. The latter meant loss of status and greater insecurity but the chance of acquiring that long-desired hold on the land. The remaining leaders of the Indo-European League (some had died in prison camps, others had left for The Netherlands) urged its members to adopt Indonesian citizenship. Wertheim sees the clamor for land on the part of the Eurasians as a cry for help coming from the marginal man who feels threatened and hemmed in without prospects for the future and who hankers after a piece of land he can call his own.[15]

That the IEV changed so completely from its Dutch-centered policy to the other alternative indicates the existence of divergent viewpoints among its members. The Eurasians had always emphasized their Dutch descent and their loyalty to the Dutch throne. At the same time, they had laughed at the *totoks*, especially the newcomers. A well-defined set of values set the "Indies" Dutch apart from the Holland-born, a gap carefully nurtured rather than ignored. This cultural ideal encompassed such qualities as hospitality, generosity, close ties between real or classificatory kin members, body cleanliness, soft speech, and gentle manners, all of which were contrasted with the supposed stinginess and mercenary characteristics of the Dutch, their loud voices, rough manners, their drinking and swearing, their excessive cleanliness with regard to the house but not to the body, and whatever other stereotypes were used to set off the good qualities of the in-group. Leaving one's country of birth and moving permanently to another with a cold climate and a society whose values were not fully accepted was a difficult decision to make.

Not only the IEV leadership but many officials of the Dutch government, as well as others, suggested that Indonesian citizenship and a career in New Indonesia would be the best choice the Eurasians could make. It was, of course, not irrelevant that the postwar years were for The Netherlands a crucial time in which the country needed to regain strength after the German occupation. Some authors, strongly in favor of Indonesian citizenship for the Eurasians, were obviously misguided in their views of both the future of Eurasians in Indonesia and the psychological forces at work.[16]

At the Round Table Conference in 1949, which was decisive for all parties concerned, the heterogeneity of the Dutch in Indonesia was again demonstrated by the presence there of three distinct groups of representatives. One delegation represented both Holland-born and Indonesia-born Dutch (including Eurasians) from a number of organizations, in total about 40,000 members. This faction advocated a long period of transition within which Indonesia-born Dutch and Eurasians could decide whether they wanted to choose Indonesian citizenship. The second faction, representing the IEV, although agreeing with the need for a long option

---

15 W. F. Wertheim, *Het Rassenprobleem* (The race problem). The Hague: Albani, Vrij Nederland-reeks, n.d., p. 111.

16 W. F. Wertheim, *Het Sociologisch Karakter van de Indo-maatschappij* (The sociological character of Eurasian society), printed lecture, 1947, p. 16. Similarly, Justus M. van der Kroef, "The Eurasian Minority in Indonesia," *Amer. Sociol. Rev.*, **18**, 492, 493 (October 1953).

period, declared that they strongly favored Indonesian citizenship for Eurasians. The third faction represented the pro-Indonesian *Indo Nationale Partij* (Eurasian National Party) which claimed a membership of 300.[17]

These delegations were given a minor role in the proceedings, and on December 27, 1949, The Netherlands transferred sovereignty over Indonesia to the Federal Republic of Indonesia. All Dutch citizens born in Indonesia or resident there for at least six months before the date of transfer were given the opportunity to claim Indonesian citizenship within a period of two years after the transfer.

From here on we discuss the Eurasians no longer as a single category but as two distinct entities according to the choice they made.

The Eurasians Who Opted for Indonesian Citizenship

According to van der Veur's calculation,[18] the number of options amounted to 13,660 and involved approximately 35,000 individuals. Of this number about 800 were widows of Indonesian or Chinese origin whose husbands had been Dutch nationals. Another 1300 options were submitted by individuals born abroad. The remaining applicants were presumably Eurasians. Although this number, which represented less than 20 percent of the total number of Eurasians, was considered disappointing by Dutch officials, it constitutes a fair representation of the actual distribution of their significant relationships with the Dutch and Indonesians. If the Eurasians had faced the same choice in 1945, before the murders of the *bersiap* period and the imprisonment of all Eurasians in Java by the new Indonesian government, the number who chose Indonesia would undoubtedly have been larger.

As it was, the choice to "repatriate" to The Netherlands was far more attractive. The idealized image of Holland, so well known from a distance but so far only attainable by a few favored Eurasians on "European leave," provided a strong inducement. There was also the attraction of greater security afforded by a stable society. The Eurasians felt they could look forward to some kind of organized support in The Netherlands, something they were not at all sure Indonesia would provide. More important, however, must have been the social factor. Those who had social ties with the Dutch in Holland could be expected to choose the mother country. After five years of ever-increasing waves of repatriates it may be assumed that nearly everybody had friends or relatives in The

---

17 For more details see Paul W. van der Veur, "Eurasian Dilemma in Indonesia," *J. Asian Studies*, **20**, 45–60 (November 1960).
18 *Ibid.*, 56–59.

Netherlands. The social importance of having satisfactory relationships was evidently not realized by the Dutch authorities, who urged the Eurasians to opt for Indonesian citizenship.

That 20 percent of the eligible people were sufficiently motivated to go through the effort of rejecting Dutch citizenship and becoming a *warga negara Indonesia* (Indonesian citizen) is in fact surprisingly high. Who were these people? According to van der Veur, only 4072 women opted independently for Indonesian citizenship, compared with 9505 men.[19] Of the women 1696 were widows. The remaining women were young and unmarried. No intensive study has been made, however, of their occupations, their education, the status and racial backgrounds of their parents, and other factors pertinent to their choice. Therefore we can only speculate about their motivations.

Among the women the Indonesian and Chinese widows of Dutch citizens, because of their origin, had obvious reasons for choosing Indonesia. It is the more surprising that there were several elderly Indonesian widows of Dutch citizens who did evacuate to Holland in spite of the fact that they could not even speak Dutch.

Among the men important considerations must have been work opportunities in Indonesia, marriage to Indonesian women, their Indonesian mothers and other relatives, the existence of strong feelings of antagonism toward the Dutch, or simply love of Indonesia. Some men who had always sympathized with Indonesian nationalism must have felt that at this crucial time Indonesia needed them more than ever before. Others were persons thoroughly assimilated into Indonesian culture, which they considered preferable to what Holland had to offer. It was an act of courage when, in early 1947, a Eurasian journalist unfurled an Indonesian flag in a Dutch neighborhood in Djakarta. He was defiantly pro-Indonesian and willing to face ridicule and social ostracism for his conviction.

In 1953 Allard initiated a study of Eurasians who were citizens of the Republic of Indonesia.[20] The main focus of her research was on the question whether the Eurasians formed a separate ethnic community within the Indonesian framework. Her conclusion was that nowhere did the Eurasians form distinct cultural groups. There was free intermarriage with Indonesians, although rarely with Moslem men. Their customs and life styles did not differ from those of the Indonesian people.

A pertinent question is whether the new citizens found satisfaction in

---

[19] *Ibid.*, 57, 58.
[20] Elizabeth Allard, "Laporan tentang Penjelidikan Kemasjarakatan dari Golongan Indo-Eropah jang dilakukan di Bogor tahun 1953," *Bahasa dan Budaja*, **3** (April 1955); **3** (June 1955); **5** (October 1956).

the new state of Indonesia. In view of the number of people who applied
for reinstatement of their Dutch citizenship because they regretted their
earlier choice of Indonesian citizenship, it appears that many were not
satisfied. In 1959 2500 applications for Dutch citizenship had been received from Indonesian citizens, almost all of them Eurasians.[21] More
followed in subsequent years. Their total number grew to 22,000. In 1962,
when the western part of New Guinea finally became Indonesian (a
belated fulfilment of the promise to transfer full sovereignty over Indonesia to the Republic) 12,000 more chose to migrate to The Netherlands
instead of remaining on Indonesian soil.[22]

Again, in the absence of relevant studies, one may only speculate
why the Eurasians who remained in Indonesia had such a change of heart.
Some reasons seem obvious. The mounting economic and political problems that beset Indonesia were felt by all its citizens, but the Eurasians
were in a more vulnerable position than the native Indonesians because
they were regarded as second-class citizens. As early as 1951 the leader of
the pro-Indonesian *Indo Nationale Partij* protested against what he de-
nounced as discriminatory practices. What was most bitterly felt was the
fact that the new citizens had not been allowed to acquire land. Land
ownership had been one of the strongest arguments in favor of Indonesian
citizenship.

The gradual and general impoverishment brought about an increased incidence of theft, robbery, and extortion on the individual level
and a neglect of all services by the city government. It was a combination
of these factors that led many Eurasians to leave Indonesia. Many out-
spoken pro-Indonesian individuals—including the person mentioned
earlier, who raised the Indonesian flag in 1947—left the country. Today
there is an unknown number of Eurasians in Indonesia, probably mostly
Eurasian women married to Indonesian citizens.

The Eurasians Who "Repatriated" to The Netherlands

It should not be assumed that those who chose to remain Dutch citizens
and left for The Netherlands never regretted their choice. Around the
end of 1949 and the beginning of 1950, when the transfer of sovereignty
had been completed, a mass exodus from Indonesia reflected the panic
that caught thousands of Dutch people, including Eurasians.

---

[21] See van der Veur, *op. cit.,* 60.

[22] Data released by the *Centraal Comite van Kerkelijk en Particulier Initiatief* (Central
Committee of Church-oriented and Private Initiative), which coordinated the social
services given to all repatriates, at the occasion of the termination of its duties in
1969.

Yet, after a few years of experiencing the uncongenial Netherlands climate, the scarcity of jobs, housing, food, and almost everything else in a country scarred and weakened by war, many Eurasians were ready to return to Indonesia under the rule of Sukarno. The Dutch government, happy to see them go, even provided free passage to those who declared that they were "rooted in Indonesia." Most of these people, however, re-repatriated to The Netherlands in one of the subsequent waves of refugees. The case histories of some of these refugees showed that, once uprooted from the home environment, they would embark on a series of moves that even took some of them to foreign countries.

The Dutch government took her commitments seriously. The authorities had not expected that the number of Dutch citizens, including Eurasians, who repatriated between 1945 and 1969 would rise to 300,000 and would cost approximately 550 million dollars in government and private aid. However, they rose to the occasion and provided provisional housing, financial support, and welfare services. In 1954 the Minister of Social Welfare commissioned the *Instituut voor Sociaal Onderzoek van het Nederlandse Volk* (Institute for Social Research on the Netherlands Population) to start a research project on the social integration into Dutch society of the repatriates from Indonesia. Although the study was expected to provide guidelines for the activities of the government and private agencies involved, the emphasis was on basic research from which later specific applications could be derived.

The focus of this research was on all repatriates from Indonesia, not necessarily Eurasians. This broad base was useful because reorientation and integration problems were not confined to Eurasians. Data collection encompassed the following techniques: (a) an extensive questionnaire mailed to 3000 families; (b) 162 interviews with repatriates, usually in their homes and therefore also involving other members of the household; (c) interviews with a number of key persons in government and other agencies; (d) data collected from published sources; (e) personal observation and casual encounters.[23]

The project aimed at three areas of information: first, a breakdown of the mass of repatriates into distinct categories of sex, age, education, previous status, place of birth, and period of migration; second, some indication of their levels of integration[24]; and, third, an interpretation of the former in terms of the latter.

It was found that the following variables played a role in the general

---

[23] Data for this section derive either from the research report by J. H. Kraak, *De Repatriering uit Indonesie* (The repatriation from Indonesia), The Hague, 1958, or from field notes I took as a member of the research team, Government Printing Office.
[24] See S. N. Eisenstadt's concept of different levels of participation in *The Absorption of Immigrants*. New York: The Free Press of Glencoe, 1955.

process of adaptation: frustrations experienced in postwar Indonesia; the image and expectations of life in The Netherlands; the possibility of realizing these expectations in terms of the opportunities offered in The Netherlands; and the psychological and intellectual potential of the repatriates.

Confrontation with reality in The Netherlands proved to be a shock to many repatriates, particularly those who had occupied positions of relatively high status in the colonies. There was a painful gap between the attitudes of the Dutch population experienced earlier during "European leave" and those now displayed by immigration officials, housing and welfare agencies, and a host of people, including relatives, who had no use for refugees. Yet more than one-third of the respondents declared that the feeling of being finally "safe" offset such drawbacks as the climate, the obvious indifference of the host country, and monetary problems.

Instrumental Adaptation. The climate figured in 42 percent of the male responses and 35 percent of the women's answers as a serious disadvantage. This factor has to be seen in connection with the monetary problems (the lack of adequate clothing and heating) and the psychological *malaise* they experienced.

There was also ignorance of the existing bureaucratic requirements and benefits and of schools and job opportunities. Differences in food habits presented no serious problems because the Dutch and Eurasians in the colonies had become familiar with Indonesian food and Dutch food was known, if not always preferred, in Indonesia. However, depending on the residential area in which the repatriates had settled, ingredients were sometimes hard to obtain and rice was more expensive than potatoes. Some social workers, trying to teach Eurasians how to match meals and budgets, complained that the latter were unwilling to give up rice and Indonesian ingredients in spite of the higher prices. In a few cases Dutch neighbors complained about the smell of Indonesian cooking.

Some language problems were encountered by older persons of Indonesian descent and young children who had been brought up in an Indonesian-speaking environment. Moreover, there are variations between Dutch as it is spoken in The Netherlands (whether standard or one of several dialects) and the Dutch language spoken in Indonesia, which may range from a pidgin heard in marginal areas to grammatically and idiomatically correct Dutch pronounced in a slightly different tone of voice or with a different melody.[25]

---

[25] Similarly, Reinecke has pointed out the existence of a continuum of language types in Hawaii rather than just a "pidgin." John E. Reinecke, *Language and Dialect in Hawaii*. Honolulu: Univ. of Hawaii Press, 1969.

Problems of adaptation to the different foods and language were not considered serious by the respondents. Financial limitations, however, and the many disadvantages it entailed, in combination with the climate, were often cited as definite drawbacks.

Participation in the Network of Dutch Social Relations. Relatively few meaningful interrelations on an individual level seemed to exist between the repatriates and their hosts. There was significantly more interaction with relatives, friends, and acquaintances from Indonesia than with newly made Dutch acquaintances. On the associational level were formal ties with organizations that dealt with the former Dutch East Indies, such as the retirement foundation and the league of exinternees.

Participation in church activities was less advanced. Although most Dutch people in Indonesia, including Eurasians, were either Catholics or Protestants, their transfer to Dutch churches was less smooth than expected. Most newcomers were unfamiliar with the numerous churches in Holland that come under the general heading of "Protestant," nor did they realize the bureaucratic aspects of church membership, such as registration for the specific church of one's choice, transfer from one church to another, and, not the least of their complaints, the many contributions required. Remarks were also made about the cold, formal character of the churches, compared with the community feeling imparted by many smaller ones in the Indies.

Much more satisfactory, both in numbers and in the degree of successful adaptation, was their participation in the occupational system in The Netherlands. For those who had problems matching their qualifications (or lack of them) with the available job opportunities the government started vocational training courses.

Analyzing the repatriation as a whole, the researchers found that this particular meeting of cultures was characterized by the fact that repatriation constituted for both sides a necessity that was accepted without enthusiasm, by the similarity between the cultures of immigrants and hosts, and finally by the existence of a deep concern on the part of the home government with the cause of the immigration.

As a result of the unforeseen circumstances of this particular immigration there had been no planning in The Netherlands nor any selection, since they were all Dutch citizens. The wide range in socioeconomic and cultural backgrounds of the immigrants made collective measures less than effective. This was reflected in considerable variation in the degree of satisfaction about these measures and about the new situation the immigrants faced. A few instances of discrimination were reported, in most cases expressed in racial terms, but there was no widespread discrimination with regard to housing or work nor to associational and recreational areas. Neither were there reports of race riots or other forms of violence.

However, even the slightest evidence of discrimination or racial labeling was resented by the individuals concerned because they had always prided themselves on being Dutch. Some labels were applied innocently. Thus many Dutch people, unfamiliar with the legal and social differences between Indonesian nationals and Eurasian Dutch, sometimes referred to them as Indonesians, thereby unwittingly hurting their feelings. The label "Indo" also raised difficulties. It is usually applied to low-status Eurasians but can have a wider range. What the connotation was in the eyes of at least one author is illustrated by the following quotation:

> Members of the Indo group do not fill top positions. The Indo who does reach such a position can in fact no longer be regarded as belonging to the Indo group, although, seen biologically, he is of mixed descent.[26]

Identification and Common Value Orientation. Because of their different social backgrounds, the third level of integration, that of personal reorientation and identification with the new society, was not uniformly reached by the immigrants. More than half of the repatriates appeared to view their future in the new country with optimism. They accepted the actual situation and adapted to it the best way they knew. Although Holland-born repatriates had few problems on the instrumental and relational levels, they were often less successful in their reorientation toward the new Dutch society. This may have been the result of the keenly felt loss of their colonial status and its concomitant comforts of living.

Looking back on 25 years of intermittent migration from Indonesia and adaptation to Dutch society, we can best conclude this section by referring to the termination of the Central Committee for church-related and other private agencies concerned with the repatriates in 1969. This committee was dissolved because there was no longer a repatriation problem. Further assistance, if and when necessary, was to be provided by the existing social services and through regular channels. Although not all problems have been solved, nor is there any guarantee that no race problems will emerge in the future, the indications are that the absorption of these immigrants has so far progressed without major difficulties.

---

26 C. Veeneklaas, *Het Rassenconflict in de Opvoeding in Indonesie* (Racial conflict in Indonesian education), Mededelingen van het Nutsseminarium voor Paedagogiek aan de Universiteit van Amsterdam, no. 44. Groningen-Batavia: J. B. Wolters, 1949, p. 83.

The Eurasians in the Eyes of the Dutch

When looking for a composite image of Eurasians held by the Dutch up until the first part of the twentieth century, we can roughly distinguish three phases. The first, running more or less parallel with the period of the East India Company, is one of tolerance and indifference. The Eurasians were seen either as irresponsible and frivolous (the women) and incompetent (the men) or as a useful source of middle-level clerical workers. The children of Dutch citizens, if they were legitimate offspring, legally recognized or adopted, were usually given adequate treatment and education and regarded as Dutch, be it of a slightly inferior level.

The second phase could be characterized as one of growing moral responsibility on the part of the Dutch. Indonesia was a Dutch colony; therefore its inhabitants, and certainly the Eurasians, became part of the "white man's burden." This collective responsibility did not change the common man's image of Eurasians as indolent, irresponsible, incompetent offshoots of a worthy stem, as trustworthy middle-level clerical workers and skilled mechanics, or again as seductive, calculating women. At the same time, however, the feeling of being responsible gradually became strong enough for the Dutch government to establish more and better schools for the local-born Dutch citizens, thereby providing better opportunities for their social mobility. The armed services and colonial administration in particular became important channels for social mobility. The top officers in the East Indies Army were frequently of mixed descent, as were several high officials in the colonial administration.

A third phase occurred in the period between the two world wars, when large numbers of Dutch men and women went to the Dutch East Indies not only in the service of the colonial government but also as private entrepreneurs. This period could be characterized as one of Dutchification. Emphasis on Holland and on Dutch culture was evident throughout the colonial society. The sprawling country houses in their extensive gardens planted with tall trees and surrounded by hedges for maximum privacy were replaced by rows of neat brick homes with glass doors and windows, where people could sit on flower-bordered front porches. Some had make-believe fireplaces! Screened bedrooms began to replace the ample mosquito nets that once hung over the iron fourposters. Because the smaller houses in the paved city streets were warmer than the old-fashioned ones, some progressive Westerners installed air conditioning, which made further enclosure necessary. Dutchification implied decreased adaptation to Indonesian ways of life, and this resulted in a widening gap between the Holland-born and the local-born Dutch (including Eurasians). There was more concern with the correct pronunciation of Dutch and familiarity with typical Dutch idiom in schools. Eurasians who spoke with an "Indies" accent frequently became the butt of ridicule.

Moreover, with the growth of private enterprise and commerce, Dutch businessmen and bankers were in more frequent contact with their British colleagues. This undoubtedly influenced their interracial behavior. Contrary to their well-established position in the armed forces and colonial administration, few Eurasians were represented on the staffs of business houses, and some companies refused to permit their employees to marry Eurasian girls.

During the late thirties, the years preceding the German occupation of The Netherlands, the Dutch community in the Indies was more Dutch oriented than it had ever been since the early days of the East-India Company. Consequently the image of the Eurasians suffered. The more lower middle- and middle-class Dutch entered the colonial society, the more unfavorable became their image of the Eurasians.

The Eurasians in the Eyes of Indonesians

Unless they had been rejected by their Dutch fathers or were of unknown Dutch parentage, Eurasians belonged to the Dutch category as far as the Indonesians were concerned. This remained true even after they had opted for Indonesian citizenship.

Yet there is the question whether this was a favorable or unfavorable image. The answer can be given only in relative terms. Eurasians who had achieved a relatively high status in the Dutch colonial hierarchy were regarded with favor, probably because they usually had a better understanding of Indonesian norms and customs than the majority of Holland-born Dutch and were at the same time in a position to be useful. Conversely, if they occupied a low status within the European community and competed with the Indonesians for the same positions, their image would be less favorable. Low-status Eurasians in particular tended to cling to their Dutch nationality and to hold a low opinion of Indonesians, not unlike the attitudes of American poor whites toward Negroes. Such attitudes contributed to their unfavorable image in the eyes of Indonesians. The Indonesians might forgive a *totok* certain transgressions of the rules of good behavior, in view of the latter's ignorance, but not a Eurasian. One might say that Eurasians are Dutch in the eyes of Indonesians, but a familiar kind of Dutch, a familiarity which might breed, if not contempt, a lower evaluation and less tolerance. Eurasian girls have always been desirable marriage partners for westernized Indonesians and still are in present-day Indonesia.

Prospects

Depending on their backgrounds and the choices made, the future seems to hold the following possibilities for the Eurasians:

1. For those who repatriated to The Netherlands the most likely prospect seems to be one of complete integration into Dutch society. The absence of legal and social obstacles to intermarriage and the few problems encountered in the occupational sphere (mainly as a result of Holland's fast economic recovery and full employment after the war) make it only a matter of time before the assimilative and amalgamative process will be complete.

2. The 20 percent who originally opted for Indonesian citizenship have meanwhile largely reconsidered their choice and have settled in Holland. Those who have remained Indonesian citizens and are now living in Indonesia have shown evidence that their integration into Indonesian society will present no problems. Their number, however, is insignificant compared with the total Indonesian population of 120 million.

3. There are other possibilities for those who rejected Indonesian citizenship, yet are unwilling or unable to identify with Dutch culture. Several have turned their attention to the creation of a Eurasian or *mestizo* culture. The driving force behind this effort was, and still is, a Eurasian writer and former school teacher. Among his writings are several collections of humorous stories characteristic of "Indo" society. This particular genre, written under the pseudonym of Tjalie Robinson, has earned him a place among other writers concerned with a specific subculture, such as Damon Runyon or Erskine Caldwell. In these stories, written in a rich creole language, he has recreated a world forever lost but nostalgically remembered by many Eurasians. Nor did he stop there. He published and edited "the only Indo periodical in the world," *Tong Tong*,[27] which has been in existence for more than 15 years. The articles, illustrations, and other items are contributed largely by a faithful group of subscribers. These subscribers are mainly Dutch people from the former colony who now live in The Netherlands or in other countries.

In these writings it is possible to trace many "Indo" values. Although

---

27 *Tong Tong* (Indonesian), a wooden signal drum, formerly used in Indonesian villages.

rooted in Indonesian soil, and borrowing heavily from Indonesian culture, the values of this subculture are embedded in the life style of the Dutch in Indonesia. They encompass courage, and a fighting spirit, as exemplified by the Dutch East Indies Army, and a relaxed style of living in which good food and a fondness for music, sports, and dancing were important features, as were generosity, hospitality, and an interest in the spiritual world. Attempts have been made to keep this subculture alive in various cultural activities, the creation of "Eurasian" art forms, and the publication, in addition to *Tong Tong*, of a number of books dealing with various aspects of life in the Indies. The continuation, or resurrection, of this subculture has been valuable for many Eurasians in search of an identity. It has also produced an interesting literary genre, but because its characteristics derive from a bygone era there is little chance of its survival after the generation that was familiar with its qualities has passed on.

4. For those who rejected Indonesia and failed to find satisfaction in the Dutch or the Eurasian patterns of culture there was still another choice. Their names can be found among the many Dutch emigrants, including Eurasians, who yearly leave The Netherlands. They have a particular preference for tropical or subtropical climates and can be found, for example, in California, Hawaii, and Australia.

SELECTED BIBLIOGRAPHY

van der Kroef, J. M., "Indonesian Eurasian and His Culture," *Phylon*, **16**, 448–462 (December 1955).

van der Kroef, J. M., "The Eurasian Minority in Indonesia," *Amer. Sociol. Rev.*, **18** (October 1953).

van der Kroef, J. M., "Minority Problems in Indonesia: The Eurasian Minority," *Far Eastern Survey*, **24**, 168–169 (November 1955).

van der Kroef, J. M., "Colonial Novel in Indonesia," *Comparative Literature*, **10**, 215–231 (Summer 1958).

van der Veur, Paul W., "Eurasian Dilemma in Indonesia," *J. Asian Studies*, **20**, 45–60 (November 1960).

van der Veur, Paul W., "Eurasians in Indonesia: A Problem and a Challenge in Colonial History," *Southeast Asian History*, **9**, 191–207 (September 1968).

Wertheim, Willem F., *Indonesian Society in Transition*. The Hague: W. van Hoeve, 1959.

Dennis Hilary Gouveia

Guyana

CHAPTER SIX

THE COLOREDS OF GUYANA

On his third voyage to the Americas in 1498 Columbus is purported to have sailed along the coast of the Guianas, a region that consisted of what is now Guyana, Dutch Guiana (Surinam), and French Guiana (Cayenne), the northern areas of Brazil, and the eastern part of Venezuela. In spite of this early reconnaissance, the Guianas apparently did not appear to be enticing enough to provide an incentive for immediate Spanish settlement. It was left to the Englishman Sir Walter Raleigh and other enterprising English and Dutch sea captains to explore these coasts in their quest for El Dorado, the legendary golden empire. Despite their failure to find a city of gold, the returning Dutch and English explorers extolled the grandeurs of the area and it was only a matter of time before it was investigated for possible settlement.

Several unsuccessful plans were projected in the first decades of the seventeenth century, and subsequent Dutch, French, and British colonizing parties at first confined their activities to maintaining trading posts for bartering with the indigenous Americans. Gradually they established cotton, coffee, and sugar plantations and colonized the riverine and coastal regions. It was not until 1616 that a group of Dutch and English settlers, under Dutch leadership, founded a secure colony on an island in the estuary of Guyana's largest river, the Essequibo. Dutch colonies in Essequibo were later extended to Demerara and Bebice, the names of Guyana's second and third largest rivers. When the Dutch declared the Demerara region open to settlement, regardless of European national affiliation, there was an immediate influx of British settlers. This

103

flow of Englishmen continued for some time, with the result that by 1760 they were in the majority in Demerara. The Dutch, however, held the three colonies with more or less firmness, now yielding to England, now to France, until 1796, when during the French Revolution they were captured by a British fleet. The territory was restored to the Dutch in 1802, but in the following year it was retaken by Great Britain and re-mained British until May 26, 1966, when Guyana achieved political independence.

Guyana today is a green subtropical country, 83,000 square miles in area, on the northeast coast of South America. It is bounded on the north by the Atlantic Ocean, on the west by Venezuela, on the south and south-west by Brazil, and on the east by Surinam (Dutch Guiana). Although its geographical position suggests that it is a Latin American country, every other consideration underlines its affiliations with the British West Indies. When one speaks of the British Caribbean or of British West Indian societies, Guyana is included, since it shares a common historical and cultural heritage with most of the West Indian islands in general and the British West Indies in particular.

THE PEOPLE OF GUYANA

The importation of laborers from various parts of the world resulted in an ethnically heterogeneous population. In addition to immigrant laborers and the indigenous Amerindian population, there were genera-tions of Dutch, French, Scottish, and English planters who, by virtue of their dominant positions, were to leave a strong impression on the local culture. Their miscegenation with the slave and later populations resulted in a residual, "mixed" category within which distinctions are commonly made in terms of degree of mixture. The interweaving strands of several diverse cultures have greatly enriched the content of creole culture.[1]

A preliminary enumeration by the Population and Housing Census in 1970 shows that Guyana's population at that date was 714,233, an increase for the decade of almost 28 percent. Nearly half of these people are East Indians, a third are Africans, slightly more than one-tenth are

---

[1] *Creole* is a French word that has been adopted into the Guyanese and West Indian vocabularies. It is derived from the Spanish *criollo*, meaning native to the locality. It was originally used by those who regarded themselves and were regarded as Spanish to distinguish their own children from Negroes and Spanish newly arrived from Africa and Spain. This meaning has now been extended to refer to any item of local origin, separating it, on the one hand, from what has been recently imported from Europe, Africa, China, or India, and, on the other, from what is aboriginal.

Coloreds, and the remaining few are indigenous Amerindians, Portuguese, other Europeans, and other Asians. The percentages are presented in Table 5.

Table 5 Percentage Distribution by Racial Groups in Guyana, 1946 and 1962[a]

	1946	*1962*
East Indians (from India)	43.5	49.42
Negroes of African descent	38.2	31.7
Coloreds and other mixed peoples	10.0	12.2
Amerindians	4.4	4.6
Portuguese	2.2	1.2
Other Europeans	.7	.5
Chinese and other Asians	1.0	.6
	100.0	100.0
$N = $	375,701	602,640

SOURCE: Census of the Colony of British Guiana, 1946 and 1962.
[a] A comparison of the Census figures of 1946 and 1962 shows racial composition and trends over the 16-year period.

The first period of historical development dates from the colonization of Guyana by Europeans in the early 1600's through 1838, when emancipation brought an end to the Guyanese slave society. This period might be termed the pre-emancipation era, during which the social structure was rigidly divided into three "classes"—the dominant white European masters, the intermediate Coloreds, and the subordinate black slaves.

The second period, which can be termed the post-emancipation—pre-independence era, dates from 1838 through 1966, the year that Guyana became a nation. Freeing of the slaves in 1838 resulted in the introduction of East Indians, Chinese, and Portuguese into an already rigidly stratified society. The situation in the few years just before independence produced a strong independence movement and a rising nationalism which had far-reaching implications for an era of nationhood.

The population of Guyana around 1800 was composed of clearly differentiated categories of persons:

1. *Whites* who were either creole (i.e., those born in Guyana) or immigrants and were all free.
2. *Free Coloreds.*
3. *Free blacks.*
4. *Colored slaves* who, together with the free Coloreds, were all creoles.
5. *Black slaves*, subdivided into creoles and African immigrants.

Because of the great expansion that took place in the population during the exploitation of the Guyana colonies at the beginning of the nineteenth century, the proportion of African-born slaves was extremely high. From comparisons with British West Indian islands whose historical development has been similar it seems reasonable to estimate that the number of whites and free Coloreds was approximately equal. Colored slaves have been estimated as being about 10 percent of the slave population, an estimate slightly lower than that of free persons of color.

The Colored "Community"

Occupying a social position intermediate between the dominant white minority and the subjugated black majority were the Coloreds, or mulattoes, as they were frequently called at that time. The Colored community was clearly distinguishable from the white and black communities. The basis for this distinction was the racial factor, which, as we shall see, became in time the most important criterion used by society to establish social groups.

Within the colored group, shades of color was, for a long time, the most important attribute of individuals because it demonstrated "nearness to whiteness."[2]

The Colored population at this time included both slave and free sections, which, from rough estimates, seemed to be approximately equal in numbers. As slaves, one section of the Colored group was denied certain civil rights, such as giving evidence against free persons in a court of law, whereas free people of color were able to do so, a right they had just begun to enjoy. Politically, however, the free Coloreds were not allowed to vote or run for political office and were ever conscious of their inferior status in relation to the whites, even when they became more affluent. The free Coloreds were permitted to bear arms and join the militia under white officers. That this was allowed is significant in that it demonstrated the implicit faith of the white elite in these "mixed-bloods," which was based on the fact that the Coloreds believed themselves too "culturally white" to be aligned with the slaves.

Even though enjoying a privileged position, the free Coloreds were faced with few occupational choices. They were not needed on the plantations, since the slaves did all the menial work, and many professions

---

[2] Pat Robinson, "The Social Structure of Guyana," in *Co-op Republic-Guyana 1970*. Georgetown: Guyana Lithographic Co., June 1970.

were closed to them, even when they could have acquired the necessary education. Most of them migrated to "urban" areas, where they became small-scale retailers, sellers of agricultural produce, skilled workers, and dockworkers. They were never fully accepted by the whites and their only avenues of mobility were within their own group. Frequently, however, preferential treatment was accorded to Coloreds to create a buffer group between the whites and the large slave population. This became even more evident as emancipation drew near and the slaves became increasingly restless.

The Coloreds were in an unenviable position. Most of them accepted the evaluation placed by the whites on blackness and tried to dissociate themselves from the black slaves. Indeed, it would have been difficult for them not to have adopted this attitude. Slavery was not a desirable status, and it was in the individual's interest to demonstrate his "cultural whiteness," since "blackness" meant degradation and subjugation. Thus consciousness of status and the desire to maximize it were typical of both sections of the Colored population; the free Coloreds unsuccessfully petitioned for increased civil and political rights, whereas the slaves sought their freedom in order to acquire the legal status of persons. Acculturation by adoption of white behavior and institutions was a prominent aspect of this preoccupation with improvement of status for Colored males and contributed to the great emphasis they laid on their differentiation as a group from black people, whether slave or free. This was clear evidence of cultural differences being confused with racial difference.

Acculturation for the Colored slaves was facilitated by plantation owners at a technical level by the traditional practice of employing them as estate craftsmen or domestics and of keeping them out of field gangs. In this way Colored slaves enjoyed greater opportunities for purchasing their own freedom than the majority of their black counterparts. Free persons of color often owned land and slaves, mainly by inheritance from their white progenitors. Some free Coloreds who had enjoyed education and training at their fathers' expense were also to be found acting as lawyers and accountants or in other clerical professions. However, the social exclusiveness of the white population served as a deterrent to free Colored males entering the medical profession. There were also no Colored overseers or managers on plantations owned by whites.

The free Colored was always on the defensive to prove his "cultural whiteness," to demonstrate that he had left behind the despised cultural attributes of the slave, hence of slavery. This was clearly evident in the harshness of free Colored owners toward their black slaves. Such treatment could be regarded as expressing, in exaggerated form, the opposition between the free person and the slave as well as between the Colored and the black. The Colored sought to make evident his "whiteness" by demonstrating the degree to which he had acquired the cultural attributes of free men, which meant the cultural attributes of men who were white.

Preoccupation with status among the Coloreds, as would be expected, expressed itself preeminently in patterns of mating and association. As I have already pointed out, free Colored women preferred concubinage with white men to marriage with free men of their own complexion, even when the latter enjoyed higher economic standings.

As an aspect of their aspirations to assimilate with the whites and dissociate themselves from the blacks, both slave and free Coloreds emphasized kinship with their white lines of descent and tended to deny and repudiate their black ancestry. There are many accounts of Colored slaves holding their black mothers responsible for their own slave status and in this way vindicating their white fathers and rationalizing preference for the white line. This behavior was to continue on into contemporary Guyanese society. Among the free Coloreds motivations were similar. Their desire to adopt white culture and thus raise their social status is indicated by the fact that they constituted the largest group represented in public worship, in proportion to their numbers, and by the greater interest taken in European cultural developments that carried prestige value, such as literature, than was usual among the creole whites.

The utility of this assimilation of white culture by the Coloreds was limited, however, by custom, which at this period ruled out the possibility of social equality; for example, competition between white and Colored women could not exist because of their marked social differences. White women accepted the fact that free Colored women dressed with greater elegance than they did themselves without any desire to compete. That white women could rest assured that Colored women could not threaten their status was readily evident, for although rigorous social taboos on extramarital sexual relations were imposed on white women they were quite friendly toward free Colored women who were the concubines of their kinsmen.

When it became certain that emancipation would soon be a reality, the whites were forced out of sheer necessity to win the

. . . alliance of at least some of the free Coloreds, in case the restlessness of the slaves, excited by rumors of coming freedom, should break out into open revolt.[3]

---

[3] F. R. Augier et al., *The Making of the West Indies*. London: Longmans, Green, 1960, p. 168.

Coloreds, frustrated by being denied entry into the white society, were forming alliances with the slaves to upset the existing social structure, as was forcefully demonstrated by the Haitin experience. The fact that the Coloreds did not unite "en masse" to overthrow the white power structure was due to the influence of the premium placed on "whiteness," a factor that effectively segmented the Colored society. Both their increase in prosperity and their token inclusion in white society proved effective in preventing any concentrated Colored attack.

Guyanese Society in the Slavery Era

The three main social sections of the population, defined primarily by legal status as "free with full civil rights," "free with limited civil rights," and "unfree," were composed in the main, but not universally, of persons who differed also in race and color. Thus the whites were all free but were internally differentiated in terms of status and power; free persons with limited civil rights were in the main Colored but included some blacks; the "unfree" were predominantly black but included some coloreds.

Guyanese society under a slavery system also demonstrated the extent to which, and the ways in which, the three principal sections were differentiated culturally; that is, by their adherence to different institutions. The whites, the free Coloreds and blacks, and the slaves differed from one another in their religious observances and concepts, their legal and political institutions, education, kinship and mating patterns, family organization, property rights, division of labor, language, occupations and technology, community organization, recreation and folklore, and general value systems. In effect, the population of Guyana at this period was culturally pluralistic.

From the description of Guyana in the slavery era it can be seen how Guyanese society was being polarized between whiteness at one end and blackness at the other. Thus whiteness and blackness in Guyanese slave society involved more than physical characteristics. The social and economic dominance of the whites began to be translated at an early stage into cultural dominance. This helps to explain why the Colored group sought to accentuate its whiteness and deny its blackness, for African biological and cultural heritage was equated with subordinate status. The African tribes had brought with them their diverse native cultures but were never allowed to exert any pervasive influence on the dominant white (European) culture.

POST-EMANCIPATION-PRE-INDEPENDENCE PERIOD
(1838–1966)

Invariably it was the people of color who filled the top positions next
to the whites, for skin color continued to be a powerful determiner of
status. Negroes, Coloreds, and English-speaking whites all came to share
a common conception of the Guyanese colonial society, one in which
"cultural whiteness" became equated with superiority and things African and "black" were little valued. All the refinements associated with
"English" culture became status symbols and their successful acquisition
demonstrated the individual's "cultural whiteness." For the Coloreds,
especially, the demonstration of "cultural whiteness" was seen by them
as an important contribution to their efforts for inclusion in white society.

The Colored group was poised uneasily between the white aristocrat
and the black "proletariat." For long a privileged group, even during
the slave period, many were highly educated and came to occupy important positions in society and the government bureaucracy. Again,
however, their position was partly defined in terms of color, and since
they themselves accepted the values on which color discriminations were
based they emphasized even the smallest color differences among themselves rather than their own common identity. When they demanded
consideration, they did so on the premise that they were English in all
but color. This meant that the Colored community, which strove consistently to align its interests and status with those of the whites and
simultaneously to exclude black ex-slaves from all political and social institutions, was also identifying with those of the whites and exchanging
responsibility for protection by denying ex-slaves their civil rights.

Guyanese of Mixed Descent

In 1962 the category "mixed" constituted 12.2 percent of the total population. This is a residual category which included all Guyanese of
mixed racial ancestry. Before emancipation the word "colored" was used
to define the "racial hybrids" that were the result of white and black
intermixture. The introduction of additional racial strains in the post-
emancipation era was to result in further miscegenation. The products
of intermixing the various races came to be called Guyanese of "mixed"
descent. These mixed-bloods, other than the original Coloreds and the
later Coloreds which resulted from Portuguese and Negro-Colored mar-

riages, never really experienced a marginal status in the Guyanese society, since they were assimilated into one or another of the groups whose biological ancestry they shared. These social combinations included Chinese, East Indians, and Amerindians. For the Colored group, however, assimilation into any one of the population segments was difficult because they strove for inclusion in white society and denied their black ancestry. Since they were never able to achieve anything more than token acceptance by the dominant white upper class and would never entertain the idea of being part of the black community, they had to settle for a marginal position between the whites and blacks. Such a marginal status has posed many problems for their integration into the mainstream of Guyanese society.

The Colored-Guyanese Community as a Marginal Minority

The history of the Colored community of Guyana is the history of a people whose existence has been characterized by a certain amount of ambiguity in that they have been destined to live in two social worlds not merely different but antagonistic as well. Because of the historical developments in which "whiteness" was equated with cultural and racial superiority, the Colored group has occupied a marginal status in Guyanese society. Coloreds held a relatively independent position between the dominant white minority and the subordinate black majority, being accommodated by but not assimilated with both whites and blacks.

Because of the premium placed on "whiteness," the Coloreds came to occupy positions next to the dominant whites. Many persons of "color" were privileged, even during the slave era, and those who had been freed or born free, usually because of the "benevolence" of their white fathers, were often found in the professions and sometimes became plantation owners. They participated in politics and held commissions in the militia. The privileges that were extended to them, however, depended on the needs of the white power structure. Quite often "qualified" Coloreds were denied upward social mobility if such progress threatened the interests of the white elite. On the other hand, "there were many instances of whites according preferential treatment to Coloreds, deliberately to create a buffer group between the white masters and the large black slave population.[4] In such situations "color" characteristics became the criterion for determining social status and the individual became obsessed with demonstrating his "cultural" and "racial" whiteness.

---

[4] Robinson, *op. cit.*, p. 52.

Even in relatively recent times, and to some extent today, when prejudice against "blackness" or such features as "hard" hair could be counterbalanced by wealth or professional prestige, the mobility for the children of a dark-skinned but successful man could be enhanced by marrying a fair-skinned woman. Hence Colored women were much in demand as wives. This is evident even today; dark-skinned male Guyanese of middle- and upper-class status invariably have spouses lighter than they are. That skin color should have counted in the choice of a spouse bears witness to the strength and degrading effect of racial snobbery, but it also shows that the system is not a closed one and that prestige is not based solely on race.

Much miscegenation between whites and black and Colored slaves and free Coloreds occurred during the era of slavery and later in the post-emancipation period. The result was a sizable Colored community. The post-emancipation era also saw the beginning of miscegenation among the many new strains of people who formed the immigrant society and further intermixing resulted in the population category "mixed." These mixed-bloods now account for a little more than 12 percent of Guyana's population. However, whenever the term "colored" is used it still carries the connotation of a Guyanese of Negro and white European mixture, or Negro and Portuguese, since the distinction between Portuguese and other Europeans continues to be made.

The decade before political independence saw the Coloreds still occupying the privileged positions accorded them by virtue of their "good" color and adhering to the cultural characteristics of their European ancestors. They still enjoyed to a great extent the protection of the British who, pressured by a rising nationalism and world public opinion, were forced to concede high status jobs to "the natives," most of whom were "people of color."

Rising Nationalism and Independence

With the coming of independence in 1966 the Coloreds' reference group, the British, no longer controlled their destiny. A Negro-based political party now exercised control over the power structure. Because the emphasis was on equality of all racial groups based on achievement, the Coloreds were offered no special constitutional privileges to assist them in adjusting to the new social order. They now faced open competition from the other segments of the Guyanese population and found themselves in a young nation bent on quickly eradicating the vestiges of centuries of white European domination. It is not too difficult to understand, therefore, why the decade before independence and the years following were such an anxious period for Guyanese Coloreds. Here was a group whose social and cultural orientations were based on the emulation and internalization of white culture traits caught in a society in which rising nationalism would prompt its black political elite to put an end to "imperialist exploitation."

This faction demanded special priority for local people, as opposed to expatriates who in this case were white. Since the Coloreds had all along been associated with the whites, one would anticipate that they would be included in the target group of "white supremacists" who had to be "purged" from the elite ranks. As Smith observes, "It is not surprising that these issues should be expressed in terms of race, especially when the Europeans have been so conscious of race themselves."[5] Despite these developments, however, there had never been, until recently, any really serious antiwhite feeling.

As the British withdrew from the scene and a black central government assumed power, the Coloreds saw their survival threatened. The marginal status they had occupied during the colonial era was now even more marginal, since the majority could not now embrace a "black" power structure that had all along been denied the privileges they had enjoyed themselves. The assurances that were made by the new structure regarding the equality of all and the social status to be earned on the basis of achievement were seen as political gimmicks by most of the Coloreds. For these people the only alternative, as they saw it, was to migrate to "whiter pastures," where they hoped at least to maintain their privileged status next to the dominant white group. England was the obvious first choice because the Coloreds' former reference group lived there. Guyanese Coloreds were soon to realize, however much to their dismay, that English society considered them as "half castes" trying to pass as "English gentlemen" and was not prepared to accept them. In fact, they were treated worse than Negroes. Other predominantly white British Commonwealth countries provided the next best prospect; Canada in particular offered favorable possibilities.

Post-independence and Its Problems

Despite recent developments in integration, it can be said that the Colored community in Guyana still continues in many respects to occupy a

---

[5] Raymond T. Smith, *The Negro Family in British Guiana.* London: Routledge and Kegan Paul, 1956, p. 138.

peripheral position in Guyanese society. Over the last decade or so the
ongoing efforts at adjustment, whether assimilative, accommodative, or
escapist, can and do indicate a period of profound social change for the
Colored community. The past bears down heavily on Coloreds, and a
reversal of the traditional value system cannot be achieved overnight, if
at all. A brief examination of the ways in which the Coloreds dealt with
their marginal status and the social and psychological effects such a
marginal existence has had on their personalities will help to determine
what the future holds for the Guyanese Colored population.

The Colored community, having accepted British patterns of behavior as their own, maintains social institutions that have been more characteristic of English than of African culture. Nevertheless, a certain
amount of African cultural influence has been felt, with the result that
the Coloreds have adopted a creole culture neither wholly English nor
African. In this sense the Coloreds are marginal to both cultures, aspiring to be integrated into a white cultural world which would grant them
token inclusion at the most and denying the black cultural world which
has nevertheless exerted some influence on their lives. The influence of
the cultures of the later ethnic arrivals was rather slight in the colonial
era, and the marginal existence of the Colored community maintained
much the same framework until recent times. The gradual evolution of
a "common" Guyanese culture arising from the fusion of various European, African, and Asian cultural elements is without doubt contributing to a breakdown of this marginal status.

The emulation of the British has been as inclusive as possible and
the Coloreds are often referred to as being "more British than the British." Although this comment is primarily intended to be derogatory and
is to some extent stereotypical, it does contain an element of truth. Even
though the Coloreds have never referred to England as "home," they
have always been sensitive about demonstrating their "Britishness," for
the more British they could be the better were their chances of upward
social mobility in a social structure in which the British were the dominant group. In a Guyanese context this also meant that the mixed-
bloods, in their association with Englishmen, strove to identify their
racial sentiments with those of the whites. In fact, one criterion of complete achievement of "whiteness" by the Coloreds was the complete identification of their racial values with those of the British. Hence the
Coloreds made sure that they avoided contacts with their dark-skinned
fellow Guyanese because such contacts were viewed as being inimical to
achieving "whiteness." This has resulted in the Colored community as
a whole becoming perennially preoccupied with the degrees of pigmentation and kinship with their black progenitors. Brothers of different
color, in such a situation, often become estranged, and dark parents may

keep out of the way of their lighter children in order not to hinder their success. Numerous are the instances reported of children disavowing their darker parents,

> . . . while lighter persons who have been rewarded in social status for their lightness became rigid and even fierce at any attempt of darker persons to recognize them publicly and familiarly.[6]

Today the reverse of such behavior is gradually being effected now that a black power structure holds the reins of government and "whiteness" as a determinant of social status is rapidly losing its appeal. The Coloreds, caught in a society in such a transitional phase, are experiencing much anxiety. The following quote from one of the calypsos of a popular West Indian calypsonian, although referring to another mixed-blood West Indian, adequately and forcefully expresses the anxieties of the marginal Colored personality in quest of national and racial identity:

> . . . you can send the Indians to India
> And the Negroes back to Africa
> But will somebody *please* tell me,
> Where they('re) sending poor me, poor me?
> *I'm neither one nor the other—*
> Six of one, half a dozen of the other,
> If they('re) serious about sending
> back people in truth
> They('re) going to have to split me in two.[7]

The stark reality of their hybrid nature, both racial and cultural, in a changing social structure has suddenly and traumatically dawned on the Coloreds following the withdrawal of the whites. Reared in a social environment in which "whiteness" was equated with cultural and racial superiority, they grew up internalizing white standards and denying their black heritage. How psychologically splintered must such a personality be, spurned by a white father who never really accepted him as a sibling and spurning a black mother whose "degenerate barbarism" in the eyes of the dominant white society was a symbol of "inferiority."

The Trauma of Marginality and Ambiguous Identity

Small wonder, therefore, that the Colored looked upward to their father's people and culture and denied their own maternal heritage. This

---

[6] Oliver C. Cox, *Caste, Class, and Race.* Garden City: Doubleday, 1948, p. 361.
[7] From a calypso by the "Mighty Dougla," a Trinidadian calypsonian. "Dougla" is a pejorative word for a person of mixed Negro and East Indian descent. Quoted from David Lowenthal, "Race and Color in the West Indies," *Daedalus,* **96,** 602 (Spring 1967).

color awareness is today still a corrosive and enervating preoccupation that hampers the efforts of the Guyanese Colored to cope with problems of identity. They are caught between two racial and cultural worlds, into neither of which can they be fully integrated. As the calypso so simply yet so forcefully put it, they cannot return to Africa or African ways. It was never psychologically possible to go back because they have all along developed ways of living alien to the country of their mothers' origin. On the other hand, they cannot accept wholeheartedly the European way of life, for their roots are still in Guyana, where European influence is gradually losing its dominance or is "creolized" to meet local conditions. Moreover, even if they make the attempt to live in the land of their fathers, they will soon have to face bitter reality. The society of their white fathers, the values of which have been internalized, does not want them. In its eyes they are "half-caste," with the "tainted blood" of a "degenerate" maternal background flowing in their veins. How severe a personality strain must all this be in an already confusing world in which social change is taking place at such a rate that the individual is left mentally floundering in his attempts at adjustment! In psychological jargon the confusion and anxiety of the Coloreds may be described in the following manner:

> They are schizophrenics who consider the part of them that is "white" good and the part that is "black" bad. The frustrated aspiration of being "white" is a frequent feature of British West Indian paranoia not to mention of everyday life.[8]

For example, "I could never love a black man," asserts a dark-colored woman. "Black and black breed children like monkeys. I always want my children to be as light as possible."[9]

Such attitudes obviously must have both sociological and psychological repercussions for the Colored Guyanese. Being colored in a society in which color is equated with social position, it is almost impossible for the Colored man to attain the status that a white man of lesser ability can achieve. Also, being regarded as white or half-white in a society that is fighting to shed its "white dependence" can be just as difficult a position. In both certain possibilities are denied the individual in some cases and in others, although he might be accepted, the acceptance is only partial. Although the Guyanese Coloreds are subject to either total or partial deprivation of functions which the Guyanese culture decrees are proper for them to perform, they, in turn, may never be able to ful-

---

[8] *Ibid.*
[9] Madeline Kerr, *Personality and Conflict in Jamaica.* London: Collins, 1963, p. 96.

fill the expectations of that culture. They will experience feelings of insecurity that will make their social relations difficult and sometimes erratic. To a great extent such has been the state of the Guyanese Coloreds and it applies even today. In such a marginal situation the Colored community is faced with two broad possibilities: to strive for assimilation and possibly integration into the present social structure or to escape the situation altogether. A number of Guyanese Coloreds have sought the latter solution by migrating to Canada.

The Coloreds in Canada

The majority of the Guyanese Coloreds who migrated to Canada before and after independence settled in Toronto, a city of diverse racial and cultural strains. After a short period of residence in apartment complexes in the central city most of them moved out into the suburban municipality of Scarborough, which had a population of 217,286 in 1961. It is not known for certain how many Guyanese Coloreds migrated to Toronto nor how many reside in Scarborough, since accurate census figures are not available. Also, before 1966 Canadian census figures included Guyanese migrants among the British because they carried British passports. Since Guyana attained political independence in 1966 national passports have not specified the racial composition of the bearers. An unofficial count of Guyanese voters in Canada in 1968 disclosed a figure of 4662—50 percent of whom were listed as living in Toronto. Since these statistics did not include Guyanese under 21 years of age nor those who could not be located, it would be reasonable to estimate that approximately 10,000 Guyanese reside in Canada, half of whom are in Toronto. It is also reasonable to estimate that the majority of those residing in Toronto would be Guyanese of "color"—a small number of Portuguese and a much more sizable community of Coloreds—since until recently Canadian immigration practices sought to keep out the dark-skinned immigrants.

The Guyanese Coloreds in Toronto are for the most part well-educated, urban middle class, with a sprinkling of upper-class members. From all appearances theirs was not a mass exodus to Toronto, for their arrival presented no major problems for absorption into Toronto society. In fact, theirs was a relatively smooth transition, relatives already there aided in their assimilation into the Canadian population. The usual patterns of migration takes the form of the male head of the household arriving first, soon to be followed by his wife. After both have "checked out" the situation, the rest of the immediate family is brought over. When these members are satisfactorily settled, relatives may join the household.

Internal Divisiveness of Colored Guyanese in Canada

Guyanese Coloreds in Toronto do share some of the characteristics of a "community"—origin, particular locality in which they now live, language and religion, and other cultural traits—but there is little evidence that they support one another beyond a limited group of family and friends or that they have expectations of loyalty to one another. In fact, there are indications that intense competition exists among them as they strive to demonstrate their "cultural whiteness" in their efforts toward integration in the numerically and culturally dominant British-Canadian society. Each takes pains to demonstrate that he is doing better than the others since moving "over here." Conspicuous consumption and the white-Canadian friends they make are pointed to as indications of such progress.

This behavior is reminiscent of the way things were in Guyana when these Coloreds sought acceptance by the white upper class. Although there is a concentration of Guyanese Coloreds in Scarborough, it cannot be said that they live in proximity. Partly because of the competition among them and partly because they see clustering together as inimical to their integration into the dominant segment of society, one will never find, for example, a predominance of Guyanese Coloreds in any one district or neighborhood. Since there is no clustering and since they are not separated by distinct cultural differences, in addition to which many can "pass" as white, they are not seen by others as a distinct community. Consequently many residents of Scarborough do not treat them differently, as, for example, is done in the large and culturally distinct Italian community elsewhere in Toronto.[10] Nor can it be said that the Guyanese Coloreds in Scarborough have a separate way of life; even on arrival in Canada they share for the most part a similar culture and speak the same language as the dominant British-Canadian society they move into.

One might conclude that the peculiar circumstances that motivated the Guyanese Coloreds to migrate to Canada would in themselves have forced this group to share a common identity, even if it had never been shared in Guyana. The divisiveness of color gradations had become so much a part of their way of life that even in the face of threatening cir-

---

[10] Clifford J. Jansen, "Leadership in the Toronto Italian Ethnic Group," *The International Migration Review*, **4**, No. 10 (Fall 1969).

cumstances these values cannot be changed so easily as a change of residence. The Guyanese Coloreds in Canada are a marginal group escaping from a society in which they had little confidence that integration could ever be satisfactorily achieved. They were escaping from a society that had seen its white power structure replaced by a black power structure. They had aspired to membership in the white society of the former dominant group and as a result had developed a great degree of "cultural whiteness." They had never really been integrated into this white social structure, but at least they had achieved "token integration" from which had accrued many privileges. With the demise of the white upper class and the coming to power of a black political elite, these "marginal men," thinking of themselves as "culturally" and often "biologically" white, preferred to migrate to another country which had an almost similar dominant white society. In this new society they hoped at least to regain and maintain their privileged status and perhaps eventually attain full integration. So they were prepared to continue their marginal existence, always with the hope that inclusion into white society was a distinct possibility and thus put an end to their marginal status.

SELECTED BIBLIOGRAPHY

Augier, F. R., et al., *The Making of the West Indies*. London: Longmans, Green, 1960.

Blanchard, Paul, *Democracy and Empire in the Caribbean*. New York: Macmillan, 1947.

Guerin, D., *The West Indies and Their Future*. London: Dobson, 1953.

Henriques, Fernando, *Family and Colour in Jamaica*. London: Eyre and Spottswoods, 1956.

Hoetink, H., *Caribbean Race Relations—A Study of Two Variants*. London: Oxford, 1967.

Jaywardena, Chandra, *Conflict and Solidarity in a Chinese Plantation*. London: Athlone, 1963.

Newman, Peter, *British Guiana: Problems of Cohesion in an Immigrant Society*. London: Oxford, 1964.

Smith, M. G., *The Plural Society in the British West Indies*. Berkeley: University of California Press, 1965.

Smith, M. G., *Cultural Pluralism in the British West Indies*. Berkeley: University of California Press, 1965.

Smith, Raymond T., *British Guiana*. London: Oxford, 1962.

Betty H. Watts
University of Queensland

CHAPTER SEVEN

THE PART-ABORIGINES OF AUSTRALIA

The earliest contacts between Europeans and the indigenous people of Australia were in the seventeenth century when various expeditions reached that continent. There they found tribes of black people.[1] During the next century numerous expeditions, mainly English, established settlements that brought both settlers and explorers into frequent contact with these tribes.

The arrival of the newcomers resulted in a confrontation between two essentially different cultures. The most prominent difference was in respect to technological development. Although the material culture developed by the indigenous people served them well in their environment, it was, by contrast with that of the new arrivals, limited and primitive. Their nonmaterial culture, expressed in religion, myth, song, dance, and ritual, was extremely rich but again quite different in its underlying philosophy and orientation from that of the newcomers. This culture came to be judged by the settlers as inferior to their own.

The contacts between the Aborigines, as they came to be called, and the Europeans were consequently not always amicable; indeed, subjugation, discrimination, brutality, even killing often characterized the treat-

---

[1] Although the Aborigines' skin color suggested a Negroid stock, blood type, facial bone structure, and hair texture all place these people closer to the Caucasoid group. Some evidence taken from language and myth structure affirm an Indo-European heritage. Nonetheless, many anthropologists consider the Aborigines a separate race.

ment of the Aborigines by the newcomers. In addition to various forms of deprivation and mistreatment, the Aborigines also became victims of diseases for which they had no effective immunity. Unable or unwilling to understand the values and behavior of the Aborigines, who often struck back revengefully, many settlers approved and practiced a policy of extermination of a people they had come to fear.

Under these conditions the indigenous population declined from an estimated 300,000 in the seventeenth century to fewer than 100,000 in recent times. As the number of conflicts between the Aborigines and Europeans increased, the settlers initiated a policy of "pacification by force," as Elkin describes the efforts of the Europeans to "teach the natives a lesson."[2] The impact of these punitive assaults on the Aborigines was to have the effect of serious impairment of their culture and social organization and to reduce them to a state of pauperism.

As early as the late eighteenth century efforts were made by the English to Christianize the Aborigines, and numerous missions were established to bring the gospel to the "heathen."[3] During the nineteenth and early years of the twentieth century many missions were established, and missionaries from overseas inaugurated programs of education on behalf of the Aborigines, including those of mixed racial heritage. In 1921, for example, a missionary society of the Anglican Church founded a mission for "cross-breeds of varying castes," later to serve "full-bloods" as well.[4] These missions and educational programs often included projects that would improve the economic condition and physical health of at least some of the indigenous people. Efforts were made to ameliorate the conditions of the Aborigines and to provide various forms of protection, although maintaining a policy of segregation. Biddle explains in detail the various official acts in the State of Queensland which were essentially protective and paternalistic.[5]

Faced with the prospect of extermination by the Europeans, the Aborigines generally undertook to come to terms with the settlers whose

---

[2] A. P. Elkin, *The Australian Aborigines.* New York: Doubleday, 1964, pp. 340–341.

[3] J. W. Bleakley, *The Aborigines of Australia.* Brisbane: Jacaranda, 1961, Chapters 6–9.

[4] *Ibid.*, p. 105.

[5] Ellen E. Biddle, *The Assimilation of Aborigines in Brisbane, Australia.* Unpublished doctoral dissertation, University of Missouri, 1969, pp. 47–55. The acts were adopted in 1884, 1897, 1901, 1934, and 1939. Acts created by the Commonwealth of Australia since 1967 have been implemented to "restore Aboriginal initiative and independence in both the social and economic sense." These acts provide needed capital and technical help and funds to the Australian states to provide housing, education, employment, and health benefits. Additional acts in 1970 provide educational grants to Aborigines 14 to 21 years of age.

firearms were more efficient in warfare than their own primitive spears. There were, of course, many settlers who deplored such violence, who were sympathetic with the problems of their indigenous neighbors, and who sought to be friendly and helpful.

In the early decades of the present century it had become apparent to officialdom and others that the policy of protection, paternalism, and segregation would result in the demoralization and probably decimation of the indigenous population. Hence increasing emphasis came to be placed on their assimilation into European culture on the grounds that this culture was superior or at least more functional. It was also recognized that the integration of the Aborigines into the social organization of the Europeans in Australia was a necessary objective if all were to enjoy the rights and benefits of full citizenship.

Yet there appeared to be little concern about the prospect or possibility that the assimilative and integrative policies would actually mean the ultimate destruction of the indigenous culture. Recent assessment of the humanitarian and protective policies has indicated a further necessary step if the culture of the Aborigines is to survive. There needs to be acceptance of the concept of a pluralistic society involving the continuance of the Aboriginal culture alongside the integration of the people into wider Australian society.

In presenting an overall view of the Aboriginal population, Elkin places the Aborigines in four categories: first, several thousand full-bloods who live in remote sections of the country and who adhere to their traditional seminomadic way of life; second, full-bloods who live and work in towns or outback settlements, including reserves, but who still observe their tribal way of life and speak a native language; third, full-blood and part-Aborigines who are detribalized but only partly assimilated into the dominant culture; and fourth, mixed-bloods, mainly quadroons or lighter, who live in or near the larger towns or cities and who seek to become assimilated and integrated into the mainstream of Australian life.[6]

Demographic Characteristics

Until recently there has been little reliable information on the distribution and composition of the Aboriginal population of Australia.[7] The 1966 census provided their first complete enumeration.

---

[6] Elkin, *op. cit.*, pp. 349–350.

[7] F. L. Jones, *The Aboriginal Population of Australia: Present Distribution and Probable Future Growth* (mimeographed), 1970a.

Separate statistics for full-blood Aborigines and people of Aboriginal descent are not available. In his analysis of the 1966 census data and his projections of estimates of fertility and mortality Jones uses two classifications:

Part-Aborigines: persons of less than half
                   Aboriginal origin
Aborigines: persons of half or more than
                   half Aboriginal origin

Table 6 is based on Jones' analysis.

Table 6   Part-Aborigines and Aborigines in the 1966 Census[a]

State	Part-Aborigines (less than half Aboriginal origin)	Aborigines (half or more than half Aboriginal origin)	Total Identifiable Aboriginal Population
New South Wales	6,382	14,219	20,601
Victoria	917	1,790	2,707
Queensland	4,037	19,003	23,040
South Australia	1,079	5,505	6,584
Western Australia	2,707	18,439	21,146
Northern Territory	1,187	21,119	22,306
Tasmania, Australian Capital Territory	116	132	248
Australia	16,425	80,207	96,632

[a] From F. Lancaster Jones, *The Aboriginal Population of Australia*, 1970, p. 8, Table 2 (mimeographed). By permission of the author.

Thus it is not possible to provide the exact numbers of mixed-blood Aborigines in Australia; the total lies between 16,425 and 96,632. In an earlier analysis Jones presents a 1966 estimate of full-blood Aborigines in Australia at 44,224.[8] It would appear then that the mixed-blood Aboriginal population of Australia is of the order of 50,000. This number would represent less than one-half of one percent of the total Australian population.

Perhaps one of the most striking characteristics of this population is its age structure. Jones reports:

In fact 45.4 per cent of the "Aboriginal" population (half or more than half) were aged under 15 in 1966 . . . but among part-Aborigines (less than half) the

---

[8] F. L. Jones, *The Structure and Growth of Australia's Aboriginal Population*. Canberra: Australian National University Press, 1970, p. 35.

figure was remarkably high, 60.1 per cent. Only 29.3 per cent of non-Aboriginal Australians were under fifteen in 1966. The median age of Aboriginal Australians was 16.1 years, almost half the figure for non-Aboriginal Australians (28.3 years).[9]

The part-Aboriginal population of Australia is extremely heterogeneous with respect to geographical location and mode of living.[10] Some live in government settlements or communities and church missions. Long estimated from 1961 Census data that well under 20 percent of the part-Aboriginal people live in such settlements.[11] Many more live in and around country towns; the term "fringe dwellers" has been widely used in Australia to describe these people who physically are a part of the community but who, from a social and cultural viewpoint, function as separate entities. Still others live in cities.

Researchers report an increasing urbanization among the part-Aborigines, although the group remains predominantly rural. An analysis by Jones shows that, of the total identifiable Aboriginal population in 1966, 8.6 percent were metropolitan, 23.6 percent other urban, and 67.7 percent rural and migratory.[12] The trend toward urbanization is indicated by Jones's 1947 data: metropolitan, 4.1 percent; other urban, 7.8 percent; and rural and migratory, 88.1 percent.

A detailed study of part-Aborigines living in the metropolitan area in Queensland showed a pattern of migration from small towns to the metropolis.[13] Only 12 percent of the family units located in Brisbane had migrated directly from government settlements. In New South Wales Beasley also reported a migration to Sydney from areas all over the state; in her sample population of 100 households almost half the people had migrated to Sydney from country areas.[14]

The part-Aboriginal population has been increasing over the last five decades. Jones shows that the total identifiable Aboriginal popula-

---

[9] F. L. Jones, *The Aboriginal Population of Australia,* 1970a, p. 21. By permission of the author.

[10] For the remainder of this chapter the term "part-Aboriginal" is used to describe those persons of some, but less than full, Aboriginal ancestry.

[11] J. P. M. Long, *Aboriginal Settlements: A Survey of Institutional Communities in Eastern Australia.* Canberra: Australian National University Press, 1970, p. 4.

[12] Jones, *op. cit.,* 1970a, p. 13.

[13] H. M. Smith and E. Biddle, *Look Forward Not Back: A Study of People of Aboriginal Descent Living in the Metropolitan Area of Brisbane* (unpublished manuscript). Cf. E. Biddle, *The Assimilation of Aborigines in Brisbane, Australia, 1965;* H. P. Schapper, *Aboriginal Advancement to Integration.* Canberra: Australian National University Press, 1970.

[14] P. Beasley, "The Aboriginal Household in Sydney," in R. Taft, J. M. L. Dawson, and P. Beasley, *Attitudes and Social Conditions.* Canberra: Australian National University Press, 1970.

tion of Australia has a rate of natural increase three times that of the non-Aboriginal population of Australia.

The levels of fertility and mortality among Aborigines are high. Jones, predicting an increase in the total identifiable Aboriginal population, writes:

> Aboriginal population growth is achieved through high fertility in the face of high mortality. The Aboriginal population has not yet begun the demographic transition to low mortality and low fertility.[15]

Style of Life

Since all available evidence suggests that the majority of the part-Aboriginal people of Australia are socially and economically disadvantaged, the remainder of this chapter concentrates on the life style of the disadvantaged sector of this minority group. An approach such as this should not obscure the fact that many part-Aborigines are pursuing a satisfying and productive life within the general Australian community, different from their neighbors in no respect other than their ancestry. This group does, however, constitute a minority, and the part-Aboriginal people of Australia have yet to develop a strong and significant middle class.

Educational Achievements. Among the part-Aboriginal adults attained educational levels are, in general, extremely low. Biddle's survey of Aboriginal adults and young people from 431 households in Brisbane in 1965–1966 revealed that 2.8 percent had received no schooling, 19 percent had been educated only to the fourth grade, and a further 65.8 percent had not proceeded beyond primary school. Beasley's 1970 survey of Aborigines in Sydney over the age of 15 years revealed a somewhat similar pattern: one-third had attended primary school only; two-fifths had attended secondary school but had not gained the Intermediate Certificate awarded at the successful completion of the third year of high school. The educational level of 13.6 percent of the sample was unknown; if this information had been available, the proportion attending primary school only would probably have been larger.

Both surveys were conducted with populations currently living in metropolitan areas in which access to schools, particularly at the secondary level, is easier. Although both Biddle's and Beasley's samples included adults who had migrated to the city from country areas, significant

---

[15] Jones, *op. cit.*, 1970a.

numbers in each sample (approximately 20 and 50 percent, respectively) were nonmigrants. One might expect lower educational standards to obtain among part-Aboriginal adults who had grown up in country areas. Schapper's report on Western Australia's part-Aboriginal population in 1966, predominantly rural, supports this expectation.

Table 7 shows that only one-fifth of the part-Aborigines of Western Australia, in comparison with two-thirds of the total population, had attended or were attending secondary school.

Table 7   Level of Educational Attainment of Part-Aboriginals and Total Populations, 1966

Highest Level Attained	Part-Aborigines		Total Population, Percent
	Number	*Percent*	*Percent*
Matriculation or higher	35	0.2	9.2
Junior Certificate	198	1.3	18.4
Attended or attending secondary school	2,665	17.2	38.7
Attended or attending primary school	6,294	40.7	29.9
Age 5 and over— no education	5,253	33.9	2.0
Not stated	1,034	6.7	1.7
Total Aged 5 Years and Over	15,479	100	100

SOURCE: H. P. Schapper, *Aboriginal Advancement to Integration*. Canberra: Australian National University Press, 1970, 170. By permission of Australian National University Press.

Examination of the school achievement levels of younger part-Aborigines shows that their achievements are somewhat higher than those of the older people; for example, in Beasley's sample the people who had attended secondary school were mainly under 40 and those who had achieved the Intermediate Certificate were mostly under 30. In Smith and Biddle's Brisbane sample it was found that at every decade, as age increased, the amount of education decreased. Schapper's 33.9 percent with no education rises to 44.4 percent when part-Aborigines over the age of 15 years are considered.

The level of achievement of part-Aboriginal children still at school remains, however, far from satisfactory. Tatz estimates that in 1966–1967, although 19,306 Aboriginal and part-Aboriginal children were enrolled in primary schools, only 2596 were attending secondary school, and a mere 120 were at a university or in technical and professional institutions.[16]

The effects that the Commonwealth Aboriginal Secondary Grants Scheme will have on Aboriginal education achievement remain to be seen. The plan is likely to result in more children remaining at school beyond the statutory school-leaving age. Yet the percentage of children attending secondary school and tertiary institutions provides only one index of the educational achievement level. Statistics on the actual performance level might well be a more significant index.

Occupational Roles. Part-Aborigines tend to be employed at jobs at or near the lower end of the socioeconomic scale. The Brisbane study by Biddle and Smith revealed that approximately 87 percent of those working had jobs classified in the three lowest ranking categories on an eight-category scale. This scale orders Australian occupations by both skill level and prestige. Approximately 93 percent held jobs in the four lowest categories; the comparable figure for all Australian workers in 1961 was 51 percent.

In her Sydney sample Beasley also found a majority of the Aboriginal men (approximately 80 percent) working in unskilled occupations such as general labor and factory work. She found a similar picture for Aboriginal women: 47 percent in predominantly unskilled, full-time factory employment, 13 percent in domestic work, but only 9 percent in full-time sales or clerical work.

In 1964 Barwick published a study of people of Aboriginal descent living in Melbourne.[17] She emphasized that until recently most part-Aboriginal people have been migratory rural workers and that the city population still has the same work habits and motivations. Those migratory workers who came to Melbourne in winter and who did not have large families had a chance to meet their expenses, but large families could not afford the cost of living and soon returned to the countryside.

In Queensland, with its large government settlements, Long found that in the four settlements in which the population is mainly part-Aboriginal the majority of the workers are employed on the settlement itself, most holding jobs of a laboring or semiskilled nature; only a small proportion have positions at the foreman or supervisory level and only a few occupy clerical positions.

The general employment picture across Australia for most part-Ab-

---

[16] C. M. Tatz, "Education for Aborigines: Present Facilities and Needs," in S. S. Dunn and C. M. Tatz, Eds., *Aborigines and Education.* Melbourne: Sun Books, 1969, p. 60.
[17] D. Barwick, "The Self-conscious People of Melbourne," in M. Reay, Ed., *Aborigines Now.* Melbourne: Angus and Robertson, 1964.

origines shows this minority to be employees rather than employers, to be characteristically unskilled or semiskilled, to be heavily concentrated in seasonal rural labor, and to suffer a higher unemployment rate than the general Australian population.

Housing of Part-Aborigines. Appleyard summarizes the way of life of many Aborigines:

> Like many minority groups, Aboriginal workers are economically under-privileged. Most are unskilled, poorly paid, and subject to periods of seasonal unemployment and, as a consequence, the general economic standard of their communities is poor and includes some individuals who can only be described as poverty-stricken.[18]

Low educational achievement, linked with a typical consequence of employment in laboring and semiskilled jobs for many, is associated with degrees of poverty. The effects of low wages tend to be exacerbated by inadequate housing and large households. The housing situation of part-Aborigines living in urban areas seems to be somewhat superior to that of their fellows who live in and around small towns and in rural areas.

Beasley reports that the range of houses available to this group in Sydney corresponds to the range available to lower income groups of the general Australian population: four-fifths of the homes were cottages or houses. Of them one-fourth were rated as poor or bad with respect to interior care and maintenance and an equal proportion received the same rating on exterior care and maintenance. In the Perth metropolitan area Schapper found one-third of the Aboriginal population living in hostels, prisons, and foster homes and two-thirds in conventional housing, of which at least one-half was substandard.

Home ownership is less frequent among metropolitan part-Aborigines than among non-Aborigines. In Sydney one-fourth of the families owned or were in the process of buying their own homes, in contrast to two-thirds of the non-Aborigines metropolitan population of New South Wales. Brisbane figures are somewhat similar: only one-fifth of the part-Aborigines owned or were buying their own homes, compared with four-fifths of non-Aborigines. Smith and Biddle make the additional comment that almost one-fourth of the homes owned or being bought by the part-Aborigines were of inadequate structure.

Overcrowding is characteristic of many part-Aboriginal homes in urban areas. In Sydney, for example, Beasley found the average number of rooms per dwelling to be lower for part-Aboriginal households than for white.

---

18 R. Appleyard, "Overview," in H. Throssell, Ed., *Ethnic Minorities in Australia: The Welfare of Aborigines and Migrants.* Australian Council of Social Service, 1968.

The degree of overcrowding is emphasized when comparisons are made between part-Aborigines and non-Aborigines. The average number of persons per part-Aboriginal dwelling in Sydney is 7.03 and in Brisbane, 5.6, compared with the national Australian average of 3.55.

Studies of Australia's rural part-Aborigines reveal an even less satisfactory situation with respect to households. In rural New South Wales Beckett studied 700 part-Aborigines quartered in and around two small townships and found that the great majority lived either on government settlements or in unsightly, unhygienic shanties on the outskirts of town.[19] Long in his analysis of part-Aborigines living on the New South Wales government settlements found the standard of housing to be higher there than in fringe camps and on other reserves but that overcrowding was a general problem. On the stations surveyed he found, overall, an average of 7.2 people to each dwelling. On those Queensland settlements in which a majority of the settlement population is part-Aboriginal Long reported numbers of persons per house ranging from an average of fewer than 6 to 8.9.

Household Units. Typically, a non-Aboriginal Australian household unit consists of a single nuclear family. Part-Aboriginal households consisting of more than one nuclear family are not uncommon. In her Sydney study Beasley found that 74 percent of the households had a single nuclear family as a basis, 18 percent consisted of two nuclear families, 7 percent held three nuclear families, and 1 percent contained a nonnuclear family unit. Figures for Brisbane showed that a smaller proportion of the sample households (59 percent) consisted of only one family unit. Two family units lived in 23 percent of the households and, in a further 17 percent there were three or more family units per household.

Across Australia a number of part-Aboriginal households is extended by the presence of relatives. In Sydney Beasley reported that 31 of 100 households contained one or more supernumeraries. Her total sample consisted of 673 persons, 72 percent of whom included the household head, spouse, and child of household head and/or spouse. The remaining 28 percent were kin, in the main related to the household head either consanguineally or affinally. Only three of the 673 persons were nonrelatives. In Brisbane Smith and Biddle found that only 36 percent of 351 regular family units were made up of a full nuclear family unit only.

The figures cited here emphasize the continuing importance to the part-Aboriginal family of kinship relations.

---

[19] J. Beckett, "Aborigines, Alcohol and Assimilation," in M. Reay, Ed., *Aborigines Now.* Melbourne: Angus and Robertson, 1964.

Among both urban and rural Aborigines in New South Wales, it was certainly customary for people to have large households, for their kin obligations required the provision of hospitality to relatives who might need accommodation. Coming to the city did not free an Aboriginal from such obligations . . . . The existing overcrowding was aggravated still further by the more or less frequent arrival of temporary visitors on holiday, attending hospitals in the city, and so on.[20]

A further aspect of household structure, important to the understanding of the part-Aboriginal people, relates to the sex of the household head. A 1967 estimate indicated that approximately 13 percent of all Australian households were headed by women. For part-Aboriginal households available figures on female household heads range from 11.4 percent in Western Australia, to 16 percent in Sydney, to approximately 21 percent in Brisbane and among nonurban Aborigines in New South Wales.

Marital instability and spouselessness are more characteristic of part-Aboriginal families than of the general Australian population. Beasley found that among 16 female household heads 10 could depend on no adult male support. In her total sample of 243 adults, 39 were single. Among the remainder one-fourth were widowed or separated. Smith and Biddle found that one in eight of their household heads was divorced, separated, or single with children; for non-Aboriginal household heads in Queensland the comparable figure is 3.6 percent.

Long, too, found evidence of instability in family life in many part-Aboriginal communities and a high incidence of desertion of women with children. In the New South Wales settlements he surveyed he found 105 "fatherless families" in a total of 340 families; the children in the "fatherless families" accounting for one-fourth of all the children on the settlements.

Marriage Patterns. Most part-Aboriginal people are the offspring of part-Aboriginal parents on both sides. Recent studies show, however, that increasing numbers of part-Aborigines are marrying white Australians. Some of these unions are *de facto*; this is true, however, also of many Aboriginal-Aboriginal unions. The proportion of unions across racial lines ranges from 16 to 39 percent.

The vast majority of these cross-group unions involve one part-Aboriginal and one white Australian. It is of interest to note that cross-group marriages are more frequent between part-Aboriginal women and white men than between part-Aboriginal men and white women. In one particular area studied the greatest number of cross-group marriages had

---

[20] P. Beasley, *op. cit.*, p. 163.

occurred since 1964. Eckermann attributes this changing pattern to improved socioeconomic standards of the part-Aboriginal community, along with approval of these changes by white people. Her data indicate increased acceptance of intermarriage. No evidence is available on the socioeconomic status of the white partners in the cross-marriages reported in the various studies.

Part-Aboriginal Culture. As indicated earlier, the part-Aborigines are a heterogeneous population. Most students of part-Aboriginal communities, however, comment on the existence of a part-Aboriginal "subculture." Calley emphasizes the essential element of this culture:

> But to the Aborigine, particularly if he is a long way removed from the old way of life . . . what marks being an Aborigine is willingness to help kin and be helped by them, to live in close day to day contact with them, to emphasize interpersonal relations.[21]

Other characteristics to be found in some part-Aboriginal groupings —on settlements and reserves, on the fringes of country towns, and in some urban settings—are basically those of the disadvantaged poor: low aspirations, a sense of helplessness, short-term and improvident spending patterns, gambling, and drinking.[22] It is this sense of kinship, however, the acceptance of reciprocal obligations, that marks out the part-Aboriginal culture.

These strong kinship ties within the part-Aboriginal communities serve as a source of financial security, which undoubtedly helps to explain the existence of extended households among urbanized part-Aborigines. Beckett has pointed out the advantage of reciprocal economic assistance in a context of irregular work and prodigality. Calley finds that the part-Aboriginal community is a greater source of security—financial and social —than the welfare state:

> If one is ill, unemployed, aged, widowed or deserted by one's husband, one is quite definitely better off among one's kin than trying to go it alone against overwhelming odds. An Aboriginal community . . . can do more for the lonely, sick or aged than can the modern welfare state with all its vast economic resources.[23]

---

[21] M. J. C. Calley, "Family and Kinship in Aboriginal Australia," in H. Throssell, Ed., *Ethnic Minorities in Australia: The Welfare of Aborigines and Migrants.* Australian Council of Social Service, 1968.

[22] In Brisbane Biddle and Smith found 68 percent had no savings, 50 percent held no bank accounts, 75 percent of the male heads of family units had no life insurance policies, and 74 percent of the household heads had no insurance policy for possessions.

[23] Calley, *op. cit.,* p. 17.

Many part-Aborigines prefer to remain in their own close-knit groups, even in substandard conditions, than to aspire to higher material standards of living that would necessitate their moving away from their own people. This preference is no doubt partly due to a sense of identification and consequential feelings of security; in many cases it is no doubt due also to expectations of hostility and perhaps discrimination from the outside white world.

Questions of value are concerned here. Gale suggested that many part-Aborigines in Adelaide have been accepted into the lower and working-class sections of the city and have acquired the relevant social values.[24] Barwick in Melbourne found that most of the dark people she studied aspired to urban standards of housing and regular employment but did not yet desire the other characteristics of urbanization: the breakdown of kinship bonds and the achievement of material success on an individual or nuclear family basis. Berndt[25] and Calley both refer to the lack of desire among many part-Aborigines for the highly competitive and stressful way of life that leads to the attainment of material success. Calley writes:

Aborigines do not set store by accumulated material possessions and the forward march of technology that other Australians do. Given sufficient food and some protection from the weather, they are often content to ignore the rat race of modern society, to live for the present.[26]

Some part-Aborigines, as might be expected, have begun to espouse the values of middle-class white society. Watts, for example, studied the verbally expressed values of part-Aboriginal and Aboriginal mothers and adolescent daughters in two large government communities in Queensland; her study included control groups of white rural and metropolitan mothers and daughters.[27] She found less sharp ethnic differences than had been anticipated; the two ethnic groups, across both age levels, tended to choose similar orderings on the positions on each of the value orientations. It was found, however, that as a group the white mothers expressed a stronger preference than the Aboriginal mothers for individuality, as against collaterality or lineality, and that the metropolitan white mothers,

[24] F. Gale, "Administration as Guided Assimilation (South Australia)," in M. Reay, Ed., *Aborigines Now*. Melbourne: Angus and Robertson, 1964.

[25] C. Berndt, "A Time of Rediscovery," in D. E. Hutchison, Ed., *Aboriginal Progress, A New Era?* Nedlands: University of Western Australia Press, 1969.

[26] Calley, *op. cit.*, p. 11.

[27] B. H. Watts, "Achievement—Related Values in Two Australian Ethnic Groups," in W. J. Campbell, Ed., *Scholars in Context: The Effects of Environments on Learning.* Sydney: Wiley, 1970.

in particular, were more firmly oriented toward the future, as against the present and past, than the Aboriginal mothers. The Aboriginal mothers, unexpectedly, placed a greater emphasis on the value of doing, as against "being."[28] Among the adolescents ethnic differences were much less marked; the two ethnic groups favored the future over the present, but the white girls expressed a much stronger preference for future over present and present over past than did the Aboriginal girls. Similarly, both groups clearly favored individuality over collaterality, but the Aboriginal girls were less clearly attracted than the white girls to the positions of individuality over lineality.

Researchers have commented on the differences that have developed within part-Aboriginal communities. They distinguish between "insiders" and "outsiders"; in some respects this distinction seems to be based on differing sets of values. The "insiders," or lower class, are those who maintain lively interest in and close contact with their own part-Aboriginal people and continue to regard themselves as Aborigines. The "outsiders," or upper class, are described by Oates:

> The "outsider" class often exists in the same areas as the "insiders," but are distinguished from them by a higher living standard and a desire to be assimilated into the White community. . . . They are ashamed of the lower class and do not voluntarily associate with it.[29]

Eckermann has recently studied the values of a sample of part-Aborigines living on a Queensland settlement. She explored not only the values held by her sample but also those that they attributed to other part-Aborigines and to whites. Her data indicated that these part-Aboriginal people identified more closely with whites than with their own group. She concludes

> . . . that Aborigines see Europeans as more predictable than their own group and . . . Europeans more like themselves than other Aborigines. This is a startling development indicating that perhaps Aborigines have internalized derogatory values about themselves, have consequently rejected their own group and identified with what they believe to be European orientations.[30]

---

[28] B. H. Watts, *Some Determinants of the Academic Success of Australian Aboriginal Adolescent Girls*. Unpublished Ph.D thesis, University of Queensland, 1970.

[29] L. L. Oates, "Assimilation and the Australian Aborigine," *J. Christian Ed.*, **9**, 2, 85–100, 1966.

[30] A. K. Eckermann, "Value Orientations and Queensland Government Settlement for People of Aboriginal and Island Descent," in G. E. Kearney and P. R. de Lacey, Eds., *The Psychology of Aboriginal Australians,* In Press.

Social Interaction Between Part-Aborigines and White Australians

Different groups of Aborigines have had a variety of initial contacts with whites. Some of these meetings have been characterized by aggression on the part of the whites and retreat, with hostility, on the part of the Aborigines; others were reasonably peaceful and amicable. On the whole there has been a generally unhappy history of culture contact. This history and the adverse effects on the indigenous people have been well documented by Berndt:

> Basic similarities were overlaid by such striking divergences that the total effect of the impact, through time, had been devastating. The Aborigines could hardly have been subjugated by a people more unlike themselves, and less in sympathy with their whole orientation toward living . . . . As their world broke up around them, and they turned for support to the newcomers who had brought this about, so their dependence in more than an economic sense increased. The state of affairs which ensued reinforced, as in a vicious circle, the charges of inferiority already levelled against them.
>
> Alert and active in the traditional scene, since their survival rested on being so, in this new situation they were accused of being inherently lazy and prone to idleness. Settled in static camps, laden with cast-off clothing which they had no means of maintaining in good order and repair, they were reproached with dirtiness as an inherently Aboriginal attribute . . . . Because their rhythm of everyday living was based on a different time perspective . . . they were accused of being shiftless, having no sense of time. Capable of sustained effort in hunting and ritual affairs, responsible in attending to their own economic and social obligations, they were censured now as undependable, unwilling to work, basically irresponsible . . . .
>
> . . . Attitudes such as these are more than a faint echo from a dead past. On the contrary, they are still very much alive, although not quite as blatantly as they were . . . . But even in places where first contact lies several generations back, where such statements are more politely phrased, the memory and anticipation of them linger on among the people most directly affected by them, to influence their behaviour today.[31]

Although some improvement has been seen in recent years in the attitudes of white Australians toward the Aborigines and people of Aboriginal descent, some degree of prejudice remains; for example, government proposals to build houses for Aborigines in white towns have frequently been met with a storm of local protest.

---

[31] R. M. and C. H. Berndt, *The World of the First Australians.* Sydney: Ure Smith, 1964, pp. 432–433. By permission of the publisher.

Western studied two communities in the South—one a city with no Aborigines and the other a small country town with a sizable Aboriginal population.[32] A follow-up study was carried out in Queensland, in a metropolis and in two country towns. More than 20 percent of the respondents in the two metropolitan samples agreed with five of the 12 unfavorable statements about Aborigines. The stereotypes were that Aborigines prefer not to mix with whites, that they need protection from their own lack of responsibility, that they are pretty much alike, that white culture is much more advanced, and that Aborigines expect to get more out of life than white people. Large proportions of the country residents also agreed with these statements, agreement sometimes reaching as high as 76 percent. In addition, almost half the country sample endorsed such statements as, "the trouble with letting Aborigines into a nice neighborhood is that they gradually give it a typically Aboriginal atmosphere"; "because the Aborigine can never escape from the limits of his culture, he will always adapt the white man's materials to his old ways"; "no matter how much one might support it on idealistic grounds, there have been too many unfortunate consequences of racial mixing for me to be willing to agree with it."

The respondents were, however, substantially in favor of Aboriginal rights. In each sample more than 70 percent, and frequently more than 90 percent, agreed that all Aborigines should possess Australian citizenship, that there should be no differences in rates of pay for Aborigines and whites, that Aborigines should be encouraged to join local organizations, and that they would vote for their political party even if an Aborigine were nominated. The statement, "Aborigines should have full use of public facilities which are used by Whites," attracted reasonable support from four of the samples (ranging from 76 to 82 percent), but in one rural sample as few as 55 percent agreed with the statement.

Western's studies show that white people are substantially in support of Aboriginal rights but still, particularly in the country, hold negative stereotypes of the Aborigines as people. A majority of the part-Aborigines are rural residents; thus many of them are likely to encounter evidence of prejudice in their daily rounds.

Taft's study in the west was conducted in three areas: Perth (the metropolis); Bigtown, a provincial city with a record of racial conflict; and Smalltown, a provincial town with no record of racial conflict and a

---

[32] J. S. Western, "The Australian Aboriginal: What White Australians Know and Think About Him—a Preliminary Survey." *Race*, **10**, 4, 411–434 (April 1969). (London: Oxford University Press for the Institute of Race Relations). By permission of the publisher.

reputation for harmonious relations between whites and Aborigines.[33] Taft's data, with respect to the personal image of Aborigines held by whites, are essentially similar to those of Western (see Table 8).

Table 8   Most Frequently Chosen Qualities of Aborigines
(percentages)

Perth		Smalltown		Bigtown	
Wasteful with money	34	Wasteful with money	54	Wasteful with money	62
Lazy	32	Unambitious	36	Lazy	58
Make good parents	28	Friendly to whites	32	Unambitious	34
Unambitious	27	Lazy	30	Unreliable	32
Superstitious	26	Dirty and slovenly	26	Drunken	32
Dirty and slovenly	22	Make good parents	24	Dirty and slovenly	30
Drunken	20	Unreliable	22	Noisy	28

SOURCE: Taft, op. cit.[14] By permission of Australian National University Press.

Taft concluded from this study:

The general stereotype of Aborigines, then, is that of an irresponsible, lazy, and dirty slob who has the redeeming features of being a good parent and a friendly, respectful, and generous person.[34]

He found, as did Western, that white people exhibited more favorable attitudes toward the civil rights of Aborigines than to their personal characteristics.

Investigators, both in Australia and overseas, have explored the correlates of attitudes toward ethnic minorities. In South Australia Gale found unfavorable attitudes toward Aborigines more marked in residents of small country towns, older and less educated people, and those with depressed economic status. In his southern samples Western found that the differences between his city and country populations, in their image of Aborigines, were not due to differences in the extent of social contact with Aborigines. He writes:

It is as if the two groups (country and city) start from a different "base line," and once this has been established, variability in response pattern can be accounted for relatively satisfactorily. But what accounts for the initial differences is still an open question. Perhaps it is something to do with rural-urban differences or perhaps, and more probably, it is due in the one instance to the presence of an Aboriginal community on the outskirts of the town and in the other to a

---

[33] R. Taft, "Attitudes of Western Australians Towards Aborigines," in R. Taft, J. L. M. Dawson, and P. Beasley, Attitudes and Social Conditions. Canberra: Australian National University Press, 1970.
[34] Ibid., p. 14.

complete lack of close contact. The implication of this hypothesis, of course, is that proximity means an unfavorable image, yet our measure of contact indicates that greater contact . . . means a more favorable image.

It is stating the obvious to say that the problem is a complex one, yet it is clear that it is. Intuitively one can see how an unfavorable image of the type found in Bush Town develops. The town's Aboriginal population is housed mainly in shanties on its outskirts; the Aborigines are mainly service and unskilled manual workers, and they have all the characteristics of an underprivileged and deprived group. It is not unusual to find communities attributing the causes of such deprivation to the groups themselves . . . . Perhaps this is the fact that accounts for the different "base lines" of the two groups.[35]

Taft, too, found beliefs concerning the characteristics of Aborigines to be relatively independent of sex, age, or educational or occupational level. He emphasized the influence of community norms and the interaction between experience and norms:

The more the behavior of Aborigines is unacceptable to the White community norms, the more unfavorable the attitudes of the Whites towards them; and, vice versa, the more unfavorable the attitudes of the Whites, the more likely it is that the Aborigines will appear to behave in an unacceptable manner.[36]

Even though the behavior and circumstances of some Aborigines attract white censure, the extent of generalization indulged in by white Australians is a likely indicator of prejudice.

Few academic studies have explored the attitudes of Aborigines toward white people and toward assimilation or integration. Dawson reports one study of urban and rural part-Aborigines in New South Wales in which he sought to determine the origin of Aboriginal attitudes toward education and integration.[37] He found the urban sample to have significantly more favorable attitudes toward education than the rural sample but was not able to establish significant urban-rural differences with respect to attitudes toward integration.

Social interactions between part-Aborigines and whites are obviously affected by prevailing attitudes. When prejudice exists, members of the minority group are assigned a particular status with attendant role expectations. One part-Aborigine has commented cogently:

I must prove myself everywhere I go. If I move into strange communities, White communities, people look at me and think, "Oh, an Aboriginal person,

---

35 Western, *op. cit.*, p. 432. By permission of the publisher.
36 Taft, *op. cit.*, p. 49.
37 J. L. M. Dawson, "Aboriginal Attitudes Towards Education and Integration," in R. Taft, J. M. L. Dawson, and P. Beasley, *Attitudes and Social Conditions*. Canberra: Australian National University Press, 1970.

he's probably a no-hoper"—and I must prove myself. People just do not accept me as a person.[38]

A further limitation on between-group social interaction is imposed by the fact that most members of this ethnic community have their major contacts with whites in relatively formalized, role-defined situations. These situations—in the main employment and interaction with officials —do not give the part-Aborigines opportunity to learn appropriate modes of relating to whites as social equals. One Melbourne part-Aborigine summed up the nature of many white-part-Aboriginal interactions:

So many people come round us—they are religious or queer or university people. Nobody ever comes round just to be friends, to talk to us as if we were people, instead of Aborigines.[39]

The Brisbane study showed that more than three-fourths of the Aborigines belonged to no clubs or organizations. Thus a majority of Brisbane's part-Aborigines do not participate widely in the general life of the community.

At the same time this lack of social interaction with part-Aborigines promotes a degree of uncertainty among members of the white group. Expectations arising from within-group interaction norms are brought by members of each group to situations of contact. Since there are real differences in these interaction norms, strain, disappointment, and confirmation of prejudices are sometimes the result of attempted between-group social contacts.

Social Change and the Future

For many of Australia's part-Aborigines the present is far from satisfactory. In many respects their life position resembles that of disadvantaged ethnic minorities in other nations. What of the future? There seem to be some grounds for a degree of optimism.

Current legislative changes are gradually creating a situation in which the part-Aborigines and other Australian citizens will be subject to one set of laws. In some states further legislative changes are necessary to achieve this end, but the climate of political and social opinion indicates their likelihood. Again at a legislative level there is recognition that special opportunities and avenues of help should be made available to

---

[38] J. Moriarty, "Development in South Australia," in D. E. Hutchison, Ed., *Aboriginal Progress, A New Era?* Nedlands: University of Western Australia Press, 1969.
[39] Barwick, *op. cit.*, p. 25.

members of this ethnic minority so that they may overcome past inadequacies. There is some indication, furthermore, that white Australians are rediscovering the Aborigines as people rather than as objects of charity, a natural resource, or curiosities like the indigenous flora and fauna. At the very least a change of this nature in the attitude of white Australians will create a climate in which increasing numbers of part-Aborigines will be seen by members of other ethnic groups as individuals rather than as unfavorable stereotypes.

The review of research evidence suggests a further ground for optimism: some of the part-Aborigines are pursuing a way of life indistinguishable from that of their white neighbors. Beasley concluded her Sydney study with these comments:

> The conclusions drawn . . . indicate that in the entire metropolitan area a sufficient number of Aborigines have effectively taken advantage of the possibilities available for social and economic advancement to encourage others, and to give cause for optimism.[40]

It is noteworthy that with respect to educational and vocational achievement the position is more satisfactory for the younger than for the older age groups.

The grounds for optimism are not, however, so strong that a satisfying future can be predicted with confidence for all or even a majority of the part-Aboriginal people. There is an obvious need for programs of intervention similar to those that are being attempted overseas: improvement of housing and neighborhood facilities; promotion of better mental and physical health; fostering of employment and occupational mobility with training and retraining programs; development of political awareness and increasing minority-group participation at all levels of government; raising educational achievements by restructuring school programs; and re-education of both majority and minority group members to promote awareness of their common humanity. Social engineering is unlikely to be effective unless intervention encompasses the total sociocultural situation of the disadvantaged.

Most, if not all, advocates of social reform would accord a central place to the role of education. Long-term social improvement is dependent in part on the extent to which schools can help each child to actualize his potentials and to grow competently and confidently to maturity. If he is to do this, he must not only master basic academic, technological, and social skills but also develop higher cognitive abilities, a sense of zest and enthusiasm for the future, and a realistic but favorable

---

40 *Ibid.*, p. 186.

evaluation of himself as an individual and as a member of his particular minority group.

Some states have begun to develop special educational programs at the preschool and primary levels. Early results of some of these programs seem promising, but there is urgent need for further research to determine how the school may promote the development of the children. The schools are only one institution of society; there are limits to their legitimate role. Moreover, the degree to which they can attain their objectives is influenced by extraschool forces in the community.

Only a comparative few of the part-Aboriginal children are being reached by the special programs that are being developed; there is need for widespread commitment and action by the educational authorities.

Educational needs extend beyond the classroom itself. My research has shown that certain of the attitudes and practices of some of the part-Aboriginal mothers do not foster the educational progress of their children. There is need therefore for some form of intervention designed to help the mothers to create conditions in their homes more conducive to the optimal development of their children. The suggestion for such intervention is not meant to imply that all elements of the part-Aboriginal culture need or should be changed. As in any culture, there is strength that ought to be preserved. The integrity of the culture is a source of support and pride to members of any ethnic group; without this pride susceptibility to mental ill health increases. The problem lies, first, in separating areas of needed change from areas that either need not or should not be changed and, second, in skillfully planning and implementing cautiously, courteously, and effectively the necessary intervention procedures.

One further area in which educational change is needed is a program in schools throughout the country. The evidence presented in studies by Western and Taft shows a considerable prejudice among white people. It is true that there are many sources of prejudice and no one simple solution to it. The schools, however, could play a role, perhaps even a major role, in combating the degree of ethnocentrism that exists, particularly in curriculum content and teacher attitudes, but it must be emphasized that the success of special educational programs alone will not lead to the achievement by the part-Aboriginal people of the goal of equality without the help of all Australian citizens.

SELECTED BIBLIOGRAPHY

Berndt, R. M., and C. H. Berndt, *The World of the First Australians*. Sidney: Ure Smith, 1964.

Bleakley, J. W., *The Aborigines of Australia*. Brisbane: Jacaranda, 1961.

Elkin, A. P., *The Australian Aborigines*. Garden City: Doubleday, 1964.

Jones, F. L., *The Structure and Growth of Aboriginal and European Integration*. Canberra: Australian National University Press, 1970.

Long, J. P. M., *Aboriginal Settlements: A Survey of Institutional Communities in Eastern Australia*. Canberra: Australian National University Press, 1970.

Rowley, C. L., *The Destruction of Aboriginal Society: Aboriginal Policy and Practice*, Vol. 1. Canberra: Australian National University, 1970.

Schapper, H. P., *Aboriginal Advancement to Integration: Conditions and Plans for Western Australia*. Canberra: Australian National University Press, 1970.

Taft, R., J. L. M. Dawson, and P. Beasley, *Attitudes and Conditions: Aborigines in Australian Society*. Canberra: Australian National University Press, 1970.

Watts, B. H., "Achievement—Related Values in Two Australian Ethnic Groups," in W. J. Campbell, Ed., *Scholars in Context: The Effects of Environments on Learning*. Sydney: Wiley, 1970.

Richard Slobodin

McMaster University

CHAPTER EIGHT

THE METIS OF
NORTHERN CANADA

The people long identified as Metis in Canadian society have in recent decades developed active political organizations in the prairie provinces of Manitoba, Saskatchewan, and Alberta. Some of their leaders have become spokesmen, more or less widely accepted as such, for all Canadian citizens of aboriginal ancestry. The problems and the plight of Metis in the provinces of Canada have in late years received public attention, in contrast to the generations of neglect since the failure in 1885 of the second Northwest Insurrection, led by Louis Riel and Gabriel Dumont, in territory that is now Saskatchewan.

In the vast area north of the provinces, and especially in the Mackenzie District of the Northwest Territories, lives a population of Metis, unknown in number, but considerable in relation to the still sparse total population of the region. The Metis sector is for the most part unorganized as such and has received little attention from social scientists or administrators. One reason for this is that, unlike those recognized as Indian and Eskimo, the Metis do not exist as a legal entity.

In 1962–1964 I conducted a study of the Mackenzie District Metis under the auspices of the Northern Co-ordination and Research Centre of the Department of Northern Affairs and National Resources, Canada. This chapter is based in large part on a monograph, *Metis of the Mackenzie District* (Ottawa: Canadian Research Centre for Anthropology, 1966). The "ethnographic present" is 1963–1964.

Social Organization

The Metis nationality, or ethnic group, evolved in Quebec and Ontario during a period from the late seventeenth to the early nineteenth centuries through the activities of *coureurs de bois* and other fur-trade functionaries who, with their offspring by Indian women, developed a way of life partly Indian, partly marginal European, but in time distinct from both. Metis institutions were peculiarly those of the early North American fur-trade frontier. On the prairies and the high plains the Metis way of life underwent a further ecological adaptation. It was here, among Metis centering on the Red and Saskatchewan river valleys, that consciousness of kind was heightened to the level of incipient nationality, a tendency culminating in the declaration of Metis nationhood and the consequent insurrections of 1870 and 1885. Among Metis of the southern Mackenzie District old traditions of Metis nationality and of the insurrections retain a surprising vitality.

The original Indian-European unions in the genealogies of south ern Mackenzie District Metis are as a rule quite remote, dating in many cases from a century ago or more. The Metis here are of French and Roman Catholic tradition, although some of the old families bear Scottish names and some families are no longer Catholic. "Country French" as well as various trade jargons and Indian languages have until recently been the preferred modes of speech.

The people of "mixed" ancestry in the northern or lower Mackenzie drainage do not share these traditions or characteristics. The very term "Metis" is little known and is seldom applied. The original Indian- or Eskimo-European unions in very few cases date back as far as a century. Nonaboriginal ancestry is much more varied than it is for the southern Metis, including a noticeable minority of non-European (Polynesian, Micronesian, American, and African Negro). However, the nonaboriginal nationality most heavily represented in northern Mackenzie genealogies is Scottish. A majority of the northern "mixed" families are Protestant.

When it is necessary to make a distinction, those families that derive genealogically, and usually in tradition, from the historic population which had its center in *la nation métisse* of the western plains are termed the Red River Metis.[1] The term includes some not of Red River deriva-

---

[1] So designated because the Red River basin of what is now North Dakota and Manitoba was a region of Metis activity and settlement in the early and mid-nineteenth century. Centering on large-scale buffalo hunting and the fur trade, a

tion who live among and have assimilated with the older Metis population. Those families deriving from miscegenation within the northern part of the Mackenzie District are termed the Northern Metis. The term "Metis," unqualified, refers to (a) the entire "mixed" population of the District or (b), for convenience, either sector of the Metis—"Red River" or "Northern"—when from the context the reference is unmistakable.

It is not enough to say that the Metis or "half-breeds" are people of both European and aboriginal American ancestry. Many Indians, that is, persons identified by themselves and others as Indian, have European ancestry, sometimes in a higher proportion than those identified as Metis. Also there are urbanized individuals and families of Indian ancestry who have moved into the general population, hence are sociologically "white." Others in this category operate now as Indians, now as whites; for example, the sophisticated and wealthy families of Oklahoma known colloquially as "country-club Indians."

Since Metis and "half-breed" are terms denoting social status, it is theoretically possible that individuals wholly non-Indian in genealogy may occupy this status, just as there were, in frontier days, the "White Indians" and "Negro Indians," usually captives or escaped slaves.[2]

Family and Household Units. Among Metis the elementary or nuclear family is the basic social grouping and forms the core of the household, as is true of the Euro-Canadian and, with some qualifications, the aboriginal American peoples who were ancestors of the Metis. Initially striking features of the Mackenzie Metis family are (a) high fertility rate and, by contrast, (b) relatively modest size of household unit. In 77 Metis households studied in the Mackenzie District the total population was 378, an average of approximately five persons per household unit.

Couples with minor offspring are the modal household type of Metis, congruent with the kinship system of Euro-Canadian society. The overwhelming numerical preponderance of this kind of household composition contrasts with the situation among native societies of the District for which information is available. The paired-family arrangement is observed nowhere among the Metis, nor is the household with a couple and one or more aged parents, as it exists among Northern Athapaskans and

distinctive subculture developed here, that of *la nation métisse.* As a result of attacks by European farmers the Red River Metis society moved westward to Saskatchewan, where it was finally crushed and its way of life terminated.

[2] A. Irving Hallowell explains why such individuals might become fully participating members of aboriginal societies, whereas Indians who lived among the whites during the period in question never became full participants in Euro-American society. See his "American Indians, White and Black: The Phenomenon of Transculturization," *Current Anthropology,* **4,** 519–531 (1963).

also in rural European and non-Indian North American society. It can hardly be supposed that the latter household form never occurs among the Metis, but it is presumably not an important arrangement or recourse for the Metis. Moreover, the evidence of older informants on household composition in their families of orientation suggests that the coresidence of a child-raising couple and one or more members of the grandparental generation has been uncommon during the last 60 years at least.

Choice of Partner: Marital and Extramarital. A woman at Fort Resolution, born in 1892, remarked of her marriage at the age of 18:

You know, we young ones, we were not the boss of ourselves. They tell us, "You marry somebody" . . . . We have been married fifty-three years now.

A Fort Smith man born in 1885, twice married, recalled of his first marriage:

I was making good money. Fur was high then. I figure, easy money. I can do it again. Spent it all quick. So, I was about nineteen, my people looked around. My mother told me, "This girl"—she's Chipewyan side, same as me: Chipewyan Metis—"that's a good family. Her father a good trapper and her mother brought her up right. You better marry her." So all right, I did. . . . Well, you know, I still have good time after that . . . but I don't spend all my money on good time now.

As in these instances, most older informants who were married in the early part of this century tend to recall their own marriages as having been arranged. Usually mothers are the initiators or the agents of family authority, but in some cases, as in that of the woman quoted above, mission influence is evident. Informants of all ages agree that in recent years the situation has been quite different: individuals select their own marital partners.

Considerable qualification must be made, however, to the simple contrast thus presented. In any society individual choice is culturally and socially determined. In small and homogeneous communities, such as those in which Mackenzie Metis have been raised, choice of spouse is based more on congeniality than on romance. Linton observed that most societies throughout the world

. . . train their young people to believe that any well-bred boy and girl, once married, will be able to live together contentedly and will in time develop a real fondness for each other. In most cases this seems to be correct.[3]

There is a congruence of choice, or a ready accommodation in most

---

[3] Ralph Linton, *The Study of Man,* New York: Appleton-Century, 1936, p. 175.

instances, between family heads and marriageable offspring on the question of mates for the latter. As a consequence marriage may be perceived with almost equal truth as having been arranged by the elders or by the young people involved.

In Red River Metis culture, however, there is another tendency that social analysts generally see as running counter to the choice of partner on the basis of community standards of congeniality.

Romantic love—a sudden, violent, ineluctable attraction—is a feature of Red River Metis life. The mystique of sexual passion, in its prevalence and importance among these people, marks a subcultural contrast with Northern Metis. This is not to say that falling in love is unknown among the Northern Metis. Among Red River Metis, however, in contrast to the Northern Metis, a strong passionate attachment is one of the common values as well as one of the common hazards of life. Such attachments are indeed regarded as "unfortunate"; they always seem to bring trouble in their train. Indeed, one gains the impression they would not be considered "normal" if they did not involve disturbance, outrage, and violence. Sometimes they also involve marriage, but it is not expected that marriage on this basis will be stable.

These attachments are regarded as bewitchments, often in a literal sense. The life history of a Red River Metis man born in 1919 included three such episodes. In at least two of these affairs he was convinced afterward that he had been the victim of love-magic.

> That girl made an embroidered shirt for me. I wore it to a dance and then she asked for it back. Said she wanted to fix it better. . . . Well, she never gave it back to me. But from then on, I wanted her all the time. When I was away, I was always thinking and dreaming of her. I had to go back to that place. I quit two jobs to stay with her, and I never (i.e., hardly ever) stay with my wife that time. Then later I stayed with a Chip (Chipewyan Indian) bunch toward the Barrens. That old lady and her daughter had medicine. I stayed with the old lady and the girl, and then I could feel they were working to keep me. It was hard to get away from them, but some people from Smith came by and I went with them very early one morning. Just hitched up and left without saying anything. . . . It was hard to keep away from those women but after that for years I never went near where any of those women lived. I tell you I was afraid of their medicine.

Primary Kin Behavior

A woman born in 1922, recalling her girlhood, remarked:

> I was lucky, because I had my mother, until I was grown up and had kids myself, both my grandmothers, and a bunch of aunts and cousins of my mother's, and my Dad's two sisters. They really looked after us girls and taught us a lot, and that's how it is I can do quillwork and—if I ever had to—make a bark canoe

and a mud stove and a lot of things that older women than me can't do. And—
what my daughters can't see—we girls had a very good time that way, learning
to do things the best way, and having lots of laughs with those old women. You
know how old women are, the old-fashioned women. Always lots of fun. . . .
Also, they told us a lot about—you know—the special women's things: about
taking care of ourselves when we went with men, and all . . .

This informant appeared to have had close relations in her youth
with an unusually large number of older kinswomen, but there is a
tendency for Metis girls to have this kind of diversified support from their
own sex, regardless of the structure of their own households. In spite of
this solidarity among women, Metis family structure contrasts noticeably
with that reported for certain other economically disadvantaged populations within or marginal to our society.

No such kin groups were observed among the Metis of other Mackenzie District communities visited, but there was evidence of interaction
patterns among adult siblings. Of 34 informants on this subject 22
reported living as neighbors, working together, engaging in noneconomic
activities together, or aiding siblings in an emergency at some period in
their lives. A common type of household arrangement among the eastern
Kutchin is the paired family, consisting of two siblings of the same or
opposite sex, their spouses, and children. This household form was not
found among the Mackenzie Metis in 1963, nor is there reference to it in
reminiscences of earlier times.

Metis children observed, at widely separated localities during the
course of several months, played with their peer-group kin more than with
nonkin. Siblings in most cases constituted the modal group of playmates.
No comparable information has yet been published on playmate distribution on Mackenzie Indians and Eskimos, but one ecological point may be
noted. Under "bush" conditions Indian and Eskimo children have found
themselves throughout much of the year in situations in which most of
the available playmates were siblings of cousins. Under settlement conditions this is less true, although interaction or close kin is by no means
unimportant in the settlement. Metis in the Mackenzie District have for
several generations been more closely associated with settlements than
have Indians and Eskimos. This lends weight to the suggestion that
sibling interaction, though important in Metis life, is less frequent and
intense than it is among northern Indians and Eskimos.

The Communication Network. A very little experience of the North
brings one into awareness of the "bush telegraph" or "moccasin telegraph," by means of which news is conveyed over vast distances more
rapidly—or so it sometimes seems—than by the most modern means of

communication. Members of all ethnic groups participate in the system, but the Metis have the reputation of being the most active news and rumormongers. A characteristic comment is that of Bishop Breynat, who relates that every time he arrived at a certain Mackenzie settlement, he was at once visited by the Metis trading-post manager; "en bon Métis, il ne manqua pas de me mettre au courant de toutes les nouvelles dans les plus menus détails."

The Mackenzie Metis, traditionally associated with travel and transport, are and have probably always been more mobile physically than most Indians and Eskimos, who are far from sedentary, and enjoy more numerous, varied, and intimate social ties throughout the District and adjacent regions than do most whites. The result is that from each Metis threads of awareness and sentiment extend throughout the Northland and, in many cases, into the South.

Changes in residence are more common among men than women and are more characteristic of Red River than of Northern Metis, but they are to be encountered frequently enough in the life stories of all Mackenzie Metis. It is sometimes the case that high physical mobility is associated with homelessness; in short, the position of political refugees and of migratory workers. The Mackenzie Metis, however, are differently situated than are such disfranchised wanderers. Whether a traveler or a stay-at-home, the Metis has his role in a fairly intensive communications network. Several overlapping local circuits of the Metis branch of the "bush telegraph" consist in visiting, letter-writing, message-sending (by travelers and by the broadcast message services), gift exchange between Metis in different localities, and by other expressions of interest—for example, in gossip and storytelling with others. Evidently a number of such local circuits in the northern provinces involve Mackenzie Metis.

Traveling around among Metis in 1963 and in 1966–1967, I not only witnessed but was made an agent of this network; at each settlement visited I was given oral and written messages, remembrances, and sometimes gifts to be passed on. In most cases the recipients were other Metis. Most of these messages or gifts passed within the local circuits, but not a few were directed farther afield.

Surname-Groups. Another widespread feature of kinship and social life among Mackenzie Metis is not easy to characterize. This is the patronymic connection. The bearers of not many more than a dozen family names constitute a majority of Mackenzie Metis, and about as many other names are slightly less common. A few were borne by ancestors of real historical distinction; all of them are well known and repeatedly encountered in the history of the northwest and the fur trade.

The student of this history feels as though he is encountering the living past as he hobnobs with people named Beaulieu, Mercredi, Mandeville, Lafferty, Bouvier, Fabien, Isbister, Jones, Flett, Hardisty, Fraser, Camsell, Hodgson, Firth, Stewart, and McKay.

The old Red River Metis name groups are so large and dispersed that they no more constitute a kin group than do the Smiths or Browns of urban society. There is more to them, however, than there is to the Smiths and Browns, taken as a whole. There is a sense of being a "Beaulieu" or a "Mandeville" as something distinct within the Red River Metis universe. This in-group sentiment is reinforced by a consciousness of boundaries. Many Indians in the southern District and in the neighboring provincial areas bear the old Metis surnames. No doubt in most cases they share common ancestry with the Metis, but, if there is any sense of unity among Indians and Metis similarly named, I have failed to discern it.

Occupations

Since their appearance on the northern scene the Metis have been characterized by the wide range of their occupations. Taken as individuals, whites have undoubtedly filled the most diverse variety of socioeconomic statuses, from satrapy to beggary, but considered as ethnic groups, whites as well as Eskimos and Indians have been involved in more restricted clusters of occupations than the Metis. Certainly this has been true until recent years. Despite their representation among trappers. deckhands, and mine workers, whites on the whole have manned the administrative and white-collar positions. Eskimos and Indians, insofar as they have operated within the national economy, have been hunters, fishermen, and trappers. Mackenzie District Metis, from trading-post hunters to trading-post managers, from mail runners and prospectors to bookkeepers and nurses, have tried most of the available kinds of work exclusive of those requiring higher education in the Western sense.

Transportation, Commercial Fishing, and Trapping. From the earliest period of the northwestern fur trade, while Indians were harvesting the renewable resources and whites were "keeping the store," Metis were engaged in these activities and also dominating, in terms of manpower, the transportation industry which was the lifeline of Euro-Canadian penetration into the North and West. Canoemen, boatmen, mail drivers, "forerunners," steamboat deckhands, stevedores, river pilots, they, especially the Red River Metis, have been truly sons of the voyageurs.

Since the advent of steam on the Mackenzie District waterways, a higher proportion of whites than before has worked the boats along with Indians and Northern Metis, some of Eskimo ancestry. Red River Metis, however, have remained the predominant group.

Two additional outdoor occupations have been important in Metis economy: commercial fishing, especially on Great Slave Lake, which at the time of the study was second to transportation as an income producer for Metis, and trapping for fur.

Most Metis have worked sporadically at trapping as well as in a number of other occupations. This has been true since the 1880's or 1890's, but there are Red River Metis traditions suggesting a much more extensive bush way of life in earlier years.

One similarity and one distinction between Indians and Metis as trappers should be borne in mind. The similarity is that in the postwar years most northern trappers have relied increasingly on the spring hunt of muskrats; few are "real" trappers. The Indians' old reproach that Metis are unwilling to "tough it out" in a winter's season of fine-fur hunting has lost whatever point it may have had, since few Indians are now willing to do so either. The distinction between Indians and Metis as trappers lies in the much greater diversity of Metis employment; trapping is likely to be a sporadic activity for Metis.

Trading. The history of the Mackenzie Metis is intimately interwoven with that of the fur trade. Red River Metis are descendants of voyageurs, creatures of the fur trade, whereas the families of Northern Metis whose European ancestry is not recent are in almost all cases descendants of Hudson's Bay Company employees. It was Company policy in the nineteenth and earlier centuries to encourage the marriage of employees in remote posts with local women—a policy that was reversed in later years under changed conditions, so that most traders who have married natives in recent generations have been independents. Their descendants have tended to work in the fur trade, many of them, especially among the Red River Metis, in transporting the fur and supplies. Until very recently almost all water transport in the district was ancillary to the fur trade, owned or controlled by trading companies.

The decline in the role of Metis as post managers is related to certain general changes in the nature of commerce in the District. The earliest of these was an increase in the facility of travel between the District and areas of the South—"Outside," as they are still known in northern parlance. Passenger air travel, coming to the fore in the 1930's, made possible more frequent rotation of personnel in commerce and other activities based in the South, thus making these occupations more attractive to a larger number of whites than had been the case. Other relevant series of changes were in the organization and techniques of trading and merchandising.

With the decline in trapping and the accelerated acculturation of District natives, the need has continually grown less for the special contributions of Metis in the northern trade: their knowledge of the local languages, local trapping conditions, and individual trappers as producers and customers. At the same time there has been a rising demand for store managers with some sophistication in modern methods of retailing.

Hourly Wage Employment. Traditionally, wage employment in the North has been of a kind that is not organized into fixed working shifts and working days. Wage employment is characteristic of Metis since their earliest appearance in the District. The nature of their work, however, preeminently in summer and winter transport, has been far removed from clocked employment at repetitive tasks. Even work at a trading post has been traditionally quite different from rationalized labor.

The nature of commercial employment has been changing since World War II, as retail trade in the larger District centers has come to approximate trade in southern Canada. Many of the sales clerks are now women—Eskimo, Indian, and Metis as well as white. This is a distinctive postwar innovation in itself, for there was little employment for women in the prewar fur trade.

Many District Metis as well as Indians and Eskimos have been employed in construction, many more, indeed, than the number of job openings available to them, for the personnel turnover has been high. The reasons for the high turnover are not hard to find; they fall into two general categories: (a) deliberate intention on the part of the employee to work for a limited period and then return to some other occupation (e.g., trapping or, as some non-Metis would maintain, to no occupation) and (b) inability of the native employee to adjust satisfactorily to the nature and conditions of the work. The second category includes not only those who cannot adequately learn required skills and work habits and are discharged as a result but also those, particularly prominent or notorious in the eyes of management, who "take off" or "go on a bender" on payday.

Some Metis informants would add a third reason for labor turnover: prejudice against natives on the part of management. No doubt this is a factor, not so much in the deliberate firing of a man because he is an Indian, Eskimo, or Metis, but in mutual distrust between District natives and "Outside" management which complicates the problem of reducing the high rate of labor turnover.

Industrial society has had wide-reaching indirect effects on northern aboriginal cultures since earliest Euro-Canadian contact, but real industrialization has reached the Mackenzie District in limited degree. By real industrialization is meant not only—or not even—the operation of industrial installations but those qualitative changes in habits of life and in outlook represented by "knowing (and caring) what time it is." Industrialization in this sense—a tendency toward the creation of a middle and a working class—has affected only a slightly higher proportion of Metis than it has Indians and Eskimos. Among Metis it has touched retail-store employees in some degree, construction workers rather more, and government white-collar workers still more. However, those steadily and successfully employed in these types of work together constitute only a minority of District metis.

Education

The Postwar Federal School Program. The rapid development of the federal school system in the Northwest Territories since the close of World War II is one of the most striking features of northern Canadian history. A considerable effort is represented in the erection and operation of a federal school in every settled locality of any size in the District, the establishment of federally constructed, church-operated hostels in the larger localities—under an agreement between government and the churches when government took over the function of education in the North—and, what is perhaps most difficult, the development of an education service for the Territories.

Among the complex problems is the discrepancy between the chronological age and school grades of most native children. Table 9 is a tabulation of age-grade retardation prepared by an official at a large elementary school in the District. Difficulty in determining the actual academic level of many pupils is that figures such as those in the table are only estimates. Nevertheless, the fact of age-grade retardation is fairly obvious. Most of the reasons given by northern educators for the underachievement of native children have to do with "poor" home environment; that is, home environment is likely to retard rather than promote adjustment to and success in schools as organized in Euro-Canadian society.

One reason given for relatively poor achievement is excessive absenteeism or truancy. This is found in particular among Metis children in the larger settlements. Indian and Eskimo children reside in hostels whose management makes sure that they attend regularly, and parents of white children, especially those in the lower grades, see to it that their

Table 9   Percentage Distribution of Age-Grade Retardation in an Elementary School, September 1963

Years Retarded	Indian	Metis	White (and others)
	N = 182	149	251
−1 (advanced)	1	5	17
0	11	26	76[a]
1	22	25[a]	4
2	32[a]	19	1
3	18	9	1
4	9	14	1
5 or over	7	2	0
	100	100	100

[a] Mean figures. There was some fluctuation in these categories.

attendance is kept up. Two teachers, however, did state that there was white absenteeism in the higher grades. It was among local Metis children, however, that absenteeism was prevalent, since they were neither under the discipline of hostel authorities nor of families conditioned to "clock time" or to recognize the value of regular school attendance.

A second obstacle to academic success is deficiency in homework preparation. This is seen as largely the result of the same "permissive atmosphere in the home" or a "total lack of concern" which is said to foster absenteeism. Here, again, Metis students in the larger settlements are the most deficient group, since all hostel children and most white children living at home must spend time daily at homework and are provided with the facilities for doing so. Few Metis children living at home are required or encouraged to do homework, nor are they given a quiet place in which to do it.

Third, the native children appear to lack "push" or "drive"; that is, the competitiveness, aggressiveness, and ambition that are instilled in most white children, certainly those of middle-class families, by conditioning of which the parents are hardly aware. This lack of aggressiveness may add to the charm of the native children, but their noncompetitiveness is a handicap in modern social life.

A fourth class of obstacles to school success is the direct effect of poverty in the home, one of which is malnutrition and undernourishment. The principal of a large elementary school had cocoa and vitamin biscuits issued at 10 A.M. "for those children who needed it." In grades 1 through 3 there were 50 children on the list, almost all of them Indian or Metis. "It was obvious that, for most of them, this was the first nourishment they had had that day. . . . Naturally, you can't expect children to do well in school under those conditions." Another effect of poverty is poor condition of clothing and personal hygiene. The same principal remarked: "The fact is, many of them smell bad. And of course they are made aware of this, if they weren't already, by the more fortunate children. In the winter, the smell in some classrooms is oppressive. Often we take them upstairs and give them a bath."

Viewpoints on Native Cultures. Most persons interviewed who were professionally concerned with education in the Mackenzie District saw indigenous culture, insofar as certain aspects of it were recognized, as an impediment from whose vestiges the young people must be freed. Two school officials, indeed, remarked that the Indians in their area "had no culture." A cleric said, "Indian social life is very low. I don't blame the white people in a way for their attitude. . . . Some Metis are even more backward than the . . ." (naming the least acculturated tribe in his area). Frequently the theme of native "childishness," "irresponsibility," and need for tutelage and close guidance would be brought up in conversations with educators.

An important distinction from the culture of the dominant society, that of language, was not mentioned by school personnel in discussions of Metis, although it was frequently cited in reference to Indian and Eskimo students. There appeared to be strong consensus among District educators that the sooner the Indian languages died out, or were rooted out, the better it would be for future generations of Indians.

It appears that the language difficulties of Metis children are not those of persons whose native tongue is quite foreign but of those who speak substandard English, the same problem faced by lower class children in urban society. For many Metis children in the Mackenzie District, English, in any dialect, is not their mother tongue, that is, the language spoken by preference in the home and the one they learned to speak as infants. For many Red River Metis the mother tongue is "country" French, Cree, or Chipewyan. Certainly most of the Fort McPherson Metis whom I knew as very small children some years ago spoke Kutchin before English, however fluent they may now be in the latter language. Similarly, most of the Delta Eskimo Metis spoke Eskimo first.

Metis students seem to have no major language barrier because, in contrast to many Indians and Eskimos, a great majority of them speak fluent English at a fairly early age. Education in a language that is not one's native tongue does, however, impose difficulties concomitant with those involved in other transcultural adjustments. Many people have succeeded academically in various cultural and linguistic settings despite these difficulties, but that fact does not negate their existence as a factor added to other school problems of Metis children. The analogy comes to mind of French-speaking Canadian children fluent enough in colloquial English to be considered bilingual in common discourse yet who suffer retardation clearly related to language difficulties in English-language schools. The same is true of apparently bilingual Mexican-Americans in the schools of the southwestern United States. Yet these situations involve languages—French, Spanish, and English—that are related historically and are incomparably closer in every aspect of structure and meaning than is any one of them to an aboriginal American language.

A Red River Metis woman, born in 1920, whose native language is Cree, commented on this point. Her remarks are of particular interest because (a) she expressed great appreciation of the quality of federal schooling in the District and of the efforts and interest of most teachers and (b) as a Pentecostal preacher she is extraordinarily articulate in English.

It is very hard to read—not the reading itself, but getting the meaning of it. Because it's not your language. That makes it very hard for the children that are not English-speaking at home. . . . They (whites) don't seem to understand —I don't think they want to understand—that it is very, very hard. I know from my own experience, because English isn't my native language. No, it may be wrong of me to say they don't want to understand. Very few white people know an Indian language, and they simply haven't the faintest idea of how different it is from English, or from French for that matter. Some white people speak a few words of Cree and then they think they know it—they think it's easy to learn. But most of them just know those few words, not really the language. People—Indian and Eskimo people—tell me the same thing happens with their languages.

Internal Relations

Social Problems. To many observers the Metis seem to be a plexus of social problems, a collection of "deviants." Indeed, there is an intellectually respectable position from which indigenous American peoples are viewed almost exclusively in terms of social problems. In the present work it has seemed best to approach the study of northern Canadian Metis with no a priori expectation of material deficiencies and behavioral deviations from the norms and ideals of the dominant culture. It is strikingly true that most northern Canadians of indigenous background have "graduated" from independent marginal subsistence economies to poverty in the terms of our urbanized society.

The Metis have not constituted an independent society—except briefly and partially, as a "nation" in the Old Northwest—but rather have constituted a rural, or at any rate a backwoods, proletariat. Nevertheless, the most valid basis for an initial study of the Mackenzie District Metis is a consideration of them as humans who have worked out and are working out some means of living within the limitations and possibilities of their ecology and culture. Some of their "problems," in terms of prevailing Canadian social norms and requirements, should become apparent from such a study.

Conditions of Life, Deviance, and Law Violation. Almost every person interviewed, whatever his ethnic or other status, referred to drinking as a serious problem. This was as true of men and women known to be heavy drinkers as it was of police officers and clergymen.

Here is a sampling of Metis comments:

That—that drinking is a big problem. If they have money, they spend it at the bar. Drinking is worse now than it used to be. Used to be, one big bust a year, and that was it . . . (Northern Metis man, born 1912).

It's all liquor! Every one that comes in there (the town jail), it's all liquor. And that's why I figure there's a reason for it. And some of their stories are— like, they didn't know what to do, they didn't know where to turn to, so they feel that after the drunk, they don't have any more worries . . . (Red River Metis woman, a jail matron, born 1920).

Womans, they're worse than men! You take like when they get their family allowance most of these people around here spend their money on liquor. They don't buy nothing for kids. And some people uptown (the whites), same thing (Red River Metis man, born 1895).

Another thing is booze. Seems to be they lose their minds. They's all weak minds for the liquor. Some guy might be a good guy when he's sober; honest. When he's drunk he's a complete loss. He hasn't got a mind at all. . . . That's how the crime, everything, comes. Any man who's done the crime, he's always influence by liquor. . . . (Red River Metis man, born 1885).

The solutions offered were many and various. They included total as well as partial prohibition, adherence to a religious faith (especially the Pentecostal), the moving of families of groups into the bush to get away from it all, or, conversely, gaining experience Outside and learning to handle liquor. There were those, especially among whites not holding responsible positions, who viewed the situation cynically, offering no solution. They professed wry amusement at the spectacle provided by periodic group treks to the post office for family allowances and other governmental assistance checks, thence to grocery stores to cash them— "but taking care not to go to a store where they owe money"—thence to the liquor store and on to an increasingly erratic social round.

A pertinent set of observations on drinking behavior was proffered by an officer of the Royal Canadian Mounted Police. These observations were based on about 10 years' experience and a special study of police records in a number of District communities. The officer's conclusion was that Mackenzie District natives probably do not drink any more than whites in the District and that their actual rate of law violation—as contrasted with their arrest rate—is probably no higher than that of whites, except in (a) violations arising from the conditions under which the natives drink and (b) petty crimes against property which stem directly from deprivation. These conclusions were largely corroborated by other experienced law officials.

The Police officer pointed out that the living conditions of natives make it likely that they will be drunk in public, hence liable to arrest. For instance, since few natives own cars, they must walk home from a party, thus exposing themselves to the possibility of arrest. Whites are able to drink in greater privacy; if guests indulge too freely, they will be driven home.

The Rationalization of Interpersonal Relations. The North has been and remains a region in which primary interpersonal relationships are pervasive and widespread. It is also true that since the earliest arrival on the northern scene of the agents of Euro-Canadian society the sources of their power and authority, and to a large extent the ultimate ends to which they have been exercised, have been remote from the experience of northern indigenous peoples. These two general conditions, of which the former may be said to characterize "personal" and the latter "impersonal" relationships, have not changed markedly. What has changed in the last half-century, and most rapidly in the last two decades, are (a) the number and the variety of Euro-Canadian agents in the North; (b) the rate of personnel turnover among them; and (c) the volume of travel and communication between the North and the Outside.

"Rationalization" in this context means a tendency to formalize and bureaucratize interactions, thus emphasizing institutional terms of reference: vendor-purchaser, doctor-patient, clergyman-communicant, welfare worker-client, law agent-citizen (or offender). This tendency is, of course, in keeping with that of urban social life. Natives or non-natives who knew the North before the effect of these changes deplore them. This is how it feels to a Red River Metis, born in 1911:

Then you know, there's another thing that bothers a guy. Guys been in the country all their lives, you know, like—sort of built up the country—they're the ones that were here when things were tough—they're being pushed to one side. A fellow don't even feel at home in his own country any more. You know all these other people, they run around like they sort of own it. Makes a man feel like maybe he should move and let them take it over. . . .

And another thing: you know, in those older days, there used to be more mixing. Everybody sort of mixed together and knew each other. Now there's very little mixing. These new people they—they don't mix with us. Us natives. Used to be much better that way.

Another Red River Metis, born in 1915, echoed this statement:

This country isn't as good as it used to be. It was more like ours before. Now we feel kind of pushed to the side. It used to be, the white people that did come down here, they had to get here the hard way. There weren't many of them, and they mostly stayed. They became part of the country, too. Now—I don't know who they are. They come and go all the time. . . .

Old-timers among white functionaries complain of what an official of the Anglican Church half-humorously called "the curse" of modern communications and travel facilities. "It used to be," this clergyman recalled, "that when the last boat had left, you were left in peace with your people for a year. . . ." A federal official, also an old-timer in the District, wryly regretted that telephone service had reached this area. Others expressed similar sentiments. These men are aware of the neglect suffered by the Northwest Territories in the past. What they now miss is, in part, the security experienced, no matter how difficult the physical conditions, in a relatively stable situation, largely under local control and dominated by the people on the spot.

External Relations

It is by no means clear that the Mackenzie Metis have ever had a distinctive external system, although some parts of the Metis population may have had one. At any rate, in recent generations the Mackenzie Metis seem to have had none or almost none. This means, among other things, that the external relations of this ethnic group, that is, its means of dealing with non-Metis, have been through the institutions of the tangential societies. To oversimplify, when Metis have dealt with Indians, it has been as Indians; with whites, as whites. Since Metis by definition are neither Indians nor whites, Metis functioning in this area have been marginal Indians and marginal whites.

The implication is that there have been no Mackenzie Metis leaders, as such, confronting the non-Metis world. There have certainly been Metis leaders in other times and places; the names of Riel and Dumont, among others, are part of Canadian history.

This does not mean that there has been no leadership within the Metis internal system; there has been and there still is. Nor does it mean that there have been no Metis men of influence nor Metis with leadership potential; but personal qualities of leadership, and the influence that may derive from them, do not in themselves constitute leadership. Leadership is taken here to mean the effective exercise of power through sanctions.

Its prerequisite is a source of power and a means of channeling it in the independent and distinctive institutions of a group, community, or society. There have been Mackenzie Metis who have exercised leadership in some aspects of an Indian social system. In so functioning these men have been Indian leaders on the one hand and Euro-Canadian leaders who were Metis on the other. They have not been leaders of the Metis.

To this lack of Metis leadership in external relations there is an instructive exception. At Fort Resolution three conditions exist that are relevant to Metis external relations: (a) a majority of the Metis population is organized in semicorporate kinship groupings; (b) the leaders of these groupings in internal affairs are also leaders in external relations; (c) the Metis sector of the town's population has definite boundaries, an identity as a community within the larger plural community. A causal relation between these conditions, in the order stated, is suggested. None of these conditions prevails in any other District community known to me.

The situation at Fort Resolution illustrates by way of contrast what is meant by the absence of Metis external relations elsewhere. The semicorporate kin groupings are "givens" in the present analysis. It is not clear why they exist at Fort Resolution and not elsewhere, nor is it implied that kinship is the only possible basis for group identity, the structuring of external relations, and the power requisite to leadership.[4] To be sure, in the precontact societies of the District the internal structuring of groups was phrased largely in terms of kinship. External relations other than war were implemented in large measure by institutions of quasi-kinship; for example, trading partnership, affinity through the marriage of captives, and, in some areas, the interband and intertribal sib system.

During the mission-fur-trade period of postcontact history the external relations of communities and ethnic groups became stabilized in a few institutions by which the dominant society exercised power. This was true not only of Euro-Canadian authority and leadership but also of indigenous leadership and of interaction among indigenous groups.

The situation of Mackenzie District Metis in relation to members of other ethnic groups is rather different from those of Indians, Eskimos, or whites. This difference is reflected in the paucity of Metis leadership in external relations. As an enclave in Euro-Canadian society, the Mackenzie District Metis during the mission-fur-trade regime occupied a circumscribed, distinctive, and fairly unequivocal position. Most Metis, who are

---

4 "Kinship" is not to be taken as a kind of prime cause. It is equally valid to say that group identity is the basis of kinship. Neither formulation is sufficient, as a matter of fact.

non-Treaty, are *de jure* undifferentiated Canadian citizens. As such, it may be said that they have no special need for a system of external relations but rather that each of them must make his way on his own, as is the obligation and right of every citizen. *De facto*, they are not undifferentiated Canadian citizens. The breakdown of the old postcontact northern society, of which they were at once creatures and agents, and the rationalization of interaction in the North leave the Metis "freer" in the classic *laissez faire* sense and also more marginal than before.

Identity

Self-Identification. Of the 124 known Metis applicants for commercial fishing licenses at Hay River, 1959–1963, 109 entered a "racial origin" of Metis, in some form or other, on the applications. Fifteen of the known Metis gave a European "racial origin," and some Metis were among the 33 applicants who made illegible entries under "racial origin" or left them blank.

A Metis is justified in identifying himself as of Canadian, or for that matter, European "racial origin." Moreover, such an entry does not mean that the applicant fails to consider himself a Metis. He may feel that his "racial origin," a matter of history, is different from what he is right now.

Although all Metis are by definition persons who consider themselves Metis, this does not mean that all Metis call themselves "Metis," or any equivalent thereof, under all circumstances. It is not without significance that 17 out of 37, or 46 percent, of the Metis applicants at Hay River failed to enter "Metis" or some similar response under this heading.

During extensive conversations, awareness of being a Metis is likely to be expressed at some point. This is relatively easy for a Red River Metis, since he has available the term "Metis," legitimized by a long history, value-neutral at the least, and in some contexts honorific. The Northern Metis are in a more difficult position of self-identification; "Metis" is not common parlance north of Fort Simpson, and "half-breed" is a term that Northern Metis avoid. It is interesting that Red River Metis not uncommonly refer to themselves as "breed" and "halfbreed" without apparent strain or pain. Most commonly, a Northern Metis will signalize his self-identification by referring to "the whites" and "the natives" in contexts from which it is clear he is excluding himself. Such contexts do not necessarily occur in daily discourse. This difference in facility of self-identification (the fact that the Red River people have an acceptable term for ethnic identification which the Northern Metis lack) is not mere chance. It derives from differences in the histories of the two subgroupings as summarized below.

Regional-Historical Variation. Some of the older Red River Metis report family traditions deriving from the Metis "nation." Several told of kinsmen who had taken part in the Northwest Insurrections.

There is a well-established folklore of famed eponyms of Red River surname-groups, especially of "King" Beaulieu. There is also a tradition, related by several people of Beaulieu and Mandeville ancestry, that at some indefinite period in the early nineteenth century each of these Metis name-groups constituted a "tribe." As one informant told the story:

> These Beaulieus and Mandevilles—there may have been other bunches, but I don't know—they each had a sort of headquarters. The Beaulieus were on the Salt River and the Mandevilles on the south shore of the Lake (Great Slave) near Buffalo River. . . . Then they would pack up, the whole bunch, men, women, and children, and go on down the Mackenzie and turn up, maybe up the Liard, trading, hunting, on a great big circuit, on into northern B.C. Then over the Athabasca and back down to the Slave. . . . No, no, they couldn't do it in one season. They'd be gone for three, four, five years. They lived in the bush, like the Indians; only they kept going more, and they kept trading. . . . They were a tribe.

In addition to these traditions of semi-independence the Red River Metis have many tales that deal with the old fur trade and some specially derived from the voyageur tradition. No attempt was made, during fieldwork on this study, to collect folklore and folksongs as such, but I have heard some songs and fiddletunes that are probably those of the voyageurs, and one specifically, "Qui en a composé la chanson?"

Metis men have, paradoxically, spent their lives "in service" and yet have valued, perhaps above all else, freedom, impulse, and style. Freedom meant freedom to live as the Metis of the voyageur tradition lived; it did not preclude a great deal of hard work. This was not steady, time-clocked toil in the sober terms of the "Protestant ethic." Rather, it constituted episodes, sometimes quite prolonged ones, of arduous, often dangerous work that required a considerable degree of skill and initiative; *par excellence*, work in the canoe brigades and, at a later period, the bateaux. These periods alternated with those in which, as the Red River man quoted earlier remarked, "I spent it all (money) quick." Another use for money within the same tradition was mentioned by a Red River Metis elder at Fort Smith:

> I've made an awful lot of money in my time. I don't have any of it to show. (He laughed.) Spent it on good times. Some of it I gave away. Helped people, like old people, people who are stuck. That's what I figured money was for. I wish I knew then what I know now. I'd keep some of it. . . . But what the hell. . . .

Within this "free" life there was room for a considerable range of individual differences. A Red River Metis might be habitually honest or dishonest, witty or slow-tongued, a reasonably conscientious family man or a libertine, a devoted churchgoer or a scoffer. If, however, he could pull his weight on the river or on the trail and knew how to enjoy himself in the appropriate ways off the river or trail, he was an authentic Metis. If he were deficient in the former respect, he was shrugged off as a *cabochon* ("duffer," "incompetent"); if deficient in the latter respect, a *lourdaud* or *lourdais* ("dull person," "clod"). In either case he was no true Metis.

By contrast, the Northern Metis have little tradition appertaining specifically to their Metis status. This is in keeping with the shorter family lines since the original miscegenation and the shallower genealogies of Northern compared with Red River Metis in the District. Northern Metis traditions are primarily traditions of the Hudson's Bay Compary in the lower Mackenzie. Reference here, as in the discussion of Red River Metis tradition, is to the generations now elderly or deceased within the last twenty years and apparently to the generations immediately preceding them. Among the Northern Metis most persons of this age range are the offspring or grandchildren of white men who were in Hudson's Bay Company employ during "the Old Days" of the monopoly fur trade. Among Red River Metis there exist attenuated traditions of the warfare between the Hudson's Bay Company and the Northwest Company, in which these Metis played a conspicuous and, at times, semi-independent role. Among Northern Metis, however, there are no historical traditions reaching back in time beyond the Hudson's Bay Company monopoly trade.

For the older Northern Metis, identification with the Company is closely related to identification with the white father-figure. As such, it is a relationship of dependence and emulation, an ambivalent one with its other aspects, more or less repressed, of hostility and resentment.

Like their Northern fellows, many Red River Metis of the older generations have been sons of Hudson's Bay Company men, and have been themselves periodically employed by the Company. However, their attitude toward the Company has been more independent than that of the older Northern Metis. Their loyalty has been to their fellows, *les compagnons de la brigade,* rather than to the Company.

Summary

Some of the major social and cultural distinctions between the Red River and the Northern Metis in the Mackenzie District are schematically summarized below.

Red River Metis	Northern Metis
Descendants of remote miscegenation.	Descendants of relatively recent miscegenation.
European ancestry: predominantly French (Canadian) or gallicized Scottish or Irish.	European ancestry: predominantly Scottish, secondarily Scandinavian, English.
American ancestry: predominantly Algonkian (Cree, Ojibwa, or Saulteaux), Iroquoian (Six Nations), or Athapaskan of the Slave region (Chipewyan, Slave, Dogrib).	American ancestry: predominantly Athapaskan of the lower Mackenzie and middle Yukon regions (Bear Lake, Hare, Kutchin, some Dogrib), or Western Eskimo.
Predominantly and traditionally Roman Catholic.	Predominantly and traditionally Anglican (European ancestors often Presbyterian or Lutheran); secondarily Roman Catholic.
Possessing autonomous Metis traditions stemming from (a) old Lower Canada; (b) the Metis "nation" of the old Northwest; (c) the voyageur way of life.	Possessing little autonomous Metis tradition. Traditions are those of (a) the Hudson's Bay Company in the northern Mackenzie District; (b) the aboriginal society to which they are related.
Recognizing few European or Indian kin.	Recognizing an appreciable number of Indian, Eskimo, and white kin.
Surname-groups large, diffuse, genealogically deeper than those of Northern Metis.	Surname-groups smaller, more cohesive, genealogically shallower than those of Red River Metis.
In terms of residence and employment, the most mobile sector of the District population.	Less mobile than Red River Metis but more so, on the whole, than Indians, Eskimos, and most whites.
Although individual employment histories are extremely varied, as a group traditionally and still largely associated with transport.	Traditionally associated with fur-trade employ but not particularly with transport.
Independence and the satisfaction of impulse highly valued. Validation through identification with Metis tradition.	Authority and hierarchy valued. Validation either through (a) identification with white father and Euro-Canadian power institutions or (b) prestige and leadership among aboriginal congeners.

The Metis Orientation. On a scale of the variation in the total northern population, including Eskimos, Indians, and whites, the majority of Metis are neither strikingly bush-oriented nor strikingly urban-oriented. This majority of Mackenzie Metis evidences another sort of orientation. For convenience it may be called regional orientation. The term "regional" is used here in approximately the sense employed in some humanistic, sociological, and geographical studies, in which a nation may be described in terms of definable regions; there are regional dialects, regional art, regional ecologies. In this sense the Western Subarctic, within which most Mackenzie District Metis reside, is a region of Canada; the Mackenzie Metis are and long have been its characteristic people *par excellence.*

Members of particular Indian and Eskimo tribes, bands, or local groups have been identified with particular subregions far more intimately than have most Metis. Insofar as Indians and Eskimos move away from their local and particularistic identities and become relatively indistinguishable from other northern inhabitants, they converge on the established Metis pattern. The same is true of whites who, as a result of lengthy residence, type of occupation and social life, including marriage to native women, and other disposing factors in some degree lose identification with "Outside" institutions and interests and become, often unwittingly, more closely identified with the North (i.e., the Western Subarctic) than with their regions of origin or with the national life as a whole. They, too, may be said to have converged on the Metis pattern from the other direction than that of Indians and Eskimos.

Several white residents to whom the purpose of this study was explained have remarked to the effect that "Hell, everyone is getting to be Metis here." There is truth in such a comment if "everyone" excludes the occupational elite among Euro-Canadians. Metis may be seen as constituting from their beginnings a regional proletariat. As other people of various ethnic origins have joined this proletariat, they have taken on in large measure a Metis style of life. At the same time they contribute cultural features, such as work habits, leisure-time activities, and religious preferences which are novel to the region and which are adopted by members of the Metis ethnic group. Whether further convergence will occur between the Metis proper and those who are "getting to be Metis" remains to be seen.

SELECTED BIBLIOGRAPHY

Giraud, Marcel, *Le Métis canadien.* Travaus et Memoirs de l'Institut d'Ethnologie, XLIV. Paris: Institut d'Ethnologie, 1945.

Howard, Joseph Kinsey, *Strange Empire: A Narrative of the North-west.* New York: Morrow, 1952.

Julian, Ralph, *On Canada's Frontier.* New York: Harper, 1892.

MacLeod, William C., *The American Indian Frontier*. London: Kegan Paul, Trench, and Trubner, 1928.

Slobodin, Richard, *Metis of the Mackenzie District*. Ottawa: Canadian Research Centre for Anthropology, 1968.

Tremaudan, Auguste-Henri de, *Histoire de la nation Métisse dans l'ouest canadien*. Montreal: A Levesque, 1935.

Anthony Gary Dworkin

University of Missouri

CHAPTER NINE

THE PEOPLES OF LA RAZA:
THE MEXICAN-AMERICANS
OF LOS ANGELES

When Hernán Cortéz initiated his conquest of Mexico in 1519, he encountered racially homogeneous peoples of Indian stock.[1] When the Spanish left after Mexico's Wars of Independence (1810–1823), approximately 60 percent of the population was Indian. By the time of Mexico's Revolution a century later, Indians constituted fewer than 30 percent of the nation's people, and although no racial census has been taken in Mexico since 1921 the *mestizo*, or mixed-race population of Mexico, is presently in excess of 80 percent, leaving less than 20 percent to "pureblood" Indians, Europeans, including "pure-blood" Spaniards, and Negroes.[2]

North of the border, in the United States, well over 80 percent of the Mexican-Americans are *mestizos*.[3] The actual percentage cannot be esti-

---

[1] In Spanish *los indios* (Indians) refer only to peoples from South Asia; *los indígenas* describe the Mayans, Toltecs, and Aztecs who controlled Mexico before the Conquest and who represent the native racial element in the Mexican American today.

[2] See Pierre L. van den Berghe, *Race and Racism: A Comparative Perspective.* New York: Wiley, 1967, p. 45; and Victor Alba, *The Mexicans: The Making of a Nation.* New York: Praeger, 1967.

[3] Several preferred ethnic terms used by Mexican-Americans to describe themselves, show regional variation. In Texas the term Latin American is prevalent; in New Mexico, Arizona, and Colorado Spanish-American is most often used, and in California the preference is toward Mexican-American. The word *Chicano*, which is widely ac-

mated, since racial categories and subcategories have never been precise. In fact, only since 1960 has an attempt been made to distinguish between those who are Mexican-Americans and those who have Spanish surnames but are Cubans, Puerto Ricans, Filipinos, or South and Central Americans. The Mexican-Americans themselves are often unable, or unwilling, to assist Census takers in differentiating between *mestizos* and "pure-bloods." Moore and Cúellar recount the difficulty of determining whether an interviewee is a *mestizo*:

> The paradox comes to the surface when a hazel-eyed, pale-skinned man talks about his "Indianness" and a dark-skinned, Indian-featured man talks about his "whiteness."[4]

Nonetheless, the Mexican-American community *does* distinguish between *mestizos* and "pure-bloods," and we soon discuss this difference, but it is more often steeped in social myth than racial reality.

The decline of the Indian population is a direct product of the hispanization, mestizoization, catholicity, and feudalism established by the Spanish *Conquistadores* and by the administrators, bureaucrats, and profiteers from Madrid, Andalusia, and Extremadura who followed them. The decline of Mexican-American fortunes north of the border has been a consequence of exploitation, discrimination, and profiteering by the *Norteamericanos*—the *Anglos*, and sometimes more appropriately the *Gringos*.[5]

The history of the Mexican-Americans is that of a people who have experienced the conquests of the Spaniards and the Yankees; it is not, however, the history of a defeated people. The Spanish land "reforms" of *economedia* and *repartimiento* and, much later, the Mexican upper-class "reforms" of *latifundismo* succeeded in depriving the Indians of their land. Disease, slavery, concubinage, serfdom, and overwork have reduced the Indian numbers and mixed the gene pool. Unlike the English, however, the Spaniards—soldiers and settlers—did not come with many of their women. Further, under Spanish law, codified from Justinian law by Alphonso the Wise in the thirteenth century, slaves and Indians were considered as human beings with rights and privileges. Intermarriage was not frowned on either by the church or the government. Cortéz himself

---

cepted by the young and the students, connotes and emphasizes pride in one's mixed-race heritage. On occasion this term is used in this chapter.

4 Joan W. Moore with Alfredo Cuéllar, *Mexican Americans*. Englewood Cliffs, New Jersey: Prentice-Hall, 1970. By permission of the authors.

5 *Anglo* (Anglo-American) is a term used by Mexican Americans to describe whites in the United States who are of European ancestry. *Gringo* is the derogatory form of the word *Anglo*.

married a Tlascaltec Indian, named Malinche, who, with her people, helped him to overthrow the Aztecs in two short years. The gene pool also contains the contributions of blacks from Africa who were brought over on slave ships in the sixteenth century to reduce the burden on the Indians, then protected *de jure*, if not *de facto*, by the New Orders of 1542–1543.

Unlike the English who settled the Atlantic coast of North America, the Spaniards in Mexico sought to incorporate the indigenous peoples into the colony of New Spain. Like the English, however, they did seek to replicate the mother country in the New World; nonetheless, they counted as citizens the indigenous peoples and thus succeeded in producing the cultural, racial, and religious hybrid that is modern Mexico.

It was this racial hybrid, the *mestizo*, who traveled from Mexico City to California, the northwestern territory of New Spain to found what is now the City of Los Angeles. Their descendants constitute the second largest minority in the United States today and California's largest minority.

The Mexican-American in Los Angeles

In 1542 Juan Rodríguez Cabrillo entered San Diego Bay with his ships to mark the first white contact with the legendary islands of California. More than a century later, in 1769, Portolá discovered Los Angeles Harbor. In the same year Father Junípero Serra, a Franciscan missionary, began to build what would ultimately become 21 missions on the coast of California.

The City of Los Angeles was officially founded on September 4, 1781, although the validity of this date will never be established. Despite the claim that "pure Spaniards" were the founders, it is now known that the settlers were from the *criollo, mestizo, indigena,* and *mulatto castas* (racial classes) and had to have a military escort to keep them from escaping from their new home as much as to protect them from the Indians.

Great Spanish and later Mexican *ranchos* developed around the small city during the decade of Mexico's fight for independence. During the third and fourth decade of the nineteenth century the Anglos began to arrive in the Southwest: first in Texas but ultimately in California. Sutter's discovery of gold in 1848, California's entry into the Union in 1850, the transcontinental railroad which made California accessible to easterners and midwesterners, and the great land booms of the 1880's and the turn of the century served to reduce the Mexican-American to a *numerical* minority. Mexico's surrender to the United States to end the

1846–1848 war, the drought of 1862–1864, which killed the Mexican-American cattle economy in Southern California,[6] and Anglo interpretations of real estate, voting, and education laws converted the Mexican-Americans into a landless *power* minority.

In the early years of the twentieth century the expanding agricultural economy of California demanded a plentiful supply of cheap "stoop" labor to harvest the crops. After initial failures with Chinese coolies, Sikhs from India, and Japanese farm workers the growers turned to the Mexican-Americans, now living in poverty in rural areas and in the *barrios* (neighborhoods or ghettos) of Los Angeles. The people who once owned the land were now asked to farm it for the benefit of the Anglo *patrón*.

Mexican-Americans had resisted the low wages and long hours with attempts at unionization since the turn of the century, but it was not until 1927, when the *Confederacion de Uniones Obreros Mexicanos* (CUOM) was founded, that large-scale coordinated strikes could be called. Not wanting to raise their overhead, the growers in the 1930's persuaded the California state and Los Angeles county governments to control the "agitators."

First the farm workers and their families were placed in compounds to keep them on fields available to harvest each day unable to leave or strike. Later, between 1931 and 1934, the County of Los Angeles realized that it could assist the growers and cut the welfare rolls by "repatriating" Mexican-Americans to Mexico. Most of the children of the strikers and many of the strikers themselves were not Mexican nationals. They were United States citizens born in California, but because they could not speak English to defend their right to live in their country they were sent to Mexico. Los Angeles County deported about 15,000 in those four years, and across the Southwest in the decade of the 1930's nearly 300,000 fewer Mexican and Mexican-Americans were living in the United States.

In the early months of World War II the American war effort in the Pacific was one of retreat more often than of advancement. Frustrations over Japanese victories and the absence of a Japanese minority on the West Coast after relocation created a need for a scapegoat. The Mexican-American teenage gang member, with his tight-cuffed trousers, long coat, high boots, and duck-tail haircut provided an easily distin-

---

[6] The drought so bankrupted the *rancheros* that most had to sell their land to Anglo speculators for a tiny percentage of its real value. The massive Rancho de los Alamitos, which stretched for 265,000 acres, brought $154 on the auction block to pay its delinquent taxes. Thus, even though the Spanish Grant Deeds were to be honored as specified in the California Constitution, ways were found to get the land from the Mexican-Americans.

guishable target group. The police harassed these "zoot-suiters" who were not in the army "fighting for their country." Finally, on June 3, 1943, with tacit newspaper support, the Zoot-Suit Riot erupted in East Los Angeles. In 1944 the Juvenile Court of Los Angeles County took action against those wearing zoot-suits, by forcing them to work for the Sante Fe Railroad as convict laborers.

Many Mexican-Americans did serve in the U.S. Army and Marine Corps during the war. In fact, proportionately more combat decorations were awarded to Mexican-Americans than to any minority in United States history.

The returning G.I.'s, the *veteranos*,[7] who went to college under the G.I. Bill, organized chapters of G.I. Forum, MAPA (Mexican American Political Association), CSO (Community Service Organization), and other groups that sought to end segregation practices in California. By 1950 these *veteranos* had overturned legalized restrictive covenants in housing, the antimiscegenation law, and laws requiring segregated schools and public accommodations.

The conditions faced by Mexican-Americans today are much improved because of the *veteranos*. However, using legalism as a strategy, they succeeded only in removing *de jure* segregation. The major difficulty faced by Mexican-Americans in the 1970's is *de facto* discrimination.

The Demographic Perspective[8]

The most recent and reliable estimates of the total Mexican-American population suggest that between five and six million Mexican-Americans live in the United States. The vast majority (79.2 percent according to the Census estimate for 1969) live in the five southwestern states of California, Texas, New Mexico, Arizona, and Colorado (in descending order of population size).

Los Angeles is the population center and possibly the cultural center for Mexican-Americans in the United States. It certainly has more individuals with Spanish surnames and Mexican ancestry living within its

---

[7] In some *barrios* the term *veterano* is also used to refer to adults who are veterans of gang warfare during their youth. This usage of *veterano* is not implied here.
[8] Census statistics presented in this section were taken from Marcia Meeker with Joan R. Harris, *Background for Planning*, Research Department of the Welfare Planning Council, Los Angeles Region, Research Report No. 17, February 1964, and U.S. Bureau of the Census, *Current Population Reports*, series P-20, No. 213, "Persons of Spanish Origin in the United States: November 1969." U.S. Government Printing Office, Washington, D.C., 1971.

borders than any city in the world, aside from Mexico City itself. In 1960 the County of Los Angeles reported approximately 576,000 Mexican-American residents, and more than 70,000 Mexican-Americans were living in the large Chicano ghetto of East Los Angeles. Los Angeles was adding new Mexican-American residents at the rate of 2250 per month. An EYOA (Equal Youth Opportunity Agency) estimate places the present (1970) Spanish-surname population of Los Angeles county at nearly 1,118,000, or about twice the size of the 1960 total. Only a small percentage of this population would be non-Mexican-American: Latin Americans, Cubans, Puerto Ricans, and Filipinos. If this estimate is reasonably correct, the monthly increase in Los Angeles county of people with Spanish surnames is greater than 4500!

Although conditions among Mexican-Americans in Los Angeles County are better than they are elsewhere, they are far from ideal. The measures of affluence—income, education, and occupation—reveal that the Mexican-Americans in Los Angeles are at a definite disadvantage compared with the Anglos. Median income for Los Angeles' Mexican-Americans was $5759 in 1960, compared with $7433 for the Anglos. Although the Anglo in Los Angeles County had completed 12.2 years of schooling (first-semester junior college level), the median for the Mexican-American was only 9.0 years and 8.0 in the large ghetto of East Los Angeles (less than a full junior high school education). In 1960 5.1 percent of the Anglos were unemployed, whereas 7.4 percent of the Mexican-Americans were without jobs. If we consider underemployment—or the placement of people in low-status, low-paying jobs despite their qualification for better positions—the Mexican-American representation was easily 40 percent and has remained so today.

The Experience of Discrimination

These statistics may be presented in a more dramatic way in the experiences of individual Mexican-Americans. At several interview periods in the 1960's and the 1970's Mexican-Americans were asked to relate the various kinds of problem they faced in the *barrios* of Los Angeles. The data gathered from these interviews are summarized in the following pages. The topics include discrimination at school, by the police, and in the marketplace as home buyer, consumer, and employee.

Education. It is a belief in American society that the only route to fulfillment of the American Dream is by perseverance and education. Ethnic minorities believe overwhelmingly that it is in the educational system—the existing one or one that has been revamped—that success, liberation, or assimilation will accrue to them. Yet the present educational system militates against such goals for minorities and especially Mexican-Americans. Principal problems include the system of *de facto* segregation, overt and covert prejudice among teaching and administrative staff, the language barrier, and the absence of Mexican-American teachers in the schools.

Although segregated education was ruled unconstitutional in California in 1945, and in the United States in 1954, segregated housing, ghettoization, and Anglo opposition to sending their children to school with Mexican-Americans have left the latter in schools that are segregated *de facto*. More than two-thirds of the population of the ghetto in East Los Angeles is Mexican-American and its high school student population is more than 80 percent Mexican-American. Children so isolated from the rest of society soon come to believe, and teachers sometimes reinforce this belief, that their segregation is due to their "inferiority to the Anglo." They see and learn only the brutality that accompanies ghetto life.

They are also deprived of the opportunity to realize the American Dream. One of the observations of the Coleman and Campbell report, *Equality of Educational Opportunity*,[9] was that although most children in ghetto schools have ambitions as high as their suburban counterparts they never learn about how to realize them. This includes procedures for getting into college, the kind of training needed for a career, and how to go about interviewing for a job. These things are rarely communicated to ghetto school children, and fewer role models are available than in the suburban schools.

Prejudice in the school is many faceted. It ranges from the absence of textbooks that teach Mexican culture and history, thereby giving the child the impression that his people have no background of consequence, to the use of derogatory racial terms and the assignment of students to college-preparatory or trade-school courses on the basis of race. One parent reported that although her son had been independently tested by a psychologist and shown to have genius-level intelligence his high school counselor repeatedly attempted to keep him from taking college preparatory courses because "Mexicans don't make good scientists." Another Mexican-American student was told by his counselor to take only manual

---

[9] James S. Coleman and Ernest Q. Campbell et al., *Equality of Educational Opportunity*. U.S. Department of Health, Education, and Welfare, Government Printing Office, Washington, D.C., 1966. See also Raymond W. Mack, Ed., *Our Children's Burden*, Random House, New York, 1968, and Roscoe Hill and Malcolm Feeley, Eds., *Affirmative School Integration*, Sage Publication, Beverly Hills, California, 1968.

arts courses with a specialization in auto shop because "Mexicans are good with their hands and can do good body work on cars."

A few teachers have confided to this researcher that the school administration would "be a lot happier if all the Mexicans were taken out of the schools." One Anglo teacher in an East Los Angeles elementary school stated in 1966:

> If you keep these Mexican kids active, you keep them out of mischief. Punishment keeps them in line, just like it does in the Army. If you keep after these damn kids on the playground, then all will be fine in the classroom. These kids are born liars; you can never tell when they are telling the truth and you can't trust them. Consistency is very important here, there is only one way to do things around here.[10]

The presence of prejudiced teachers and counselors in the *barrio* schools is due to the fact that truly dedicated teachers are rare in most ghettoes. Minority people are hired infrequently, and only neophytes in teaching or those who are incompetent can, as a rule, be found in minority schools. Suburban schools and the wealthier districts in the city that pay higher salaries hire away the best teachers assigned to the *barrios*. There are some eminently qualified and dedicated teachers in the *barrios*, most of whom are Mexican-Americans, but extraordinary teachers are not plentiful. Nonetheless, they are seriously needed.

In 1966 few of the Anglo teachers in the East Los Angeles schools spoke Spanish and few of the children entering the schools for the first time spoke English. In some classrooms children and teachers said nothing to one another, since neither could speak the other's language. Since the mid-1960's attempts have been made to teach Spanish to the classroom teachers, but the efforts have often been more token than effective.

Until recently teachers in most of the school systems in the Southwest, and especially in Los Angeles, punished children for speaking Spanish in the classroom or school yard. Teachers sometimes assumed that Mexican culture, and the language that reinforces it, were major deterrents to assimilation and the future success of the children. Other teachers, unable to speak Spanish themselves, felt that the use of Spanish by the children reduced the control the teachers could have over them. By speaking Spanish, some teachers feared, the pupils could more effectively plot against them. One teacher stated the following:

> Mexican Americans want to be different. They don't want to be American.

---

[10] Quoted from Anthony Gary Dworkin, "No Siesta Mañana: The Mexican American in Los Angeles," in Raymond W. Mack, Ed., *Our Children's Burden*. New York: Random House, 1968, p. 389. By permission of the author and publisher.

They insist on speaking Spanish in school. Don't they think American is good enough for them? If you ask me, it's too good for them![11]

In 1966 of the 4000 teachers in the Los Angeles City school system only 80 were Mexican-Americans. Although the schools have attempted to recruit more Mexican-American teachers, they have had relatively little success. School is still seen as a place in which one experiences failure. Anglo prejudice and the absence of Mexican-American teacher role models makes the problem circular. With only prejudiced Anglos and few Mexican-Americans available to emulate in the schools, the pupils do not seek to identify with that status position and in so doing deprive the next generation of available role models.

The consequence of these problems is that despite the token efforts attempted in the *barrio* in East Los Angeles the drop-out rate among Mexican Americans has remained fairly constant throughout the 1960's. A member of the Los Angeles Board of Education announced in 1963, "Twenty percent of the Mexican-American youth drop out before the eighth grade, and three out of every four are gone by the time of high school graduation."[12] The percentages have undergone little change since then.

Police and the Community. Several respondents contended that police brutality is a frequent problem in the Mexican-American community. Even middle-class suburban Mexican-Americans indicated that they believed police-initiated violence to be excessive. The data suggest that stereotypes of the "dangerous" Mexican are given credence by some police officers. Patrolmen interviewed by this investigator in the early 1960's seemed to rely on the Ayres' imagery of the knife-wielding Mexican-American.[13]

One of my Mexican-American respondents in 1966, a newspaperman, observed:

The police approach the Mexican with the fear of the unknown. Police believe the old stereotypes that a Mexican will stick a knife into your back if you don't watch out. They see the Mexican as potentially violent. The police believing these old stereotypes walk into the Mexican community and act bel-

---

[11] Dworkin, *op. cit.*, pp. 404–405. By permission of the author and publisher.

[12] *Ibid.*, p. 430. By permission of the author and publisher.

[13] Captain E. Duran Ayres was the Los Angeles Sheriff's Office chief of the Foreign Relations Bureau during the time of the Zoot-Suit Riots. He attributed Mexican-American gang violence partly to discrimination and deprivation but mainly to "racial instincts" and "inborn characteristics" which cause him to let blood and kill with the knife he carries. See Carey McWilliams, *North from Mexico.* New York: J. B. Lippincott, 1949, or Greenwood Press, 1968, Chapter 13.

ligerent. They feel they have to show the Mexican that they are tough. As such, you get a self-fulfilling prophecy of violence. There are two levels of brutality: (1) verbal manhandling and aggressiveness, and (2) if the suspect reacts with any resentment to the insults shouted by the police, the police hit him, thinking that the suspect was about to attack the officer.

Although the Los Angeles Police Department has made several attempts to improve police-community relations, including the establishment of citizen review boards and the hiring of Chicano policemen, the events of the summer of 1970 in East Los Angeles (including the killing of three Chicanos, among whom was the newspaper and television reporter Reuben Salazar) suggest that law enforcement in the county may be less progressive.

Many instances of police brutality may well be fabrications or misinterpretations of standard police behavior. Nonetheless, both the Mexican-American community in general and many law enforcement officials believe the mutual negative stereotypes of the other. When both groups stereotype one another and rely on those stereotypes to guide their interactions, violent confrontations are frequently unavoidable.

The Economic Sphere. Mexican-Americans frequently complain about the quality of housing available to them. The 1960 Census indicates that in East Los Angeles 29 percent of the homes were deteriorated or dilapidated, compared with 22 percent in the black ghetto of Watts, and 6 percent in the Anglo neighborhoods. Some individuals reported paying $70 to $100 per month for apartments that had no plumbing and where some landlords required their tenants to share a common outhouse. Frequently, Mexican-Americans who attempted to buy into better neighborhoods in the Anglo suburbs were turned away. Several interviewees of this researcher reported being told by real estate agents, "Sorry, no Mexicans allowed here."

Individuals complained that welfare recipients were frequently forbidden to purchase automobiles with their welfare checks. The absence of an automobile in Los Angeles, which spreads over 4100 square miles and lacks a rapid transit system, forces Mexican-Americans living in the *barrio* without transportation to rely on local employment and ghetto merchants. In the *barrio* the corner store charges considerably more for a given item than a supermarket in the Anglo suburbs. A dollar's worth of cornmeal in the *barrio* would likely cost only 65 cents in a suburban store.

The higher prices in the ghetto are a consequence of three intersecting variables: (a) the high unit cost of wholesale items purchased by a low-volume corner store (supermarkets are rare in the *barrios*); (b) the high insurance premiums ghetto merchants must pay because of numerous incidents of vandalism, shoplifting, and robbery in ghetto commercial areas; and (c) the opportunity afforded ghetto merchants to exploit their captive consumers. A Mexican-American newspaperwoman once recounted to me that some Anglo merchants are not above selling secondhand items at new-product prices. In one extreme case, a 1949 black and white television set, its picture tube tinted with glass stain, was sold in 1966 for $300 as a new color set. As Caplovitz and Marx each document, "the poor pay more."[14]

Like the blacks, Chicanos are frequently victimized in the labor market. In November 1969 unemployment among Mexican-Americans was 6.2 percent, compared with 2.7 for Anglos. Estimates for 1971 suggest that compared with 7.5 percent unemployment for the city the Mexican-American figure is closer to 10 percent. Only 18 percent of the Mexican-American males are in white-collar occupations, compared with 41 percent for the Anglos.

In a very narrow interpretation of civil rights legislation the Chicano is considered white (the Census once termed Chicano "Spanish whites") and thus is not eligible to complain about job discrimination. Although, in fact, cases have been brought before the FEPC and the Civil Rights Commission's Mexican Affairs Division, some employers, when faced with the mandate to hire more ethnics, fire Chicanos and hire blacks to comply with the civil rights laws. Other employers pit Chicanos and blacks against one another. One employer asked a Chicano if he would work for a given rate, and, when the Chicano said "yes," the employer asked a black if he would work at a lower rate. When the black agreed, the employer returned to the Chicano with the black's agreement and asked if the Chicano would undercut the black. This continued until the black decided the rate was too low and so the Chicano was hired—at less than one-half the State of California's minimum wage.

A Frequent Cultural Explanation

Recently in *El Grito*, a Chicano scholarly journal, Nick C. Vaca examined systematically the portrayal of Mexican-Americans in social science throughout the twentieth century.[15] His conclusion was that a cultural

---

14 See David Caplovitz, *The Poor Pay More: Consumer Practices of Low-Income Families*. New York: The Free Press, 1963. Also Gary T. Marx, *Protest and Prejudice: A Study of Belief in the Black Community*. New York: Wiley, 1968.
15 Nick C. Vaca, "The Mexican-American in the Social Sciences," *El Grito*, 3, 3–24,

determinism model still prevalent in social scientific writing served ul-
terior motives in the comparison between Mexican-Americans and Anglos. It has been a frequent method of researchers to compare the two
groups, pointing out how more closely the Anglo adopted the progress-
oriented "Protestant ethic" values and how the Mexican-American
more often endorsed values that militated against success in a technolog-
ically advanced urban society. In such comparisons Redfield's folk-urban
dichotomy is employed. Mexican-Americans are assumed to come from
a society which is

> . . . small, isolated, non-literate, and homogeneous, with a strong sense of group
> solidarity. The ways of living are conventionalized into that system which we
> call a "culture." Behavior is traditional, spontaneous, uncritical, and personal;
> there is no legislation or habit of experiment and reflection for intellectual
> ends. Kinship, its relationships and institutions, are the type categories of ex-
> perience, and the familial group is the unit of action. The sacred prevails over
> the secular; the economy is one of status rather than of market.[16]

As a "folk" people, Mexican-Americans are pictured as emotional,
complacent, fatalistic, superstitious, and unsanitary. The Anglo, in contradistinction, is said to be more scientific, rational, ambitious, orderly,
and a host of other characteristics that Anglos prefer to be thought of as
possessing. Many are Anglo stereotypes of the Mexican-American that
some Chicano scholars believe are held by Anglo researchers to rationalize Anglo discrimination. Although some of the images held by those
social scientists who endorse the "folk" model for Mexican-Americans
appear to have racist motivations, unconscious subject bias and overem-
phasis on rural samples provide better explanations for the Anglo researchers' findings and interpretations.

It is true, however, that reliance on cultural determinacy models to
account for differentials between Anglo and Mexican-Americans may
have the unintended consequence of minimizing Anglo culpability for
Mexican-American misery. Although it is true that there are several real
dimensions on which cultural differences exist, the assumption that the
"characteristics" of Mexican-Americans predestined them to ghetto life
and that Mexican-American culture is to blame is far from reality. It is
a fact of American society that the major difficulty faced by Mexican-

---

17–51 (Spring and Fall, 1970). See also Octavio I. Romano V, "The Anthropology and
Sociology of the Mexican-Americans," *El Grito*, **2**, 13–26 (Fall 1968).
[16] Robert Redfield, "The Folk Society," *Amer. J. Sociol.*, **52**, 294 (January 1947). By
permission of the University of Chicago Press, publisher of *The American Journal of
Sociology*.

Americans (or any minority group) is not their culture but the racist beliefs of some Americans on whom they are forced to depend.

Many of the differences attributed to culture ought properly be attributed to social class. The principle of "ethclass" developed by Gordon and tested by Landis, Datwyler, and Dorn operates here[17]; that is, comparisons of peoples cross-classified by ethnicity and social class reveal that like-positioned members of different ethnic groups share common values, interests, and life styles. We find that the middle-class Anglo and the middle-class Mexican-American share more in common than either does with its lower class counterpart. This is true also in comparisons that hold lower-class or upper-class status constant while letting ethnicity vary.

In some instances we find elements attributed to Mexican-Americans also equally present in Anglos, regardless of social class. One such element is the pattern of *machismo* or male dominance. Dworkin, writing on the traditional picture of the Mexican-American male and the cult of *machismo*, comments as follows:

The Mexican family, like the Catholic Church, is patriarchal and authoritarian. There is a double standard in which the restrictions upon the male are significantly less. Education is for the man, sexual liberties are for the man, material comforts are for the man, and politics are for the man. The woman is subordinate. She must be faithful to her husband and her children. She is controlled by her parents until she marries; then she is dominated by her husband.[18]

Madsen adds the following:

The young husband must show his male acquaintances that he has more sexual energy than his wife can accommodate. To prove his prowess, he often continues the sexual hunt of his premarital days. . . . The most convincing way of proving *machismo* and financial ability is to keep a mistress in a second household known as a *casa chica*. Few men in the lower class can aspire to such luxury, which constitutes the height of manly success among middle- and upper-class husbands.[19]

An examination of the mass media in the United States casts doubt on any claim that *machismo* is exclusively Mexican-American.

---

[17] See Milton M. Gordon, *Assimilation in American Life*. New York: Oxford University Press, 1964, and Judson R. Landis, Darryl Datwyler, and Dean S. Dorn, "Race and Social Class as Determinants of Social Distance," *Sociol. Soc. Res.*, **51**, 78–86 (October 1966).

[18] Dworkin, *op. cit.*, p. 401. By permission of the author and publisher.

[19] William Madsen, *The Mexican Americans of South Texas*. New York: Holt, 1964, p. 49. By permission of the author and publisher.

Grebler, Moore, and Guzmán recently contended that *machismo* is declining in the *barrio*.[20] The data suggest, however, that it has shifted from a rural model to an urban model, rather than disappearing. A conference on the status of Mexican-American women dealt with the issue of *machismo* and concluded that the double standard based on sex, the central concept in *machismo*, is still a pervasive problem for Mexican-American women.

Some Real Differences

Despite the danger of crediting too much to cultural factors, it is important that we examine certain extrinsic cultural characteristics that often provide the basis of Mexican-American stereotypes. The image of the Mexican-American as lazy, fatalistic, or short-run hedonist is little more than a stereotype. It has been utilized to rationalize inferior treatment of Chicanos. The activities of Mexican-American labor and political leaders throughout the Southwest and the efforts of the *veteranos* after World War II deny the validity of the stereotype. Nonetheless, some elements of Mexican-American culture have been functional for the survival of the people. These are the use of Spanish as the primary language, the stress of the family unit over the individual, and the unifying concept of *La Raza*.

Spanish: The Medium of a Cultural Heritage. One of the most efficient ways to destroy a cultural heritage is to eradicate a language. Educators frequently felt that Mexican-American culture was antithetical to the "Americanization" of the children. As stated by Milton Gordon, assimilation in American society is predicated generally (especially if the minority is of low status) on the acceptance of the norms of Anglo conformity or the renunciation of one's own culture for that of the dominant society.[21] Spanish provides for the Mexican-Americans a familiar cultural heritage on which to depend. It provides a private language, a sense of security, and a sense of being and of history. To give up Spanish is to say that one's ancestors accounted for nothing and that one's ancestors made no impression on the history of the Southwest. Not only would this be erroneous, it would be tragic. Furthermore, when Spanish is spoken at home, it becomes easier to express the ideas laden with special, personal meaning in that language. Finally, since Spanish is seen

---

[20] Leo Grebler, Joan W. Moore, and Ralph C. Guzmán, *The Mexican-American People: The Nation's Second Largest Minority.* New York: The Free Press, 1970, p. 363.
[21] Milton M. Gordon, *loc. cit.*

as the "culprit" by the Anglo educator, it becomes a symbol of pride to speak the language. I have known several Mexican-Americans who, before running for local political office, have attempted to sharpen their comprehension and fluency in Spanish, to prove to the people that they are not simply Anglo dupes—or *Tio Tacos.*

The Stress on Familism. Extended familism with geographical propinquity is a highly functional practice among poor people. Although it implies more mouths to feed, it also guarantees that there will probably be at least one person in the household unit who has a job at any one time. For the poor an extended family unit living within a single household, or in nearby households, guarantees that advice, babysitting, home medical care, life insurance, and some degree of financial security will be available. The Mexican-Americans in the ghetto frequently cannot afford a substantial insurance policy with a large organization; they must rely on their own resources and resourcefulness. One consequence is that the family unit becomes sacred. Reinforced by the sanctity of the family stressed in Catholicism, Mexican-Americans often place greater emphasis on the family than on its individual members. This is a functional adaptation. There are, of course, exceptions, especially with an increase in family affluence. Nonetheless, the relative absence of the stress of the family unit over the individual in middle-class suburban Anglo families causes many Mexican-Americans to assert that Anglos have "poor family life" or "little family loyalty."

Middle-class Anglo teachers, government officials, policemen, and others who do not recognize the significance of the family unit are frequently dismayed by the failures of an educational system and the Poverty Program to dislodge the Mexican-American individual from his family. The schools and the Poverty Program projects tell Mexican-American teenagers that their realization of the American Dream is contingent on leaving the ghetto and their relatives who are bound to that ghetto. Individual achievement, even at the expense of one's friends and family, is stressed; for example, when Maria is faced with the choice of continuing in school or helping her mother care for her younger siblings she feels obligated to her parents. Although an Anglo in a comparable situation might experience Maria's dilemma, if the family were affluent enough, someone could be hired to assist the mother and thus release the child to attend school.

La Raza. The third cultural element is the unifying concept of *La Raza,* or race. The concept was formulated by the Mexican writer, statesman, and philosopher, José Vasconcelos as "La Raza Cosmica."

Summarized by Grebler, Moore, and Guzmán, Vasconcelos argued as follows:

> . . . the *mestizos,* a racially mixed people of the New World with Indian and Mediterranean-European strains, would some day form the "cosmic race," because tropical climates had historically nurtured more of the higher civilizations than did the temperate ones. Ultimately, the *mestizos* of the New World would achieve their rightful place in the universe.[22]

La Raza today is a counterideology to the Anglo superiority and Manifest Destiny themes to which Mexicans and Mexican-Americans have been exposed since initial Anglo contact in the nineteenth century.

La Raza has been used to account for the prosperity of Mexico over the last three decades, but in the Southwest it has been known only to the middle and upper classes. One example of the *La Raza Cosmica* theme can be observed in the zealous statements made by a prosperous Mexican-American who lives in an Anglo suburb:

> If you show the prejudiced Anglos what an advanced culture the Mayans and Aztecs had and prove to them that the Mexican has a great cultural heritage, they will wish that they were Mexicans and respect us. In fact many will want to leave the North and move to Mexico to live.[23]

Madsen, describing the poverty-striken Mexican-Americans in South Texas, describes another form of *La Raza.* One might term this form *"La Raza* Gone Astray":

> In Texas, the history of discrimination and economic subordination has modified the concept of the ultimate destiny of *La Raza.* Many Spanish-speaking Texans would say that God had originally planned a glorious future for the Mexican-American but it probably will never be attained. The failure of *La Raza,* he would continue, is due to the sins of individual Latins. Some believe that *La Raza* is held back by the sins of all Mexican-Americans, "The only ones among us who are surely free from sin are the little children." Other Latins think that only the worst sinners are holding back *La Raza,* "We could meet with God's favor again if the drunks and thieves would reform. We all suffer because of the sins of a few." I once asked a Latin if he thought the Anglos were in any way responsible for holding back the Mexican-Americans from their God-given destiny. "Of course not," he replied, "If we lived by God's commands we would be so strong that no one could block us. Of course, the Anglos take advantage of our weaknesses but it is we who make ourselves weak, not the Anglos."[24]

---

[22] Grebler, Moore, and Guzmán, *op. cit.,* p. 379. By permission of the authors and publisher.
[23] Dworkin, *op. cit.,* p. 401. By permission of the author and publisher.
[24] Madsen, *op. cit.,* p. 15. By permission of the author and publisher.

The popular acceptance of *chicanismo* and the Chicano movement with its press for civil rights is changing this form of *La Raza* into something more reminiscent of the type described by Vasconcelos.

Hispano and Chicano: A Salient Dichotomy

La Raza has not been completely successful in unifying Mexican-Americans. There still persists a distinction between those Mexican-Americans who claim that their lineage is "pure Spanish" and those who emphasize their Indian or *mestizo* heritage. The distinction, with its invidious evaluations, dates back to the pre-1800's when the Spanish required that complex racial distinctions be noted on birth records. The landed aristocracy who possessed the great *ranchos* considered themselves *Hispanos* and *criollos*, of European or American-Spanish descent. They generated hostile and negative stereotypes of the *mestizos*, so that when the Anglos came to the Southwest they discovered two radically different sets of Mexican people with different images of one another. *La gente de razón* (the people of reason), the aristocracy, were pictured as romantic, generous, friendly, cerebral types, whereas the *mestizo* peasants were seen as lazy, sloppy, immoral, and stupid. These were the images held by the aristocracy and accepted without question by the Anglos as they entered the Southwest.

Historically the *Hispanos*, especially in New Mexico, Arizona, and southern Colorado, allied themselves with the Anglos, thereby retaining power against the *mestizo* peasants and the Comanches and Apaches. They referred to the peasants as *cholos*, *Mejicanos*, or *Mexicanos* and discriminated against them. The concept *Chicano* evolved among those who took pride in their mixed-race heritage. It is the truncation of *Mexicano*, the derogatory term used by *la gente de razón*, the *Hispanos*. The lingering dislike between *Hispanos* and *Chicanos* is evident in the following interaction situations. When asked to state what the term *Hispano* meant to him, one Chicano in his thirties replied:

> *Hispano* is a dirty word. *Hispanos* are people who pretend to be Spaniards because they think they are too good to be Mexicans. Actually *Hispanos* want to be Anglos. They are against *La Raza*.

Another man, a wealthy suburbanite who referred to himself as *Hispano*, objected to his daughter's dating a Mexican-American because "he's a *cholo*." This father preferred his daughter to date "Anglos or some persons of refinement."

Anglo Images: A View from the Dominant Perspective

In part to rationalize the taking of the Southwest from Mexico by violence, early images of the Mexican were negative.[25] We noted earlier that the Anglo portrayed the *mestizo* as lazy, greasy, cruel, and cowardly, especially on the Anglicized version of how Mexico took the Alamo. Popular writers of the era described the Mexican peasant as loose-living and immoral. Other writers pictured the *Hispano* as romantic, friendly, and fun loving. Each of these images has persisted, especially the negative ones, to serve as a reliable vocabulary of motives to rationalize ghettoization and low wages. As Ozzie Simmons succinctly states:

> . . . if Mexicans are deceitful and immoral, they do not have to be accorded equal status and justice; if they are mysterious and unpredictable, there is no point in treating them as one would a fellow Anglo-American; and if they are hostile and dangerous, it is best that they live apart in colonies of their own.[26]

Twenty-five years ago, when Ruth Tuck wrote *Not with the Fist*,[27] a seminal study of the attitudes of Anglos toward Mexican-Americans in San Bernardino, California, she reported her respondents referred to a Mexican-American as a "Mex" and indicated only negative images of such a person. Eugene Richards, enumerating stereotypes held by college students in 1950, found a preponderance of negative images similar to those used in the nineteenth century.[28]

In 1967 I collected the images of Mexican-Americans held by Anglo college and noncollege individuals between the ages of 18 and 24.[29] The stratified random sample of Los Angeles produced the following percentages of stereotypes: Mexican-Americans were seen as "lazy" (36),

---

[25] The images of the Mexican-American held by Anglos are primarily stereotypes. Allport provides us with the most commonly accepted functionalist definition of stereotypy: "A stereotype is an exaggerated belief associated with a category. Its function is to justify (rationalize) our conduct in relation to that category." Gordon W. Allport, *The Nature of Prejudice*. Cambridge: Addison-Wesley, 1954, p. 191.

[26] Ozzie G. Simmons, "The Mutual Images and Expectations of Anglo-Americans and Mexican-Americans," *Daedalus*, **90**, 292 (Spring 1961). By permission of the author and *Daedalus*, Journal of the American Academy of Arts and Sciences.

[27] Ruth Tuck, *Not with the Fist*. New York: Harcourt, Brace, 1946.

[28] Eugene S. Richards, "Attitudes of College Students in the Southwest Toward Ethnic Groups in the United States," *Sociol. Soc. Res.*, **35**, 22–30 (October 1950).

[29] Anthony Gary Dworkin, "Prejudice, Discrimination, and Intergroup Perceptions: Exploratory Research into the Correlates of Stereotypy." Unpublished Ph.D. dissertation, Northwestern University, Evanston, Illinois, 1970.

"emotional" (35), of "low intelligence" (31), "dark skinned" (30), from "large families" (24), "uneducated" (23), and "dressing sloppy" (22). Social distance statements suggested that, second only to the black American, the Mexican-American was an undesirable group to these Anglos.

Chicano Images: A Changing Perspective

It is difficult to imagine that a people can be defined negatively for generations and not have it affect their own self-conception. Madsen[30] reported that his informants rationalized Anglo discrimination as acts of God designed to punish them (the Mexican-Americans) for their sins. Simmons[31] observed that most Mexican-American stereotypes of the Anglo accounted for relative superordinate status of this group over the Mexican-American. My own research[32] reflected both the hostility of the Mexican-American toward his suppressor, the Anglo, and his own despair at the social position in which he found himself.

In 1963 Mexican-Americans, especially those born and raised in the East Los Angeles *barrio*, were asked to characterize Anglos.[33] Percentagewise they saw them as "education-minded" (100), "materialistic" (100), "tall, thin, and light complexioned" (96), "prejudiced" (90), "snobbish" (88), "tense, anxious, and neurotic" (82), "conformists" (80), and "puritanical" (78).

Percentagewise they described themselves as "emotional" (100), "unscientific" (94), "authoritarian" (92), "materialistic" (92), "old-fashioned" (88), "poor and of low social class" (84), "little care for education" (78), "mistrusted" (78), "proud" (78), and "lazy, indifferent, and unambitious" (78). Grebler, Moore, and Guzmán reported similar images in a sampling three years later in both San Antonio, Texas, and Los Angeles.[34]

---

30 Madsen, *op. cit.*

31 Simmons, *op. cit.*

32 Besides the study cited in Footnote 29, see any of the following by Anthony Gary Dworkin: "Stereotypes and Self Images Held by Native-Born and Foreign-Born Mexican Americans," *Sociol. Soc. Res.*, **49**, 214–224 (January 1965). "Epilogue to Stereotypes and Self Images held by Native-Born and Foreign-Born Mexican Americans: Mexican American Stereotypes Revisited," in John H. Burma, Ed., *Mexican Americans in the United States.* New York: Schenkman, 1970, 397–409; "National Origin and Ghetto Experience as Variables in Mexican American Stereotype," in Nathaniel Wagner and Marsha Huag, Eds., *Chicanos: Social and Psychological Perspectives.* St. Louis: Mosby, 1971, Ch. 8; "Patterns of Mexican American Stereotypy," in Hector L. Cordova, Ed., *Perspectives on Mexican American Studies.* New York: Holt, Rinehart and Winston, in press.

33 Dworkin, 1965, *loc. cit.*

34 Grebler, Moore, and Guzmán, *loc. cit.*

However, by 1967–1968, in a subsequent study, changes occurred in the images.[35] Many of the same words were used by the Mexican-Americans, but they were often qualified by the statement that it was Anglo discrimination that had caused this unfavorable stereotype rather than, as Madsen had seen, God's punishment for Mexican-American sins. The onus of the blame had shifted to the more culpable target. Furthermore, some images, previously defined as unfavorable, were redefined; for example, in 1963 "wild," "daring," and "emotional" were seen as unfavorable, as by middle-class suburban Anglo standards they might well be; but in 1967–1968 they had become favorable qualities, connoting sensitivity and "soul."

The images of the Anglo had also changed, if not denotatively, then connotatively. Although high social position and materialism were once favorable qualities, they were later reinterpreted to imply that the Anglo attained his status by being part of the "establishment" and by suppressing minorities for self-advancement.

There are several reasons why the stereotypes of the Anglo and the autostereotypes of Mexican-Americans have changed in the last 10 years. The Chicano movement may account for much of this change. Mexican-Americans, especially the younger generation, have announced a manifesto: that to be of La Raza, to be a Chicano, in the United States is to be proud of oneself, to be proud of one's history, and to be vigilant against discrimination. A second factor, not unrelated to the first, is that as a consequence of the Chicano movement, Mexican-Americans have learned not to accept the Anglo uncritically. This applies not only to the promises made by Anglo salesmen who go door to door through the barrio, but of Anglo teachers and textbooks that interpret the history of the Southwest in terms of Mexican villains and Yankee heroes. As such, stereotypes that the Anglos have been teaching the Mexican-Americans for a century are now being questioned, and those images that have been retained are redefined within a Mexican-American perspective.

The Chicano Movement and the Future

The Chicano movement, which developed at Loyola University in Los Angeles in 1966, is only the latest in a series of attempts to resist and overcome Anglo domination of the barrios and Anglo discrimination. Although it is not solely a student movement, it is heavily populated by the young. With a cadre of better educated supporters and with the

---

[35] Dworkin, 1970a, 1970b, loc. cit.

assistance of New Left organizations it is more likely to achieve its goals than previous groups in the Mexican-American community. It has its roots in the efforts of those who built the CUOM in the 1920's to resist the Anglo farm operators; it also has its roots in the efforts of the *veteranos*.

The movement is made up as much by such people as César Chávez, Reies Tijerina, and "Corky" Gonzáles as by college-age Chicanos on campuses. Through a century of resistance against the Anglo has come the powerful ethic of the Chicano movement: that the culture of the Mayans and Aztecs, combined with the culture of Spain, has produced a mixed people, a hybrid with a destiny in this land, who will continue to resist those in the United States and elsewhere who place individual wants and Anglo superiority above human rights.

Jacobs, Landau, and Pell are correct in stating that Chicanos and *chicanismo* is of the "third world."[36] The cultural heroes of the Chicanos include Mexican historical revolutionaries such as Juarez, Zapata, and Villa, who not only opposed the power of rich landlords in Mexico but also the United States when it interfered with Mexican affairs. Additional heroes include Chicanos of the present era, including César Estrada Chávez, Reies Tijerina, Rudolpho "Corkey" Gonzáles, and even Huey Newton of the Black Panthers (despite the tendency for Chicanos and blacks to fight one another and to oppose one another's advances).

Chávez, labor leader, shrewd political actor, and dedicated humanitarian, became a national figure in his successful grape strike in Delano, California, in 1965.[37] He is probably the leading civil rights leader among the Chicanos, and his nonviolent orientation reminds one of the late Dr. Martin Luther King, Jr., a comparison that has often been drawn and acknowledged by members of the Chicano community. During the Delano strike considerable community support in East Los Angeles was generated. Residents of the *barrio* refrained from buying grapes and other fruits that were not picked by National Farm Worker's Association members. In fact, support of the Delano strike was one of the first widespread collective acts by the East Los Angeles community and clearly indicated that conditions were feasible for a large social movement.

Tijerina and Gonzáles are less nonviolent in their strategy for Chicano liberation. The former was involved in the abortive violent attempt in Rio Arriba County, New Mexico, by *La Alianza Federal de Mercedes*

---

[36] Paul Jacobs and Saul Landau with Eve Pell, *To Serve the Devil: Natives and Slaves* (Volume I). New York: Random House, 1971.

[37] See John Gregory Dunne, *Delano: The Story of the Grape Strike*. New York: Farrar, Straus, and Giroux, 1967; and Rev. William E. Scholes, "The Migrant Worker," in Julian Samora, Ed., *La Raza*. Notre Dame University Press, 1966, pp. 63–94.

(Federal Alliance of Land Grants) on June 5, 1967, to make a citizen's arrest of the Anglo-controlled county district attorney in the town of Tierra Amarilla and to reclaim lands historically owned by Chicanos, but presently part of a U.S. National Forest.[38] The result was the arrest of Tijerina on federal kidnapping charges. This incident aroused the support of Chicano communities throughout the Southwest. Gonzáles, supporter of Tijerina, is a leader and influential poet.

The cries of *chicanismo* resound through an increasing number of newspapers and organizations. Among the more prominent news organs in the Southwest are *El Malcriado, La Raza, El Grito de Norte, El Gallo, El Inferno, Inside Eastside, Carta Editorial, El Papel, Basta Ya!*, and the scholarly journals in the social sciences and the arts, *El Grito* and *Atzlán*. Organizations include revolutionary groups such as *El Lado* and the Brown Berets and student organizations that include MECHA (*Movimiento Estudiantil Chicano de Atzlán*), MAYO (Mexican American Youth Organization), UMAS (United Mexican American Students), and MASC (Mexican American Student Confederation).

Conclusion

The image of the passive, accommodating Mexican-American resting against a building with his *sombrero* over his face is far from an accurate description. Too many years of Anglo discrimination plus the beginnings of hope as a result of the actions of Mexican-Americans since World War II have shattered forever the myth of a passive people. Six years ago I observed that Mexican-Americans in Los Angeles would not be sleeping much longer—that they would no longer tolerate the treatment inflicted on them by Anglos. At that time I noted one Mexican-American source who stated that in the 1950's if one were to encounter a Mexican-American on a *barrio* sidewalk and you were in his path he would get off into the street and let you pass. In the 1960's he would insist on his right to walk on the street too. In the 1970's he may well contest your right to be in his neighborhood and on his street. Because Anglo-Americans appear to understand violence best and because nonviolent strategies of the past have been met only with Anglo violence, many Chicanos of today are not unwilling to take arms against their Anglo tormentors, be they the cop on the beat, the Anglo teachers in the ghetto schools, or

---

[38] See Nancie Gonzáles, *The Spanish Americans of New Mexico: A Heritage of Pride.* Albuquerque: University of New Mexico Press, 1969.

government bureaucrats in their offices.[39] Within a week of this writing I spoke to a Chicano community leader in the Midwest. She lamented that the time for talk had passed, and she feared that continued discrimination against Chicanos ". . . will only mean fighting, bloodshed, and violence." Even if violence is not the prospect for the future, a more active and critical evaluation on the part of Chicanos of their own role in history and that of the Anglo is unavoidable. Blind acceptance of Anglos or even of Anglo social scientists is behind the Chicano. He will demand the rights enjoyed by Anglo-Americans. He will demand that his schools teach more than about John C. Fremont, the Alamo, and the American victories over Mexico. He will demand his rightful access to an accurate picture of history and his place in that history, and he will demand that he be taught by his own people, the people of *La Raza*.

SELECTED BIBLIOGRAPHY

Dunne, John Gregory, *Delano: The Story of the Grape Strike*. New York: Farrar, Straus, and Giroux, 1967.

Dworkin, Anthony Gary, "Stereotypes and Self-Images Held by Native-Born and Foreign-Born Mexican Americans," *Sociol. Soc. Res.*, **49**, 214–224 (January 1965).

Dworkin, Anthony Gary, "No Siesta Mañana: The Mexican Americans in Los Angeles," in Raymond W. Mack, Ed., *Our Children's Burden*. New York: Random House, 1968, Chapter 8.

Dworkin, Anthony Gary, "Epilogue to Stereotypes and Self-Images Held by Native-Born and Foreign-Born Mexican Americans," in John H. Burma, Ed., *Mexican Americans in the United States*. New York: Schenkman, 1970, 397–409.

Dworkin, Anthony Gary, "National Origin and Ghetto Experience as Variables in Mexican American Stereotypy," in Nathaniel Wagner and Marsha Huag, Eds., *Chicanos: Social and Psychological Perspectives*. St. Louis: Mosby, 1971, Ch. 8.

Dworkin, Anthony Gary, "Patterns of Mexican American Stereotypy," in Hector L. Cordova, Ed., *Perspectives on Mexican American Studies*. New York: Holt, Rinehart and Winston, in press.

Gonzáles, Nancie, *The Spanish Americans of New Mexico: A Heritage of Pride*. Albuquerque: University of New Mexico Press, 1969.

Grebler, Leo, Joan W. Moore, and Ralph C. Guzmán. *The Mexican American People: The Nation's Second Largest Minority*. New York: The Free Press, 1970.

Madsen, William, *The Mexican Americans of South Texas*. New York: Holt, 1964.

McWilliams, Carey, *North from Mexico*. New York: Lippincott, 1949.

---

[39] The militant Chicano Liberation Front (CLF) has taken credit for the bombing of 28 buildings in Los Angeles between March 1970 and August 1971. College campuses, high schools, banks, supermarkets, and city buildings were included in the bombings.

Moore, John W. with Alfredo Cuellar. *Mexican Americans*. Englewood Cliffs, New Jersey: Prentice-Hall, 1970.

Simmons, Ozzie G., "The Mutual Images and Expectations of Anglo-Americans and Mexican-Americans," *Daedalus*, **90**, 286–299 (Spring 1961).

Tuck, Ruth, *Not with the Fist*. New York: Harcourt, Brace, 1946.

Vaca, Nick C., "The Mexican American in the Social Sciences," *El Grito*, **3**, 3–24, 17–51 (Spring and Fall 1970).

Brewton Berry
The Ohio State University

CHAPTER TEN

AMERICA'S MESTIZOS

In the eastern United States there are some two hundred communities of people whose racial ancestry is uncertain and whose lives are profoundly affected by that uncertainty. Most of them insist that they are white and covet the prestige and status accorded to white people. The whites, however, suspect that there is some black ancestry, however small and remote, and are unwilling to accept them. The mixed-bloods vehemently deny black ancestry but will often confess to the presence of an Indian strain. Indians—those, at least, who enjoy some official recognition as such—are skeptical of the mixed-bloods' claim and acknowledge it only reluctantly.

They are known by a wide variety of names. In New York and New Jersey they are called Jackson Whites; in Pennsylvania, Pools; in Delaware, Moors and Nanticokes; in Maryland, Wesorts; in West Virginia, Guineas; and in Tennessee, Melungeons. There are many groups in Virginia, where they are known as Ramps, Issues, Cubans, and Brown People, and where there are also those who claim descent from old Indian tribes, including the Chickahominy, Mattapony, Pamunkey, Nansemond, and Rappahannock. They are especially numerous in North Carolina, where, in addition to the 30,000 Lumbees of Robeson County, there are smaller groups of Haliwas, Portuguese, and Smilings. In South Carolina we find Brass Ankles, Croatans, Redbones, Redlegs, Buckheads, and Yel-

This chapter was written with the support of a grant from the American Philosophical Society.

lowhammers. Louisiana swarms with them. In the southern part of the
state, along the bayous and deep in the marshy fringes near the Gulf of
Mexico, there are the Houma Indians, known locally as Sabines. In
western Louisiana are a numerous people known as Redbones, who first
gained attention in the 1850's when Frederick Law Olmsted attributed
the lawlessness of the frontier to the presence of a "large number of free
negroes and persons of mixed blood." Alabama has its Creoles and Cajuns, Florida its Dominickers, Ohio its Carmelites, Rhode Island its
Narragansetts, and Massachusetts its Gay Heads and Mashpees.

Nomenclature

These names are usually anathema to the people who bear them. There
are exceptions, however. The Nanticokes of Delaware and the Narragansetts of Rhode Island are proud of those ancient Indian names and strive
continually to gain wider acceptance for them. So it is with the Shinne-
cock, the Poosepatuck, the Montauk, and the Matinecock, all of Long
Island, the Waccamaws of North Carolina, and the Chickahominy and
other Indian groups in Virginia. These are all strongly suspected of having little Indian blood, and they have retained almost nothing of their
ancient language and culture; but there is an unbroken thread that binds
them to the past, and they cling tenaciously to their tribal identity,
guarding their old Indian names as priceless possessions.

Not so with the others. Worst of all, as these folk see it, are those
names that explicitly identify them with blacks. Thus the Jackson Whites
loathe the term "Blue-eyed Negroes," which they sometimes hear; the
South Carolina Brass Ankles detest "Red Niggers"; and the Virginia
hybrids cringe at the sound of "Issues," a shortened form of "Free Issues," a name by which the free colored, before and after the Civil War,
were differentiated from those blacks whose freedom derived from the
war.

Occasionally the name applied to these people is descriptive of some
physical characteristic they possess or are thought to possess. Thus there
are the Brown People of Virginia, the Yellowhammers of South Carolina,
and the Black Andersons, who live in the North Carolina mountains.

It is quite common for entire communities to be known by the fam-
ily name that is most prevalent among them; for instance, there are the
Van Guilders and the Clappers of New York, the Laster tribe in North
Carolina, the Coe clan in Kentucky, and the Chavises and Creels of

South Carolina. The most common surname is Goins, or some variation thereof, and in not a few places this is the term applied by outsiders to the entire community.

Sometimes it is some peculiar habit of the group that serves as the basis for a name. In a remote quarter of South Carolina the mixed-bloods are known as Clay-eaters. Whether or not they deserve this label is beside the point. The strange custom of geophagy does occur in many parts of the world, and it would not be surprising if it appeared in one of the mestizo communities. In one part of the Virginia mountains the common name applied to the hybrid population is "Ramps." The local explanation is that it comes from "rampion," a wild, onionlike plant gathered and eaten by these people.

Elsewhere it is some aspect of the geography that furnishes the name; for example, Kentucky has its Pea Ridge group, Pennsylvania its Keating Mountain group, and West Virginia its West Hill Indians. Their names may be taken from the towns near which they live, such as the Summerville Indians of South Carolina, the Carmel Indians of Ohio, and the Adamstown Indians of Virginia. In North Carolina those who live in Person County are called the Person County Indians, and those who inhabit the borders of Halifax and Warren counties have come to be known as the Haliwa Indians. Elsewhere they are called Cubans, Moors, Turks, or Portuguese, and fanciful stories are told about how their ancestors reached these shores.

Finally, there are those names that are truly mysterious—Brass Ankles, Melungeons, Guineas, Wesorts, Redbones, Redlegs, Bushwackers, Pondshiners, Buckheads, Sabines, and Dominickers. These names have great antiquity, their origins forgotten, but the myths accounting for them are numerous and fantastic.

Those who have studied these hybrid groups are at a loss to know what to call them. One hesitates to use the popular, local names, so offensive are they. Many writers simply refer to them as mixed-bloods, racial hybrids, or mongrels. The term "triracial isolates" has enjoyed a certain vogue, and in the literature they are often called "raceless people," "racial orphans," "mystery people," "half-castes," "half-breeds," or merely "breeds." The term "mestizo" has been proposed and seems to be gaining acceptance. It has the advantage of being noncommittal. Literally it means "mixed," and these folk readily admit that they are mixed. The term is widely used in Latin America, where it is applied to those of European and Indian ancestry, but is often applied to other mixtures as well. In the Philippines it is used for those of Chinese and native racial ancestry. The dictionaries define "mestizo" as "a person of mixed blood," so it would seem, therefore, to be a fitting label for the folk we are describing.

Origins

The origin of these American mestizos is unknown. There is evidence that they were present in colonial times, and some of them participated in the Revolutionary War. General Thomas Sumter used them effectively in his guerilla assaults on the British, and after the war allowed them to settle on his estate, where their descendants still reside. The records show that in 1790 a group of mestizos petitioned the South Carolina House of Representatives for exemption from certain laws applicable to blacks, and their petition was granted. There is documentary evidence, though admittedly scanty, that before the Civil War there were groups of people here and there who set themselves apart from both the black and the white populations.

Although history has ignored them, myth and legend have flourished, and stories explaining their origin are legion. It is often said, and widely believed, that the Lumbees and certain other North Carolina groups are the descendants of the celebrated "Lost Colony." Tradition has it that in 1587 Sir Walter Raleigh dispatched an expedition of 120 men and women, under the leadership of John White, to establish a colony on Roanoke Island, off the Carolina coast. The settlement was made and a fort was built. Thereupon White returned to England for supplies but ran into certain obstacles, and it was not until 1591 that he finally returned to Roanoke. The colony by that time had disappeared, and the only clue was the word CROATOAN, carved on a tree. The probability is that disease, starvation, and hostile Indians account for the colony's disappearance, which had proved too much for earlier attempts. It is more romantic, however, to accept the legend that the desperate and discouraged settlers sought refuge with the friendly Croatan Indians, who received them hospitably and eventually intermarried with them.

The Jackson Whites profess to be descendants of the Tuscarora Indians, who were driven from their North Carolina home by the encroaching settlers. Early in the 1700's, they say, the whites began invading their territory, even making slaves of them. In 1711 the Indians took to the warpath, but were defeated. Thereupon they began their trek northward, and were eventually adopted into the League of the Iroquois. Some of the stragglers, however, made it only so far as the Ramapo Mountains, where they mixed with the remnants of other tribes, and together they spawned the present-day Jackson Whites. Down in North Carolina the Haliwas insist that they are descended from those Tuscaroras who remained behind in their homeland.

Local historians, although not denying that some Indian blood flows in the veins of the Jackson Whites, tell a different story. During the Revolutionary War, when the British occupied New York City, an enterprising man by the name of Jackson conceived the idea of bringing in 3500 women to satisfy the lust of the troops who were quartered there. The British commanding officer fell in with the idea, being convinced that by thus guarding the virtue of their daughters he would curry favor with the local population, which was largely Tory. He demanded only that the women be loyal subjects of His Majesty. Jackson thereupon set sail for England, where he succeeded, by devious methods, in obtaining his quota. On the return journey, however, many of the young women died and their bodies were tossed into the sea. One ship, with 50 aboard, was lost altogether. Jackson, finding himself short of the number specified in his contract, hastily dispatched a ship to the West Indies, where he readily secured the necessary number of females. True, they were black, but Jackson pointed out that his contract had nothing to say about color, but only that they be subjects of the Crown.

At the war's end provision was made for the evacuation of the British troops, but no mention was made of Jackson's ladies. The New Yorkers, however, demanded their expulsion. What became of the blacks nobody pretends to know, but the white women, with their bastard children, crossed the Hudson and headed for the Ramapo Mountains, where, they had been told, outcasts such as they might find a refuge. There they were welcomed by the motley crowd already living in that secluded spot —Indians, outlaws, Tories, deserters, and runaway Negro slaves. This story has enjoyed wide popularity, but, unfortunately, it has no basis in fact.

There are numerous other myths, also without visible means of support, which purport to explain the origin of the mestizos. In the mountains of Tennessee the story is told that the devil was driven from hell by his domineering wife, and for a time he roamed the face of the earth. Eventually he came to the hills of Tennessee, which so reminded him of his old haunts that he decided to settle there. He took to himself an Indian squaw as a wife—and from that unholy union came the race of Melungeons. Elsewhere the mestizos are traced back to shipwrecked sailors, Moslem princes, Spanish ladies, English noblemen, and pirates.

Some of the mestizo groups have a valid claim to descent from certain Indian tribes that once inhabited the Atlantic seaboard. Thus the group at Mashpee, Massachusetts, properly insist that among their ancestors were the Mashpee Indians, though, admittedly, there have been no full-bloods for centuries. Several of the Virginia groups, too, are doubtless descended from the Indian tribes whose names they bear, although there has obviously been much Negro admixture. The Nanticokes are probably a remnant of the tribe that remained behind when the majority had been forced to migrate. So with the Gay Heads of Martha's Vineyard and the Choctaws of Mississippi. Many others, of course, insist that they are descendants of the aborigines, but evidence is wanting and even the tribal affiliation is conjectural.

Most mestizo groups, in all probability, represent an amalgam of Indians, adverturers, traders, runaway slaves, outlaws, deserters, and deviants of all types, both white and black. The Lumbees are a case in point. In the 1730's, when the first European settlers arrived in that region of North Carolina now known as Robeson County, they found living there a race of mixed-bloods. These people lived in houses, not wigwams, cultivated crops, spoke an English dialect, and had the manners and customs of the frontier. In a document written in the year 1754 no mention is made of Indians living in the territory, but it is stated that "a mixt Crew, a lawless People, possess the Lands without patent or paying quit rents." White settlers moved in nevertheless, and the two races had as little to do with each other as possible. In time they developed a pattern of coexistence and managed to live together harmoniously, except when some crisis arose to disrupt the truce; for instance, the mestizos were allowed to vote and to send their children to schools with the whites, even though they were designated in the census as "free persons of color." However, when the state constitution was revised in 1835, the mestizos were denied the franchise and were excluded from the white schools. Resentment mounted, for they insisted that they had rendered service in both the Revolutionary War and the War of 1812. Thereupon they set about to build their own schools and to hire their own teachers. Another crisis developed during the Civil War, when the Confederacy, in its desperation, drafted the mestizos, not to bear arms but to do manual labor along with slaves and free blacks. This they refused to do, with the result that three of them were captured and executed as deserters. There followed many years of turmoil until, in the 1880's, the mestizos embarked on their long and arduous struggle to establish their identity as Indians.

An isolated section of West Virginia known as "The Narrows" has, since the earliest times, been the home of a people who bear telltale mestizo surnames. Through that section of the state flows the Tygart River. It follows a northeasterly course until it approaches the border between Barbour and Taylor counties, where it changes its direction, making a sharp U-turn. The peninsula formed by this loop provides an ideal hideout for man and beast. Guarded on three sides by the deep glades of the Tygart, and on the fourth by almost impenetrable laurel thickets, it has long served as a haven for refugees of all kinds. As recently as 1900 this region was accessible only on horseback. Nearby there ran an old Indian trail—Horseshoe Run Trail—along which bands of Shawnees, Cherokees, Delawares, and Hurons were in the habit of traveling. The abundance of game in "The Narrows" could hardly have failed to attract the attention of these wanderers, and the isolation doubtless served as a magnet for the misfits of society. The Guineas, however, who have long made this area their home, maintain that their ancestors included Dutch settlers, English colonists, veterans of the American Revolution, and a beautiful Delaware maiden by the name of "Pretty Hair."

Migration has always been seen by the mestizos as a means of improving their economic situation and of escaping the humiliations of the racial caste system. In an earlier age the frontier beckoned to them, and many of them were in the forefront of the westward movement. The Sabines are believed to have lived originally east of the Mississippi River but, when the French and Spanish arrived, began to move steadily toward the southwest. They settled for a time at Lake Ponchartrain and then drifted south along the bayous until they reached their present home a century or more ago.

In the mountains of Tennessee, in the county of Hancock, there is a remote spot known as Newman's Ridge which has long been the home of an enigmatic people known as Melungeons. They were the earliest settlers in that region, having come from Virginia and North Carolina in the 1790's. They were classified at one time as "free persons of color" but in 1834 were deprived of the franchise. For a century and a half the prolific Melungeons migrated in all directions from Newman's Ridge, and there are now communities of them in Virginia, Kentucky, Ohio, and 15 other Tennessee counties. Neither in their culture nor appearance are they distinguishable from other mountain folk.

Migration to some distant place, however, is not the most characteristic adjustment that mestizos have made to their situation. They share with their Indian cousins the disposition to react to an unpleasant experience by withdrawal. They have, accordingly, chosen to segregate themselves from their oppressors by moving into the nearby hills or swamps, or onto the less desirable land, where they have established their separate communities, usually referred to in the literature as "racial islands." Contacts with the unfriendly outside world have been kept to a minimum, and they have attempted in their isolation to find for themselves a relatively self-sufficient existence.

Interrelations with Whites and Blacks

Isolation, however, has never been complete and some contact with outsiders has been unavoidable. The nature of such contacts depends largely
on the attitudes and beliefs entertained by those involved in them.

Most white people in the eastern United States are oblivious of the
fact that all around them there are thousands of individuals who are not
quite white, nor black, nor red. Perhaps they have heard of Jackson
Whites, Lumbees, or Brass Ankles, but these people they regard as a
peculiar, local phenomenon, little realizing that similar groups exist in
most of the eastern states and certainly unmindful of the fact that they
are so numerous. Those who have heard of such folk have seldom had
any dealings with them or, if they have, their meetings have been casual
and impersonal. In short, few white people have any genuine knowledge
of mestizos.

It is not surprising, therefore, that in their attitudes and beliefs
whites are ambivalent. There is no little disagreement about just what
blood flows in the mestizo's veins. There are those who insist that they
are simply a cross between Indian and white. "There's not a drop of
nigger blood in those people," said one informant. Others hold that
they are mulattoes—Negro-white hybrids—who refuse to admit it and
try to pass themselves off as Indians. "They are not *real* Indians, you
know." Most whites, however, are of the opinion that mestizos are a
mixture of Indian, white, and Negro, although they differ in their estimates of the relative amounts of each of these basic stocks. Occasionally
one is told that a certain individual is a "full-blooded Indian." Others
accept goodnaturedly, but skeptically, the mestizo's claim to Indian ancestry and will refer to them as "so-called Indians," or "Indians by courtesy."

If the whites are equivocal regarding the racial make-up of the mestizos, they are no less so regarding their character, habits, and tempera-
ment. Many insist that they are dirty, lazy, sexually immoral, mean,
lawless, and unambitious. Their poverty is attributed to their lack of
industry and education. Said a Virginia registrar of vital statistics: "Their
moral standards are low, as evidenced by the fact that 21 per cent of their
births are illegitimate. . . . Their ambition seems to be limited to secur-
ing recognition first as whites, and, if that fails, as Indians." On the
other hand there are many whites, including those who know them best,
who describe them as "innocent and friendly" and who maintain that
they are clean, hard-working, honest, law-abiding, patriotic, and loyal to

their friends and relatives. "All the meanness that they are accused of goes right back to the whites."

This ambivalence on the part of the white man manifests itself in the interracial etiquette. Wherever unlike groups of people live together, there invariably develops a body of rules and customs for the purpose of regulating and facilitating their relations with one another. Sometimes these laws are enacted by legislatures and enforced by the courts, but usually they are unwritten customs and traditions. One who violates these norms finds himself the subject of gossip and is likely to be reviled, shunned, ridiculed, harassed, or worse. The code of interracial etiquette which regulates the relations between whites and blacks is rather well recognized in most of the regions in which mestizos are found, though, of course, it changes with the passage of time.

How does the etiquette apply, then, to one who is neither white, nor black, nor red? Just as there is a lack of consensus in regard to what the mestizo is, so there is confusion about how one ought to relate to him. Customs vary widely from place to place. In some communities mestizos are accorded most of the privileges customarily reserved for whites. They have always been permitted to sit downstairs in movie houses, not upstairs with the Negroes; they have used the white rest rooms at filling stations; they have been served at restaurants and soda fountains. Even in these "liberal" communities, however, the line has been drawn at intimate social relationships and at membership in lodges and civic associations. Elsewhere, however, mestizos are subjected to most of the rules of etiquette applied to Negroes. They are not welcome at white barbershops, swimming pools, churches, or eating places. Titles of respect are withheld, shaking hands avoided, and personal interaction is brief and cool. Everywhere, however, whites differ from one another about how rigidly to apply the local rules of etiquette.

The black's image of the mestizo is more accurate than the white man's. It shows greater insight into the nature of the problem and deeper understanding of his aspirations and frustrations. Moreover, there is often a suggestion of charity and tolerance, which are all too rare among whites. This is not to say that blacks hold mestizos in high esteem or look up to them even slightly. They know full well that they are a racially mixed people, but are uncertain about the mixture and are not vitally concerned. Miscegenation is not regarded by them as a catastrophe as it is by the whites. Blacks know that mestizos aspire to be white and are continually rebuffed. They know that mestizos feel that they are superior to blacks, and this they resent but not deeply. To them it is rather a pathetic gesture, which they dismiss with a shrug. Blacks, however, are quite prepared to take the mestizos in, to admit them to their schools, to permit them to live in their neighborhoods, to worship in their churches, to dance with them, to eat with them, and even to intermarry with them. Many mestizos have chosen to do so.

Identity and Self-Concepts

Important as it is what the whites and blacks think of the mestizos, it is more important what the mestizos think of themselves. One's self-concept is crucial in determining one's aspirations, expectations, and achievements.

A few of the mestizo groups have never categorically denied having some black ancestry. Darke County, Ohio, is the home of a unique group which admits to being black, but they "are not like other colored folks." Here, on the frontier, an aggregation of free colored people found refuge early in the nineteenth century. Tradition has it that the first to settle was a man of Indian-white-black mixture from Virginia, who fled from that state when rumor had it that free colored people were to be re-enslaved. He was joined by others of similar racial stock from North Carolina. Still later, mixed-bloods from Tennessee arrived and were accepted. They flourished, purchased land, built comfortable homes, established schools and churches, and became well-to-do by frontier standards. Although they do not deny their black ancestry, neither do they take pride in it. One confessed, "There is a lot of blood in our relation—Indian, Scotch, Irish, Dutch, and a little bit nigger."

The community has seen better days than the present, but the homes they occupy today testify to the fact that they once enjoyed a high level of prosperity. They take pride in the achievements of their sons and daughters who have gone away to college and have made good in various professions. Many indeed have gone, some passing over into the white race, others rising to prominence in the black world.

In Cumberland County, Kentucky, on an isolated spot known as Coe Ridge, overlooking the Cumberland River, there once flourished a community of Indian-white-black hybrids known as the Coe clan. They were brought as slaves to that frontier settlement by a certain John Coe, of North Carolina. After the Civil War, when they found themselves free, they acquired land on the ridge, adopted their master's surname, and proceeded to establish their community. They prospered, for the country was rich in timber, and they were skillful at logging and rafting. Their numbers increased.

The Coes never pretended to be other than black. The Cherokee strain in their make-up, which was never great, became more and more diluted, and the Indian culture failed to survive. They lived harmoniously with the neighboring whites, whom they seldom saw. There were occasional encounters, however, with certain rough elements of the white population.

Things went quite well with the Coe clan until around 1910, when the timber supply became exhausted. The land was poor and eroded, agriculture was not feasible, and moonshining seemed the only profitable occupation. This brought them into continual conflict with the local authorities, converted the industrious Coes into a lawless group, and the community itself began to lose its cohesiveness. The members began to drift away, going to Dayton, Chicago, and several Indiana cities. By 1958 the community had entirely disappeared.

There are other mestizo groups whose members identify themselves as black. Gouldtown, New Jersey, began in colonial times as a refuge for Indian-white-black hybrids, and from that community many have gone forth to achieve prominence in American black society. The number is doubtless greater for those who have left the village and been absorbed into the white population. These people, however, are hard to trace, for they burn their bridges behind them, fail to return for family reunions, and neglect to tell their progeny the romantic story of their eccentric forebears. Frilot Cove, Louisiana, is still another mestizo group whose members have never denied their black ancestry, even though they do not boast of it. Nor have they made any claim to Indian ancestry, though they might if they chose to do so. They do, however, draw a clear color line between themselves and the surrounding black community.

Most mestizos doubtless think of themselves as white people, aspire to status as whites, and resent any inference that they are other than white. They declare themselves to be white whenever the opportunity presents itself—when they purchase hunting and fishing licenses, when they obtain driver's licenses, when births and deaths are recorded, when they enter the military service, and when the census is taken. Marriage to a white person is highly approved, whereas marriage to a black leads to ostracism. When they move to a new community, as they are doing in increasing numbers, they invariably seek shelter in a white section, affiliate with a white church, and send their children to white schools.

Many mestizos, however, perhaps despairing of achieving white status, have chosen to identify themselves with Indians. The Sabines, in Louisiana, insist that they are Houma Indians. They cultivate contacts with those whose status as Indians is more secure than their own. They search the papers for items about Indians, which they clip and preserve. When they learn that a meeting of Indians is to be held anywhere, they collect money and send representatives. It is much the same with the Narragansetts, the Haliwas, the Lumbees, the Nanticokes, the Chickahominy, and the Gay Heads. When, in 1970, the white people of Massachusetts were preparing to celebrate the 350th anniversary of the arrival of the Pilgrims, the Mashpee Indians became miffed when they were not invited to participate in the ceremonies. They proceeded, therefore, to stage a celebration of their own, commemorating the 100th anniversary of the recognition of their community as an independent, self-governing town. They used the occasion to publicize the fact that their ancestors were hunting and fishing on the Cape when the Pilgrims arrived, that they had good grounds for their numerous grievances against the whites, and that they were determined to retain their identity as Indians and to preserve their heritage. It must be noted, however, that by no means all members of these mestizo communities share this enthusiasm, much to the distress of their fellows who see their salvation in Indianness.

The classic example of a group which has long striven to achieve an Indian identity is the North Carolina Lumbees. As mentioned above, the white settlers who first encountered them on the frontier in the early 1700's regarded them, not as Indians, but as "a mixt Crew, a lawless People." For a century and a half there were intermittent conflicts between the two races. Then, in the 1880's, Hamilton McMillan, a white man who lived near them and knew their problems, discovered their legend of descent from the Roanoke colonists and the Croatan Indians. He was able to persuade the state legislature to pass a bill designating them as Croatan Indians. What an effect this had on the community! At last they were officially Indians, tribal name and all. Theirs was a glorious and romantic past, linked with the first Europeans. They grew proud and self-confident, proceeded to build schools and churches, and even established a college of their own.

Their high spirits, however, were soon deflated. The proud name Croatan began to lose its glamor. Whites and blacks would pronounce it with a sneer, and eventually shortened it to "Cro." Even the dictionaries began to define "Croatan" as "a people of mixed Indian, white, and Negro blood living in North Carolina."

Once again the Indians took their grievance to the legislature and succeeded, in 1911, in having the word "Croatan" stricken out, making them simply "the Indians of Robeson County." This involved their repudiation of the romantic tradition of descent from Sir Walter's colonists, but the name had become so abhorrent to them that they gladly paid the price for its removal. Even so, to this day they have not succeeded in expunging the word from the language.

The ambiguity of the new name proved an embarrassment to them, for it was tantamount to admitting that they had no idea who they were nor whence they came. So, in 1913, the lawmakers, playing fast and loose with history, passed "an act to restore to the Indians of Robeson and adjoining counties their rightful and ancient name" and gallantly dubbed them Cherokees. Nobody, however, ever took this seriously except the Cherokees themselves, who protested loudly at this flagrant desecration of their cherished name.

Thereupon the poor nameless mestizos tried another tack. They undertook to have the federal authorities designate them "the Siouan Tribes of the Lumber River" and to grant them status accorded to other Indians. The Bureau of Indian Affairs balked at the suggestion. The Bureau of the Census did report them as Indians for a time, but in 1950 classified them simply as "Other Non-whites."

The search for an acceptable name continued until in 1953 the ever-agreeable state legislature formally designated them Lumbee Indians and in 1956 the Congress of the United States followed suit. Now at last they had a name they could bear with pride and which neither whites nor blacks have yet learned to pronounce with scorn.

The success of the Lumbees in establishing their identity as Indians prompted other mestizo groups in North Carolina to follow a similar course. Near the northern border of the state, in the counties of Halifax and Warren, there lived another community of mixed-bloods who called themselves the Haliwa Indians. Despite the fact that they have long maintained that they represent a remnant of the Tuscaroras, the whites in the neighborhood were disposed to regard them as mulattoes. A leader appeared among them in the 1950's, and an organization was formed which began to exert political pressure. As a result, special schools were established for them, separate tax rolls were set up, birth certificates were changed from "colored" to "Indian," and in 1965 the state legislature officially recognized and designated them Haliwa Indians.

Not all mestizo groups, however, have sought to resolve their identity problems by striving for recognition as Indians. The Tennessee Melungeons have always been an especially elusive group, for they are virtually indistinguishable, both culturally and physically, from their "white" neighbors, though some of them have rather dark complexions. Traditionally they have been identified chiefly by the surnames they bear— Goins, Collins, Delp, Bunch, Harris, Sexton, Gibson, Mizer, and Johnson. They have never taken pride in their possible Cherokee ancestry nor fostered the myth of their Portuguese origin. They abhor the term "Melungeon" and never employ it. Many of them have moved from the community, doubtless merging into the white population. In recent years some of those who remained behind have sought to develop group pride, to promote a better image, and to make the term "Melungeon" respectable. To that end they engaged the services of a playwright, Kermit Hunter, who wrote a play entitled "Walk Toward the Sunset: The Melungeon Story," which was presented with some success at Sneedville, Tennessee, throughout the summer of 1969. Most of the roles were played by students from nearby Carson Newman College. Many Melungeons, however, are unhappy about this experiment and would prefer to bury the past.

Life Style

Group loyalty and a sense of community are not strongly developed among mestizos. Ethnocentrism is hardly one of their characteristics. Those who succeed in escaping from their rural ghettos, for example, by marriage to a white person or by obtaining a higher education, are seldom motivated to return and serve their fellows.

Their communities are continually rent by a variety of cleavages. Those who have managed to accumulate some property and to enjoy modest comforts are the objects of the envy and malicious gossip of those less fortunate. Their shades of skin color are a perpetual source of discord. Those who have Caucasoid features feel superior to those whose features are more Negroid and often blame the latter for the discrimination suffered by the entire community. Even in the home partiality is shown to those children who have "good" hair and whose skin is fair. Teachers report problems of discipline when certain of their mestizo pupils hurl the epithet "nigger" at their darker cousins. In those communities in which deliberate efforts are being made to achieve recognition as Indians there are some whose indifference to such efforts is still another cause of friction.

Even so, it is in those communities that have chosen to seek Indian identity that one finds the strongest sense of community—those that have a name of which they need not feel ashamed and a body of tradition and myth to which they can point with pride. Here, also, is the inclination to form voluntary associations and to work for community betterment. Thus we have the Chickahominy Indian Association, the Nanticoke Indian Association, and the Sons and Daughters of the First Americans (Narragansett). The members of these organizations periodically arrange "powwows," festivals, and councils, strive for association with other Indian groups, publicize their activities, and endeavor to perpetuate the few Indian cultural traits with which they are familiar. Elsewhere whatever solidarity is found in the mestizo communities is developed around their churches and schools. Today, however, the special schools are giving way to the forces of integration, and the church, with its adjoining cemetery, remains the only institution around which the group can coalesce. Many mestizo communities, however, do not even have a church.

It is not surprising that the vast majority of mestizos are impoverished rural folk, for they have tended to follow the notoriously unprofitable occupation of farming and, what is more, do so on land that is rocky, hilly, rough, and eroded. The Lumbees are an exception, for they are capable farmers and own much of the good land in Robeson County. For most mestizos, however, their plots of land are small and of little value and only a bare existence can be derived from the maize, truck, or tobacco they raise.

Not all of them, of course, are farmers. The Sabines devote themselves to their traditional occupations of fishing and trapping but nowadays are finding them less and less rewarding. The Cajuns of Alabama support themselves by lumbering and gathering turpentine, and the New Jersey Pineys earn a living from the cranberry bogs. Many Melungeons have become coal miners in Kentucky and Tennessee. From Newman's Ridge some have migrated into Virginia, where they have appropriated the steep hillsides for their cabins and cornfields and where their presence is tolerated, for when the need arises they provide a source of cheap farm labor. Most of them supplement their paltry irregular earnings by hunting and fishing and by digging for ginseng, yellowroot, and sassafras, which they sell to local dealers. Some, here and there, capitalize on their reputation for being part Indian and make a little money by weaving baskets, making crude pottery, and by hiring out as guides to hunters and fishermen. Mestizos, almost everywhere, are suspected of manufacturing and selling illegal whisky, and there is abundant evidence that the suspicions are well founded.

Since World War II many mestizos have found their way into other occupations and have achieved a measure of economic security hitherto unknown to them. Those who lived near military installations succeeded in obtaining employment, usually unskilled, in the warehouses or motor pools. Some operated trailer parks. Increasing numbers are finding steady employment in textile mills or as automobile mechanics, carpenters, painters, and truck drivers. Mestizos have always avoided those occupations that tended to identify them with blacks. Domestic service they shun, though the Maryland Wesorts are so employed and the West Virginia Guineas are occasionally found working as household servants. The great majority, however, continue, as they have in the past, to make their living from the soil.

The participation of the mestizos in the life of the larger community is minimal. They are, of course, admitted to the local hospitals but in somewhat smaller proportions than their numbers in the total population. Wherever racial segregation prevailed, as it generally did until recently, the difficulties were frequent, for the mestizos insisted on being assigned to white wards, despite the objections of the other patients. Similar problems have occurred in the jails. Public Health nurses complain that expectant mothers fail to attend their clinics, school principals deplore their lack of interest in P.T.A., Red Cross officials make futile efforts to interest them in classes in nutrition and first aid, county agricultural agents despair of organizing 4-H clubs among them, and librarians say that they make no use of the facilities they offer. Their failure to participate in the community's activities and to utilize its resources is customarily attributed to their ignorance, depravity, and apathy. Few suspect that it might be their pride.

In military service the situation is quite different. Mestizo boys are called up as readily as those whose blood is "pure." They almost certainly served in the Revolutionary War, and there are many today who boast that their grandfathers wore the uniform of the Confederacy, for they have documents to prove it. These documents have at times been submitted in court to prove white blood, and in certain southern courts no clearer evidence is needed.

World War II again raised the question of their racial classification. Draft boards here and there took a cavalier attitude toward the matter and enrolled them as white, even when their color was quite dark. Some boards simply passed the problem of classification on to the induction centers. Records show numerous examples of the assignment of mestizos to black units from which they exerted every effort to have themselves transferred. Some succeeded, but others served their time, bitter, resentful, and frustrated. Others deserted and hid out in their isolated and inaccessible homes. A few were surprised to discover that their buddies accepted their claim to Indian ancestry and because of it enjoyed a certain distinction. Most mestizos, however, have entered the military service as whites and have had the rare experience of finding themselves accepted as such.

On the whole, military service has had a profound effect on mestizos. It has broadened their horizons and destroyed their provincialism. Many look back on their military experience with nostalgia and talk about it with obvious relish. They associated with white men, dated white girls, and quite a few married them. They learned that by getting away from home they could escape the stigma that weighed so heavily on them. Many never returned.

For several generations the mestizos, unlike the blacks, have enjoyed the privilege of the ballot, although not until after the Civil War. The Melungeons were denied the right to vote in Tennessee in 1834. The Lumbees for many years had the ballot, but when the state's constitution was revised in 1835 it was taken from them. Elsewhere it was the policy to regard mestizos as "free persons of color" and to deny them the ballot. For many years now, however, the mestizos have been voting. In West Virginia the Guineas traditionally have been Republicans, as are the Wesorts and the blacks thereabouts. The whites are Democrats. In South Carolina the Brass Ankles have long voted in the Democratic primaries, even when that privilege was reserved for white men. Tradition has it that they even supported General Wade Hampton and his Red Shirts when in 1877 they succeeded in throwing out the carpetbaggers, scalawags, and blacks and reinstating white supremacy in South Carolina.

How the mestizos won the ballot would be difficult to say, but it is a safe guess that it came not as a result of their own efforts but rather through the machinations of politicians who believed that here was a block of votes they could control. Nor have the mestizos used the franchise effectively. The Lumbees, 30,000 strong, are an exception, for they hold the balance of power in their county, and the success they have had in persuading legislatures to grant them their tribal names is testimony to their political influence. Others, however, partly because of their small numbers, have exercised no such power.

Oppressed and underprivileged groups have often found in religion a bond that holds them together and a philosophy that makes life tolerable. This is hardly true, however, of the mestizos, for religion seems to rest lightly on their minds. The problem of their identity has been uppermost, and, in fact, affects their relations with the church. The religious affiliation of mestizos tends to follow that of their neighbors. The Wesorts of Maryland are Roman Catholics, as are the whites and blacks among whom they live. Those at Frilot Cove, as well as the Sabines along the coast, are nominally Catholic. In the Carolinas, Tennessee, and Kentucky they incline toward the Baptist faith, but turn Methodist when their status improves.

The various sects have looked on the mestizos as proper objects for their missionary efforts, but their success has been negligible. The Baptists have made gestures toward the Sabines, the Presbyterians toward the Melungeons, and the Episcopalians toward the Issues and the Summerville Indians. These efforts have usually proved futile because the missionaries failed to appreciate the vulnerable spot in mestizo psychology. In one community the minister, who had worked among the Indians of Arizona, let it be known that he did not regard the mestizos as "real Indians," and they left the church in a body. The South Carolina

Turks for many years attended the High Hills Baptist Church, where they were permitted to sit downstairs with the whites (but across the aisle), while the Negroes sat in the balcony. Then came a minor snub by some of the white parishioners, and the Turks resigned and set up their own church. Mestizos are usually not welcome in white churches, and devious methods are used to exclude them when, as occasionally happens, they express an interest in affiliation.

Into this situation, in which discrimination and neglect have been so conspicuous, have come the small emotional cults which have won many converts. In one community the mestizos deserted the Episcopal mission and went over to the Pentecostal. In another they abandoned the Baptists and established their own Holiness Church. No one, however, not even these purveyors of the fundamentalist gospel, pays much attention to them.

The public school has been the major battleground of the mestizos. Until recently, in most of the states in which the mestizos live, the schools have been strictly segregated. When the time came to enroll their children, therefore, the mestizos came face to face with the question, "Are you white or black?" In most areas of life, however, it was not put to them quite so bluntly. They did not have to work at jobs in which they were not treated with respect. If the churches snubbed them, they simply absented themselves or started their own. Whether they voted or not was never a major concern. They could refuse to patronize restaurants, barbershops, merchants, swimming pools, and movie houses where they were not accorded the treatment they craved. If people chose not to speak to them, shake hands with them, or show them the common courtesies, they had only to turn aside. Military service was another matter, but they always found that the armed forces were never too concerned with the fine points of racial classification.

The schools were different. When a child reaches a certain age, both law and custom decree that he must go to school, and for most mestizos that meant either a white or black school. From the one they were barred, and the other they refused to attend. "I'd ruther my chilluns grow up ig'nant like monkeys," said one mother, "than send 'em to that nigger school."

It is only within the last three or four generations that this has been a problem for them. Before the Civil War the southern states did not regard the education of children as one of their responsibilities; later on, when they did assume it, they made a distinction between their obligations to whites and to nonwhites. In the ensuing controversy the mestizo was left to shift for himself. Most of them attended no school at all.

Into this vacuum there often came a primitive type of institution—

small, ill-equipped, irregularly operated, and poorly staffed. They were sometimes called "Indian schools" or "mission schools," but the professionals in the field of education referred to them as "special schools." In the published reports they were enumerated with the white schools, for the mestizos would have rebelled if they were to discover that they had been listed otherwise.

These special schools came into existence in various ways. In a few instances the mestizos used their political power, which is small, to obtain a school for their children. Often they reached into their own pockets to erect a building and to hire a teacher. Several churches undertook to provide a minimum of education for those who were totally without it; mission schools were operated by the Methodists, Baptists, Episcopalians, Presbyterians, and Roman Catholics. Elsewhere they came into existence through the efforts of some charitable individual; for example, in the 1890's, a kindly New Englander by the name of Dr. Shepard became interested in the Summerville Indians and opened a school for them. For 30 years it was conducted as a mission by the Episcopalians before it was taken over by the state and operated as a "special school." Finally, in the 1940's, it was discontinued, and the children were admitted to the white schools.

The history of education among the Houma (or Sabines) is one of controversy and bitterness. From the earliest times they were excluded from the white schools of Terrebone Parish, where many of them live, on the basis that "Indian" is equivalent to "Negro." In 1918 a member of the group took his grievance to court, demanding that his children be admitted to the white schools. In the course of the testimony the plaintiff was forced to admit that one of his grandfathers had been a slave and the court ruled against him. Even today many in the adult population are illiterate and the remainder are functionally so. Most Indians over 40 years of age sign documents with an "X." It was not until 1937 that they had any school at all. At that time Baptists and Methodists began working with them, with the result that many deserted the Catholic Church. Eventually the parish erected schools exclusively for them. It is interesting to note that just across the bayou, in LaFourche Parish, the Indians are considered white and are permitted to attend the white schools. It was not until 1957 that a high school was provided for the Houma in Terrebone Parish. Before that time, if they chose to continue their education beyond elementary school, they had to travel some distance, which few of them were able to do. It is not surprising that the dropout rate has always been high, that the schools are not accredited, and that parents and teachers have little respect for one another.

There have been many changes since World War II. Special schools for mestizos are still to be found, but one by one they have been discontinued and the children have been admitted to white schools. Nor can these changes be attributed only to the historic decision of the Supreme Court of May 1954. Fifty years ago New York abandoned its special school for Jackson Whites and New Jersey did so in 1945. Other states have followed, including many in the South. The trend toward the consolidation of rural schools has been a major factor in bringing this about, though the school integration movement has doubtless had its effect. The special school for Haliwas was disbanded in 1966, and the elementary school was phased out in 1969. As recently as 1969, however, Brass Ankle parents in Dorchester County, South Carolina, were rebuffed when they sought to enroll their children in a public school instead of in the small special school that had served them for many years. On the other hand, in September, 1970, a group of Lumbees filed an omnibus lawsuit against the school board, Governor Scott, and the Department of Health, Education, and Welfare, in response to a federal desegregation decree that would have required them to send their children to an integrated public school rather than to the special Indian schools they had long attended. The Lumbees declared that they had no objection to attending schools with whites, but they would not attend with blacks.

Desegregation and integration, of course, are not synonymous, and the transfer of mestizo children to white schools has not resulted in their acceptance as equals. They often find themselves isolated and alone. They have not been welcomed into the school's activities. Senior trips have been cancelled, and social events have been called off, or scheduled at times unlikely to be convenient for the mestizos. "If the spooks start coming to our dances," said a high school girl, "we just won't go." Teachers are reported to have shown resentment at their presence. Small wonder that the dropout rate is exceptionally high, academic performance is poor, and discipline problems severe. Some mestizo parents say it was better when they had their own schools.

Stability has never been a characteristic of mestizo communities, but nowadays the forces for change are operating with added vigor. The young men have been drafted to fight in a series of wars, and those who return home bring with them greater expectations and new concepts of their identity. Paved highways have been built through their hitherto inaccessible hills and swamps. The depression of the 1930's forced them into various relief programs and into closer contacts with whites and blacks. The schools, poor as they are, have nevertheless increased the group's literacy. Radio and television have made them aware of the world beyond their small settlements and increasing numbers have moved into occupations that provide them with greater income and security.

Some communities have disappeared altogether. The Coe clan has been widely dispersed, and none remains in the former locality. One group, presumably a Yamasee remnant, long resident on the banks of the Savannah River in Georgia, has disappeared, some having moved to Michigan, others to Arkansas. A Goins community in South Carolina, once quite numerous, has dwindled to a few families, and even they are only waiting for an opportunity to leave. Some 3500 Lumbees have moved to Baltimore, and 1000 Wesorts are now living in Washington. Today there are more Melungeons in Ellicott City, Maryland, and in Kokomo, Indiana, than there are on Newman's Ridge. Guineas have gone to Akron, Brass Ankles to Florida, and Jackson Whites to New York. Some who leave home eventually marry into, and become identified with, the Negro community, but most doubtless pass into white society.

Mestizo communities, however, are not expected to disappear in the near future. The most viable, and the most likely to survive, are those that are large enough to support a community life, where there is an adequate economic base, where there is a body of tradition to give cohesion and a name of which they can feel proud, and in which the obstacles to acceptance by whites have not been surmounted.

SELECTED BIBLIOGRAPHY

Beale, Calvin L., "American Triracial Isolates," *Eugenics Quarterly*, **4**, 187–196 (December 1957).

Berry, Brewton, *Almost White*. New York: Macmillan, 1963.

Cohen, David S., *They Walk These Hills: A Study of Social Solidarity Among the Racially Mixed People of the Ramapo Mountains*. Unpublished Ph.D. dissertation, University of Pennsylvania, 1971.

Estabrook, Arthur H., and I. E. McDougle, *Mongrel Virginians: The Win Tribe*. Baltimore: Williams and Wilkins, 1926.

Evans, W. McKee, *To Die Game: The Story of the Lowry Band, Indian Guerillas of Reconstruction*. Baton Rouge: Louisiana State University Press, 1971.

Gilbert, William H., Jr., "Surviving Indian Groups of the Eastern United States." *Smithsonian Report for 1948*. Washington: Government Printing Office, 1949, pp. 407–438.

Hudson, Charles M., Ed., *Red, White, and Black: Symposium on Indians in the Old South*. Southern Anthropological Society Proceedings, No. 5. Athens: University of Georgia Press, 1971.

Johnson, Guy B., "Personality in a White-Indian-Negro Community," *Amer. Sociol. Rev.*, **4**, 516–523 (August 1939).

Levine, Stuart, and Nancy O. Lurie, Eds., *The American Indian Today*. Deland, Florida: Everett Edwards, 1968.

Montell, Lynwood, *The Saga of Coe Ridge: A Study in Oral History*. Knoxville: University of Tennessee Press, 1970.

Price, Edward T., "Mixed-Blood Populations of Eastern United States as to Origins, Localizations, and Persistence." Unpublished Ph.D. Dissertation, University of California, Berkeley, 1950.

Stern, Theodore, "Chickahominy: The Changing Culture of a Virginia Indian Community," *Proc. Amer. Phil. Soc.*, **96**, 157–225 (April 1952).

Weslager, C. A., *Delaware's Forgotten Folk: The Story of the Moors and Nanticokes.* Philadelphia: University of Pennsylvania Press, 1943.

Bernhard L. Hormann

University of Hawaii

CHAPTER ELEVEN

HAWAII'S MIXING PEOPLE

The Problem of Identity

"I don't know . . . what 'Hawaiian' is—I feel it is the place, not the *race*," a woman of mixed ancestry—Hawaiian, Caucasian, and Chinese—married to a Caucasian, wrote to me recently. In a conversation not long before that she had told me that she cannot profess an interest she cannot feel in gleaning old Hawaiian traditions from interviews with aged Hawaiians nor in preserving them in her teaching. What does concern her is the story of all the people who have become a part of modern Hawaii. This caused her to look into the coming of her Chinese great-grandfather as a merchant from China. She has told me that in teaching the Hawaiian language she had sought to instil in her students some enthusiasm for the ethnic languages and customs of Hawaii and to record the way these languages have become mixed in the day-to-day conversation of people of various origins in the little rural and urban neighborhoods where they and their children have mingled.

This person of aboriginal Hawaiian ancestry mixed with the Asian and European represents an honest attempt to come to grips with the problems of her ethnic identity. There is a sort of identification with all the people of Hawaii—and with those beyond its shores. Let her represent the fact that the many people of pure and mixed origin are right now in process of defining who they are. For the time being they still present somewhat uncertain and at times contradictory ways of defining their major identities. Their groping will be reflected in my own groping in this chapter for an articulate answer to the question of how the people of Hawaii, mixed and unmixed, identify themselves.

The Problem of Concepts

A new book is being acclaimed in Hawaii. Called simply *The Hawaiians*,[1] it uses this term to include all the people living in the Islands, much as one speaks of Californians and Virginians. However, there is a special problem in Hawaii in the presence of a sizable proportion of ethnic Hawaiians and part-Hawaiians, descendants of the aboriginal Polynesian population. To refer to the resident population, the clumsy term "Hawaii's people" has been frequently used. This is the title selected by Andrew W. Lind, the sociologist whose researches in Hawaii extend back more than 40 years, for one of his recent books. He employed it to suggest that a process described by his predecessor and colleague, Romanzo Adams, the founder of modern sociology in Hawaii, in his monograph, *The Peoples of Hawaii*, had reached a state advanced enough to justify the singular *Hawaii's People*.[2] Adams had begun his study with the words, "There is abundant evidence that the people of Hawaii are in process of becoming one people. . . . But, while they are becoming one people, they are still many peoples." Lind defended his change of title, which he had first applied to the 1955 edition, in this way:

> Notable developments which had occurred in the intervening years, especially those associated with the wars in the Pacific and in Korea, had so radically altered the Island situation and the relationships among the various ethnic groups as to justify a shift in the title of the study.

For these peoples of Hawaii the term race has been commonly used. The connotation is similar to ethnic group, nationality, ancestry, or cultural group. When race is used in Hawaii, physical traits are only one possible element of the accepted connotation. This is similar to what the U.S. Bureau of the Census accepts when it declares:

> The concept of race as used by the Bureau of the Census is derived from that which is commonly accepted by the general public. It does not, therefore,

---

[1] Robert B. Goodman, photos; Gavan Daws and Ed Sheehan, text; Jo Rinehart, editor. Sydney, Australia: Island Heritage, 1970.

[2] Andrew W. Lind, *Hawaii's People*. 3rd ed. Honolulu: University of Hawaii Press, 1967. Cf. Romanzo Adams, *The People of Hawaii*. Honolulu: Institute of Pacific Relations, 1923.

reflect clear-cut definitions of biological stock, and several categories obviously refer to national origins.[3]

The term subnation recently proposed by Petersen[4] will, in my judgment, prove unacceptable, and we will have to continue to allow terms like *race, ethnic group*, and *minority group* to serve discussions of race relations and interracial mixing. The term *peoples*, as used by Adams and Lind, does, however, refer accurately to the Hawaiian situation and points to the central question of this chapter: Are the many peoples of Hawaii indeed becoming one people? Are they a "new people" in the sense that Hughes had in mind?

To the extent that they (any variety of tribes or other component groups of people) begin to feel themselves one for the purpose of gaining and maintaining a new political standing at home and in the world, they become a new people. A new people is one only recently or scarcely even yet come to the kind of self-conscious unity in which it is capable of political expression and/or action.[5]

Hughes raised some highly suggestive questions about what enters into the making of a new people. He considers such matters as race in the biological sense, language and territorial distribution, the arts pursued by the people and their history, and the kinds of leaders, education, occupations, and political positions found among them.

In the present discussion we are concerned with the ethnic Hawaiians and part-Hawaiians, the immigrant ethnic groups, still counted separately and still largely unmixed, and the various mixtures among these immigrant ethnic groups. There is no established term for the mixtures of these nonaborigine-descended groups. They consist mainly of Caucasian-Oriental mixtures and of mixtures of the people of the Far East: Filipino, Japanese, Chinese, and Korean. Popularly, they are often referred to as cosmopolitan, and there are those who feel that a designation for this growing part of the population is important. For our discussion they are important and fortunately we have ways of determining their numbers.

---

[3] U.S. Bureau of the Census. *U.S. Census of Population: 1960*. Final Report PC (2)-1c. U.S. Government Printing Office, Washington, 1963. p. x.

[4] William Petersen, "Classification of Subnations in Hawaii: An Essay in the Sociology of Knowledge," *Amer. Sociol. Rev.*, **34**, 863–877 (December 1969). Petersen has obviously misunderstood the use of the term *Other Caucasian* in Hawaiian demographic statistics. This and other misunderstandings make his exercise in the sociology of knowledge difficult to follow.

[5] Everett C. Hughes, "New Peoples," in Andrew W. Lind, Ed., *Race Relations in World Perspective*. Honolulu: University of Hawaii Press, 1955, pp. 96–97.

That all the people of Hawaii together, including unmixed as well as mixed, have some of the characteristics of a "new people" is also important. I refer to them as *Hawaii's people*.

THE COMPONENT PEOPLES OF HAWAII

Geographical and Historical Background

In the framework of what the people of Hawaii are becoming we can think first of the ethnic groups that, at one stage or another, entered the scene and are still to a decided extent identifiable, statistically, as well as culturally and socially, as reference groups. These groups, disenchanted with their ancestral identities and traditions, are becoming, in the language of the twenties, thirties, and forties, Americanized or, in the language of more contemporary sociologists, are now acquiring a new ethnic pride in a pluralistic society.

So, before dealing more particularly with the mixed people, we shall review the arrival of the various peoples who today make up the heterogeneous population of Hawaii within which this mixed element is becoming increasingly important.

Hawaii geographically is one of the most remote communities in the world, about 2400 miles from its nearest neighbor. This is the reason for its late discovery, prehistorically, by Polynesian seafarers, probably between A.D. 500 and 700, who came from Tahiti, 2700 miles away. It also accounts for its late historical discovery in 1778, two and one-half centuries after Magellan's transpacific crossing and only two centuries ago. These Polynesians, who represented elements of the three basic stocks of mankind, after centuries of migration from the western Pacific and Asia settled Hawaii and became ethnic Hawaiians. They had a preliterate neolithic way of life, getting their subsistence from agriculture and fishing. Having no trade, money, cities, or system of writing, they nevertheless had a complex social and religious system and a number of highly developed skills and crafts.

The arrival of Captain James Cook quickly made the Islands a lucrative port of call for pioneers engaged in the fur trade, the China trade, and whaling. The disruption, caused by the seething activity in Hawaiian society and its way of life, made it possible for Western enterprisers to develop "factories in the field" to produce commodities for the world's markets—sugar, later pineapples, some coffee, rubber, sisal, rice, and even silk. To supply laborers for these plantations people from peasant villages were imported from South China, various Pacific islands, Portugal, Japan, Norway, Germany, Puerto Rico, Korea, Spain, the Philippines, and Russia. About 400,000 people were brought in, primarily between 1875 and 1925. Many of the Asians returned to their homelands, and among all there was a continuous movement to the Mainland. Independent pioneers came too—beachcombers, missionaries, and merchants —from northern European countries, the eastern United States, and China. Most recently American Negroes and Samoans have joined the small numbers already in Hawaii.

The native Hawaiians declined steadily in population from the moment of contact with the first arrivals, when they numbered perhaps 300,000, but until the late 1880's they continued to be in the majority. Since then no ethnic group has had a majority. The total population of the Islands reached its lowest point (50,000) about 1875, and since then there has been a steady increase, due to continued immigration and a high rate of natural growth, in all groups except the "pure" Hawaiians who now number fewer than 10,000. Part-Hawaiians probably number about 140,000. The total population is about three-quarters of a million, including more than 100,000 military personnel and their dependents.

All this demographic movement and heterogeneity applies to a group of islands about 6500 square miles in area, or a little smaller than the State of New Jersey. The main and central island, about one-tenth of the total, has more than 80 percent of the population. This is Oahu, politically the City and County of Honolulu, with a density of 1018 per square mile. In contrast, Hawaii, the "Big Island," has only 15 persons per square mile, although its area is two-thirds of the total and seven times that of Oahu.

Politically the Islands were independent until annexation by the United States in 1898. Hawaii became the fiftieth state of the United States in 1959.

Ethnic Composition

At the time of writing the best available statistics on ethnicity are those issued by the Hawaii State Department of Planning and Economic Development in 1968 as its estimates for July 1, 1966 (see Table 10). These estimates were derived from sample surveys which contained a question on race of parents and which, it was believed, reduced the uncertainties regarding ethnic numbers in the U.S. Census of 1960. In this count the Puerto Ricans had been "lost," probably mainly to the white category, many part-Hawaiians had put themselves into the pure- or some non-Hawaiian category, including Caucasian, and people of non-Hawaiian

Table 10   Resident Population of Hawaii by Ethnic Heritage, 1950 and 1966[a]

	April 1950 (%)	July 1966 (%)	Change 1950–1966 (%)
MIXED:			
Part-Hawaiian	14.8	17.1	+ 72.5
	(73,885)	(127,418)	
Non-Hawaiian	4.1	8.3	+ 204.2
	(20,337)	(61,872)	
Total mixed	18.9	25.4	+ 100.9
	(94,222)	(189,290)	
UNMIXED:			
Total unmixed population[b]	81.1	74.3	+ 36
	(405,972)	(552,077)	
Not reported		0.3	
		(2,581)	

[a] Includes persons in barracks and institutions. SOURCE: Hawaii State Department of Planning and Economic Development.
[b] Hawaiian, Caucasian, Chinese, Japanese, Korean, Filipino, Puerto Rican, Samoan, Negro.

mixture had not been counted separately at all, as in the 1950 Census. This last group, the so-called "cosmopolitans," showed an increase which was more than 200 percent of their numbers 16 years earlier, in the 1950 Census, whereas the Caucasians had increased by only 80 percent and the part-Hawaiians by about 70 percent. However, since 40 to 50 percent of all Caucasians are in the military, in uniform or as dependents, and the military population experiences rapid and continuous turnover, it is clear that the significant increases in resident population have been among persons of mixed ancestry. The Report also notes that "Caucasian totals for 1960 included an unknown but sizable number of part-Hawaiians and Puerto Ricans."[6]

Mixing: Extent, Process and Significance

If these data are reasonably accurate, as I believe they are, a quarter of Hawaii's present population is mixed, up 134.4 percent from the 18.9

[6] Department of Planning and Economic Development, State of Hawaii, Statistical Report 55, March 15, 1968. Table 10 is based on the Report. The sources cited are U.S. Census of Population: 1950, Bulletin P-B52, table 9; estimates by Hawaii State Department of Health and Hawaii State Vocational Rehabilitation Plan; and 1960 U.S. Census data on barracks population.

percent of 1950. Two-thirds of these mixed people are part-Hawaiian; the other mixtures do not involve Hawaiian ancestry.

Mixed Births. One way in which we might determine how these non-Hawaiian mixtures are distributed is to examine the birth records by race of father and mother. For 1969, of the known mixed births, 6463 in number, or 70.3 percent, were part-Hawaiian; 18.6 percent were born of Caucasian parents on one side and non-Caucasian and non-Hawaiian parents on the other, that is, mainly "Eurasian" (a term not used in Hawaii); and 11.1 percent were born of intra-Oriental mixtures. For the five-year period from 1960 to 1964 these percentages were 71.8, 16.6, and 11.6, respectively.

Thus it is clear that in the mixing process today the part-Hawaiians dominate at a little more than two-thirds, whereas the smallest third is more heavily weighted in the direction of part-Caucasian mixtures than of non-Caucasian, non-Hawaiian mixtures.

These mixed births represent about two-fifths of all births in recent years, as shown in Table 11. The table omits births by unknown fathers and births by "other" fathers and mothers because they are unclassifiable as mixed or unmixed. It is known, however, that children born to part-Hawaiian mothers by unknown fathers inevitably belong to the part-

Table 11   Mixed and Unmixed Births, State of Hawaii, 1960–1964 and 1969, by Known Fathers

	1960–1964 (%)	1969 (%)
MIXED:		
Part-Hawaiian	71.8	70.3
Caucasian, non-Hawaiian	16.6	18.6
Non-Caucasian, non-Hawaiian	11.6	11.1
	100.0	100.0
Total mixed	38.0	41.6
	(31,249)	(5,958)
UNMIXED:		
Total unmixed[a]	60.4	57.6
	(49,647)	(8,203)
Other	1.5	1.1
	(1,237)	(153)

SOURCE: A. W. Lind, *Hawaii's People*, Table 27, p. 114; table supplied by Hawaii State Department of Health for the 1969 data. Births by "other" fathers and mothers unclassifiable. Births by unknown fathers have been omitted. These have been between 5 and 9 percent.
[a] Hawaiian, Caucasian, Chinese, Japanese, Korean, Filipino, Puerto Rican, Samoan, and Negro.

Hawaiian category and are therefore mixed. If this not inconsiderable number of births (505 for 1969) were added, the proportion of mixed children in 1969 would rise to 44.1 percent. Since all mixtures except the part-Hawaiian have for many years been classified by one of their "unmixed" parents, these mixed persons, when adult, represent an unknown but ever-growing number who are being counted as unmixed but who are actually mixed. It is certain that today there must be a considerable number of births that appear to be unmixed but in reality are mixed—for this or several other plausible reasons. Thus in Hawaii about one-half of all births are mixed.[7]

Mixed Marriages. These mixed births reflect interethnic marriages. A look at them and their trends is therefore in order.

The Department of Health of the State of Hawaii and its governmental predecessors have issued annual reports over a period of about six decades which list marriages by race of groom as against race of bride and which have been repeatedly analyzed by a succession of sociologists. There is no doubt that the proportion of out-marriages has been going up, as Table 12 bears out. By groups of years, Lind, for instance, listed 11.5 percent of out-marriages for 1912–1916, a gradual increase in subsequent periods, and finally 37.6 percent for 1960–1964.[8] To these percentages we can add the later ones issued by the Department of Health for the years since then; 38.1 percent for 1966, the highest point to date, and a decline in the annual percentages of out-marriages to 33.7 in 1969. This decline might, on the surface, indicate that the recent tendency toward reassertion of ethnicity noted by some researchers on the Mainland, and suggested by a few as about to occur in Hawaii, had indeed reached the Islands.[9] A closer look, however, indicates that *Caucasian* out-marriage rates *only* have been coming down from 27.3 percent of *all* Caucasian brides and grooms in 1961 to 18.9 percent in 1969. At the same time the proportion of all brides and grooms who were Caucasians increased from 32.3 percent in 1961 to 51.2 percent in 1969, and this at a time when the Caucasians were only 32.0 percent of the population (1960).

How are we to explain this curious dominance of Caucasians among

---

[7] See also Newton E. Morton, Chin S. Chung, and Ming-Pi Mi, *Genetics of Interracial Crosses in Hawaii.* Basel and New York: Karger, 1967. This elaborate study by geneticists, using birth records of children and their parents and serological and other evidence, finds the extent of mixing even greater than elementary statistical analysis seems to indicate.

[8] Andrew W. Lind, *Hawaii's People*, 1967, p. 108.

[9] This is suggested by Elizabeth Wittermans-Pino, *Inter-Ethnic Relations in a Plural Society.* Groningen: Wolters, 1964, and William Peterson, *loc. cit.*

Table 12   Percentage of Out-Marriages in Hawaii for Certain Ethnic Groups

	1912–1916	1930–1940	1950–1959	1969
Out-marriages for total population	11.5	22.8	32.8	33.7
Hawaiian brides	39.9	62.7	81.5	93.9
Hawaiian grooms	19.4	55.2	78.9	81.7
Part-Hawaiian brides	66.2	57.9	58.4	54.7
Part-Hawaiian grooms	52.1	41.0	41.3	65.0
Caucasian brides	11.7	10.7	16.4	18.5
Caucasian grooms	17.3	22.4	37.4	19.4
Japanese brides	0.2	6.3	19.1	33.8
Japanese grooms	0.5	4.3	8.7	29.3
Chinese brides	5.7	28.5	45.2	68.4
Chinese grooms	41.7	28.0	43.6	59.9
Korean brides	0.0	39.0	74.5	87.6
Korean grooms	26.4	23.5	70.3	76.8
Filipino brides	2.8	4.0	35.8	50.3
Filipino grooms	21.8	37.5	44.8	53.4

SOURCES: Lind, *Hawaii's People*, 1967, Table 24, 108; Reports of Hawaii State Department of Health.

those getting married in Hawaii? The obvious explanation is that in the 1960's an increasing number of marriages involving military personnel took place, many of them on "R and R" (Rest and Recuperation) from Vietnam. Of all designated areas for "R and R" Hawaii has been the most popular because it is closest to the continental United States. A brief sojourn in Hawaii makes possible a reunion with parents, wives, and fiancées. Although these "R and R" marriages are registered and therefore counted in Hawaii, they will not contribute to the permanent population of the state. How large a proportion—more than 40 percent—is represented by military personnel and their dependents in the resident Caucasian population of Hawaii was mentioned earlier. We can plausibly assume that when the present peculiar military situation of the United States abates the influence of this military component will decline and the more permanent residential population of Hawaii will continue to participate in the upward trend of Hawaii's interethnic out-marriage rates. To this trend Caucasian men in uniform have contributed because of the relative lack of Caucasian women, and it is their contribution, noted above, that is reflected in the higher proportion of mixed births with one Caucasian parent than of non-Caucasian, non-Hawaiian mixed births.

More fully identified with Hawaii are the Japanese, whose number is large enough to give us a clue to what is happening among the resident ethnic groups. Because of their more recent immigration than the Chinese and Portuguese and their relative closeness to their powerful homeland, they have been slow in getting on the out-marrying bandwagon. In 1912–1916 only 0.5 percent of the grooms and 0.2 percent of the brides were marrying out. In the fifties these percentages had risen to 8.7 and 19.1, respectively, but by 1969 the number of Japanese marrying out had risen to 29.3% for the grooms and 33.8% for the brides. The percentage of Japanese grooms marrying out more than tripled from the decade of the fifties to 1969, whereas that of brides, already higher, increased by more than half.

Many more than half of all Chinese grooms and brides married non-Chinese in the 1960's, a sharp increase from the preceding decade. For the Koreans the percentage has been higher than 70 since the early 1950's and more than 50 percent of the part-Hawaiians, already mixed, and becoming a sizable group, have married outside the part-Hawaiian group.

It should also be remembered that persons from Hawaii in military service or in colleges and universities away from the Islands may marry out and then return to Hawaii to live. Such out-marriages are not counted statistically in Hawaii but they are reflected in births.

Up until the recent occurrence of "R and R" marriages my judgment had been that the proportion of all interethnic marriages was approaching 40 percent. If we had a way of counting marriages of local residents only, I am confident that this judgment would still be accurate and that the proportion might well be more than 40 percent today.

The Context of Mixing

Historical Context. Historically the context has been quite favorable to interracial mixing from the time of the discovery of Hawaii almost two centuries ago. The men on all the first ships from 1778 on were extended sexual hospitality. The offspring thus ensuing were easily absorbed into the Hawaiian community; they and their mothers were accepted without shame, for illegitimacy was a concept inapplicable to the Hawaiian way of life. Some of the men from these ships stayed in Hawaii and those who had the character and skill that won them recognition among the chiefs were invited to have "chiefly" women as their wives. Thus almost from the beginning interracial marriage was sanctioned by Hawaiian royalty. So, for instance, Queen Emma, the midnineteenth century consort of Kamehameha IV, was a granddaughter of an English-man who married the niece of the first Kamehameha. Queen Liliuokalani, the last reigning monarch, married to an American who had become a Hawaiian citizen, was childless and designated her niece Princess Kaiulani as heiress to the throne. Kaiulani's father was a Scot. There has never been a law in Hawaii against intermarriage under any government.

The foreigners who came to Hawaii to make a living, whether white Europeans and Americans, or imported laborers from China and else-where, were men, seldom accompanied by wives—the missionaries and later importees from Portugal and Japan were major exceptions. Grad-ually women of all groups came in as immigrants. This unusually high sex ratio of foreign men was also conducive to intermarriage. The Chinese concubinage system made such marriages with Hawaiian women har-monious with Chinese custom. As a "hybrid" population developed and was accepted, it acted as a bridge for all the groups entering the Hawaiian social scene and as an example more favorable than unfavorable to further intermarriage. The many groups, none of them after the late 1880's in the majority, also allowed greater ease of association, par-ticularly as those of the laboring class developed a sort of cosmopolitan "pidgin" language and way of life among themselves. Politically, parties stumbled into balanced tickets and racial electioneering was avoided. This association started among adults at work on the plantations and was encouraged in the classes and on the playgrounds of the schools that children of all groups attended, starting in the eighties and nineties of the last century. The year-round outdoor life and the community-wide interest in sports also furthered such interracial contacts in a small insular community in which people inevitably faced inward toward one another. Intimate relations, friendships, and even marriages developed easily in this atmosphere.

Social Barriers. The force of social barriers cannot, however, be denied. Class barriers, starting with the distinction between "chiefly" and "commoner" Hawaiians, were given another dimension when Caucasians (Haoles), who built the sugar and other industries, became the economic rulers and the social elite. Even today there survives among some of them a kind of paternalistic condescension, which is reciprocated either by marked anti-Haole feeling or by extreme deference among Hawaiians and non-Caucasian immigrant ethnic groups.

There have, of course, also been ethnic ghettos, although no "solid" ones, and ethnic institutions, such as afternoon foreign-language schools, temples and shrines, movie theaters, benevolent associations, shops and restaurants that sell ethnic foods, foreign-language newspapers, clubs built around Old World places of origin or Old World cults, such as judo, Chinese drama, and Portuguese Holy Ghost celebrations.

Above all there has been the strength of Chinese, Japanese, Portuguese, and Filipino families and those of other ethnic groups. This pride of family involves status in the competitive struggle in each ethnic community. It also involves a sense of reputation of each ethnic group in the wider community. The out-marriage of children, both of sons and daughters, was and still is often vigorously resisted on grounds that the name of the family within the ethnic community will be shamed and that the family will not have close and natural associations with the family of the other ethnic group, for in the Old World view marriages have been unions between families rather than between individuals. So, although marriages among "local" people, born and reared in Hawaii, but often of different ethnic ancestries, are in many respects "in-marriages," the resistance to them is clearly to be reckoned with.

The Case of the Japanese. Sometimes the Japanese of Hawaii are pointed to as having the strongest sense of ethnic pride as well as the greatest degree of separatism. The fact that they have been from the beginning of this century the largest of Hawaii's ethnic groups, with a peak of 42.7 percent of the population in 1920, although never in the majority, has made it easier to maintain ethnic ways and a kind of ethnic solidarity. The data on their relatively low out-marriage rates bear this out, but the recent increases, already mentioned, also indicate a steady decline of solidarity. In addition, the closeness of Japan, its strength as a nation before World War II, and its rapid recuperation after its disastrous defeat, making it today one of the most productive countries in the world, inevitably were reflected among some of Hawaii's Japanese in a kind of self-assurance, at times showing aggressive or complacent overtones, about the quality of the Japanese people.

The pride of many Japanese, as well as Chinese, families, under strain to maintain the unsullied integrity and to strengthen them through the education of their children and through the most delicate marriage negotiations, may be likened to the pride of the royal houses of Europe in the last century. The strength and unity of these Oriental families are also reminiscent of the strength and unity of many Jewish families. There is, however, a difference in the integration—namely, in the Jewish strength of the religious element and their sense of being a people. For the Japanese and Chinese family solidarity is based on a cult of ancestors through the male line. The Jews, on the other hand, involve the family's identification with a people, historically one, although found in many parts of the world. The difference can, I believe, be seen in the relative ease with which the Japanese and Chinese of Hawaii have become Christianized, a process we do not see occurring among, say, the Jews of New York City. In an unpublished study of liquor consumption patterns done in 1960 a random sample of the adult population of Oahu was asked a question about religious identity. Among the Japanese in the sample 35.3 percent identified themselves as Protestant, Catholic, or Mormon Christians. Among the Chinese more than half, 55.9 percent, so identified themselves.[10]

Another development in the immigrant communities, especially the Japanese, has produced a deep sense of at-homeness in Hawaii. This is the growth of kinship groups, wider than the nuclear family, which relate three or four living generations as well as a number of households through the ties of sibling and cousin relationships. As these wider groups of kin appeared ties with the homeland weakened and, during World War II, were completely suspended. At the same time the need for Hawaii-based ethnic institutions to provide a variety of warm social relationships became weaker and has been increasingly supplanted, first by the wider family and then by various interethnic institutions, an interethnic community life, and the pursuit of nonethnic interests.

Continuous weakening of the ethnic communities, their traditions and institutions, has been encouraged, paradoxically, and at times even overtly, by tolerance; over the years this has allowed the Japanese, Chinese, and all immigrant groups to establish ethnic institutions of the sort mentioned as existing in Hawaii's ethnic ghettos: afternoon foreign-language schools, Chinese temples eclectically combining Taoism, Buddhism, Confucianism, and the cult of the ancestors in the manner congenial to peasant folk, Japanese Buddhist temples, Shinto shrines, and faith-healing new religions from Japan, Portuguese societies of the Holy Ghost, Filipino Rizal Day or Flores de Mayo celebrations, and traditional restaurants and movie theaters. However, attendance at public and private American schools, in which the tenets of American public life and patriotism are taught, was enforced, and American movies and magazines were already more appealing in the twenties and thirties than the ethnic ones. Christian churches were more dynamic and understandable than Asian religious institutions. The attrition of young people from the ethnic ways has been persistent and continuous, but in general it has not split families.

---

[10] Data supplied by Harwin L. Voss and used with permission of the Liquor Commission of the City and County of Honolulu and the Economic Research Center, University of Hawaii.

I should like to mention another force that has tended to weaken the assertive ethnocentrism of Hawaii's Japanese people, namely, their experience in World War II, in which their country of long-time residence and livelihood, the country of their citizenship in increasingly large proportion, was at war with their country of origin. This possibility occurred to me when I read the analysis of the Germans in New York City by Glazer and Moynihan. That their ethnic strength and identity are relatively weak in New York these authors attribute to the two world wars and to the intense criticism of the Nazi regime by Americans in general. Sensitive Americans of German ancestry muted their German background.[11]

In the tense international situation of the 1930's the loyalty of Hawaii's citizens of Japanese ancestry, referred to as AJA's, was a constant subject of discussion in which suspicions and allegations were openly voiced and also vigorously denied—usually by "Haoles," some of whom were sociologists, who knew them well. The story of the mass internment of Japanese on the Mainland, although fewer than two thousand of Hawaii's 160,000 Japanese, alien and citizen, were interned or relocated, is well known. The young men of Japanese ancestry in ROTC units in Hawaii were activated, then deactivated, then allowed to volunteer, first for a nonuniformed unit which provided various services for the armed forces on Oahu, then for the 442 Regimental Combat Team and the 100th Infantry Battalion which later became famous for their outstanding performance in Europe and elsewhere. The Japanese population of Hawaii was apprehensive for a while, but quick recognition by military leaders, including Admiral Chester Nimitz, head of all armed forces in the central Pacific, of the "success of Hawaii's experiment in race relations and in democracy" helped allay apprehension on all sides. Nevertheless, this whole experience hastened disenchantment with the ethnic homeland.[12] From a peak in 1934, when 85 percent of the Japanese children of school age attended Japanese-language schools, the proportion in 1960 was down to about 30 percent.[13]

Since the victory of the Communists in China in 1949, the Chinese of Hawaii have been in a somewhat analogous position.

Today there is a new influence from the Mainland, namely, a re-

---

[11] Nathan Glazer and Daniel P. Moynihan, *Beyond the Melting Pot: the Negroes, Puerto Ricans, Jews, Italians, and Irish of New City.* Cambridge, Massachusetts: The M.I.T. Press, 1963, 131 ff.

[12] Andrew W. Lind, *Hawaii's Japanese, Experiment in Democracy.* Princeton, New Jersey: Princeton University Press, 1946.

[13] Yukuo Uyehara, "Some Aspects of the Teaching of the Japanese Language in Hawaii," *Social Process in Hawaii,* **24,** 84–88 (1960).

vival of interest in the various ethnic groups of America, starting of course with the blacks. On the West Coast black studies programs have become ethnic studies programs, to which Japanese, Chinese, Mexican, and sometimes American Indian have been added. Each group seems to be doing mainly "its own thing" in these courses and in the ethnic organizations, which are taking on the shape of political interest groups. Whether these new approaches will be enthusiastically accepted in Hawaii, it is too early to tell. I doubt it, although there are some indications of change in the *Zeitgeist* of youth reaching some of the youth of Hawaii, as this excerpt from a paper written in the spring of 1968 by a Japanese woman student suggests:

What we "want" is to protest, to march, to stand up and be counted, against the massiveness of power and society. But this is impossible to do. Why? Because it hurts innocent people. Our parents do not understand. They were raised, and they hold, and they have raised us, on different values. What we believe, what they believe, and what they think we believe, are three different things. To yield externally to them robs us of nothing. So we make this sacrifice. And there is harmony in the family. As long as one is part of the household, obligations exist. Maybe later, later. . . .

In this case, however, there is influence against rather than for Japanese ethnicity.

For the time being the tolerant pluralism of Hawaii seems associated with a steady and mutual assimilation, whereas on the Mainland the stress on pluralism and ethnic power suggests a retreat from those of our national programs of cultural assimilation that have not been accompanied by social acceptance and, at times, from recent programs of forced integration that have under some conditions created more tensions and problems than solutions of race relations.

Enough has been said to point to steady decline—up to now—in the strength of the ethnic communities of Hawaii. This is a genuine counterpart of the process of mixing described earlier.

Where Do the Mixed People Belong?

The pertinent questions now are these: What direction will these mixed people take as they join existing groups or form groups within which they can easily achieve a sense of belonging? What are their reference groups? Are they, in any sense of the sort Hughes had in mind, becoming a new people?

Sociologists have long pointed to two possibilities: mixed people are absorbed into one or the other parent group or they become a new ethnic element, clearly identified as biologically and culturally mixed. Although there is evidence, already referred to, of mixed people being absorbed into one of the several component groups and for other mixed people to regard themselves as mixed, it is my observation that both the "pure" and the mixed have been in the process of becoming a single local community, a Hawaiian variant of American society and culture.

In order to illustrate these points, I have introduced the case histories of a few of my students in the last three decades. Some part-Hawaiians speak first.

Part-Hawaiians. First is a male student who attended Kamehameha School, a private institution established by the will of the last surviving descendant of Kamehameha I, supported by her estate which consists of 9 percent of all the land in Hawaii and maintained for children of some Hawaiian ancestry. Although it has a typically American curriculum, it has put some emphasis on Hawaiian studies. Its student body is extremely mixed, running in appearance from blond Caucasian through off-white and brown Oriental to light and dark brown Polynesian and having surnames that are Japanese, Chinese, Hawaiian, and all the nationalities of Europe. At the same time it is segregated in that all students must have at least some Hawaiian blood. There is continuous discussion of the best ways the institution can serve the Hawaiians, whether it has helped to improve their way of life, whether it has merely isolated a small number of the bright ones from the Hawaiian community to which they never return, even as leaders, or whether it has excluded the Hawaiians from the wider community and thus hampered the development of interrelationships. This student wrote in 1965:

> I did not know the effect Kamehameha was to have upon myself, my family, and my friends. Before entering Kamehameha I felt like a nothing. "All Hawaiians are no good. They're stupid. Look at all the land they had and gave away. You're all fat and lazy, only eat, drink, and sleep." You tell me. Who wouldn't feel inferior after being subjected to such disparaging remarks? To top it off, I applied three times; after the third attempt but before knowing of my acceptance I was really depressed.
>
> After my first year everything changed. I felt something funny when I returned home for Christmas vacation. My brothers and sisters looked up to me. They asked me questions about the school; they said I acted "different." My friends reacted the same way. They were all interested in Kamehameha's heritage. Those who had made disparaging remarks against the Hawaiians began changing their stories; a lot of them respected Kamehameha.
>
> I returned to school with a new attitude. I felt confident; I was proud. I told my friends about the experience and to my amazement a couple of them felt the same pride. They themselves had experienced the same reaction during

their vacation. . . . Kamehameha had something special, people thought. It advanced the Hawaiians.

A girl in another of my classes (1960) also discusses her Hawaii background. After first giving her very mixed ancestry (English, Hawaiian, Scottish, and Japanese), she tells of the Hawaiian and Christian influences in her home. Then, getting into the question of her Hawaiianness, she writes:

I have not always been proud of my Hawaiian blood. There was a time back in the elementary school when I violently denied my Hawaiian heritage. Many of the Hawaiians I knew then, outside my immediate family, were either sloppy, uncouth, or alcoholics. In school, I was in the "A" class which was composed almost entirely of Japanese with a small percentage of Haoles and Filipinos. The Hawaiians, who were concentrated in the "C" and "D" sections, came from poor and disorganized families.

The Japanese in my class were a smug majority who had definite prejudices toward other nationalities in general. I was determined to be liked and accepted (by them, but) I was not Japanese as far as they were concerned, so that I was never quite one of the bunch. One of my school experiences illustrating the prejudices of a few Japanese occurred when I was in seventh grade. Our class was divided into two debate groups, each of which was to choose two persons to represent it. I was to represent our group along with a bright Puerto Rican boy. The next morning I went to school with a page full of notes for the debate, only to overhear one of the class ringleaders convincing the others in our group to choose another boy and girl because they were Japanese. It was not until I attended school in Honolulu that I began to identify myself with Hawaiians.

The newly found pride may, however, be in the fact and extent of mixture rather than in preoccupation with Hawaiian identity. When this happens, the interest will be in the contributions made by the various heritages to the person's upbringing and the pride in the fact of mixture. So one girl states in her first paragraph: "I am of Hawaiian, German, Chinese, and Maori background." She then concludes, "These races and their certain customs have influenced my upbringing, Hawaiian being the most dominant." At the end she announces that she is married and expects to bring up her children "to be proud of their mixed heritage."

Non-Hawaiian Mixtures. Since mixtures containing no Hawaiian element have for the most part not been counted separately, it is not easy to consider them. Yet these "cosmopolitan" mixtures are recognized from time to time. A contest for ethnic queens each year at the University of Hawaii has among its categories "cosmopolitan." A person mixed in this way is normally not offended by being asked what his ancestry is, and although some new arrivals from the Mainland find this an exaggerated attention to "race" the attitude in Hawaii is rather that mixed ancestry is a "conversation piece."

I remember, for instance, the paper of a girl of mixed ancestry, Filipino on her father's side, Japanese on her mother's. She told how her parents met in the plantation area of one of the outer islands and had married against the wishes of her mother's Japanese parents, who, however, after several years and with the arrival of grandchildren, had become reconciled to the union. Her father being a Catholic, her mother coming from a Buddhist family, they had "compromised" by sending their children to a Protestant Sunday school. When they visited her Japanese grandparents on a neighboring plantation, her Filipino father insisted, although he himself refrained from participating, that the children join their grandfather in paying their respects at the Japanese family shrine. At home her mother prepared Japanese dishes, her father, occasionally, Filipino ones and each teased the other. Her father referred to her mother's cooking as "shoyu-sugar" cooking, she to his as "bagoong" (a salted fish paste) cooking. The daughter gave a picture of a contented family. Soon after I had had her as a student she told me that she was seriously dating a Haole from the Mainland.

Well known to me is a young school teacher whose father is Portuguese and whose mother is Japanese. Her mother became a convert to Catholicism and has taken her new religion very seriously. The daughter was enrolled in an education class in which a man recently arrived from the Mainland bemoaned the loss of Hawaiian culture and was all for organized attempts to revive it. The school teacher reported to me how she had challenged his position by asking him what his possibly mixed European ancestry was and how much he retained of the various ancestral cultures. She also told of her own mixture. She stressed the fact that she regarded herself as primarily American, although she recognized and appreciated the Portuguese and Japanese cultural influences in her upbringing, but also felt that she had benefited by the cultures of other ethnic stocks that were not in her ancestry.

Cumulativeness of Mixing. Once a precedent of successful mixing has been established in a family of whatever unmixed ancestry, further intermarriages occur more easily and a cumulative process is started. A young Chinese from another island wrote that his major friendships had been with Japanese boys. Several members of his family had married Japanese, and he also would marry one.

A girl of complicated mixture describes a similar process in her family:

My mother is of Japanese and Hawaiian ancestry, her mother being pure

Hawaiian and her father being a native of Japan. When my mother married my father she had accumulated a conglomeration of customs of various racial groups through education and the mingling with other people, but Japanese customs were still predominant.

Although her mother's Japanese father had returned to Japan "because he had a premonition that he was going to die," his influence prevailed over that of her gentler and less educated Hawaiian mother. In high school she became a Christian because she no longer received "personal gratification" from Buddhism.

My father is of pure Chinese ancestry, his father coming from China and his mother being born in Hawaii. Daddy is the oldest son after five girls, in a family of sixteen children, and so he was the "prized" child in that family. His family followed strictly Chinese customs, and so my father was typically Chinese. Naturally my father's parents wanted him to marry a pure Chinese girl, and so after they had already selected his mate for him, and he still continued to see my mother (in a romance that had started in high school), they took drastic steps. They forbade my mother ever to enter their house; they continuously hounded my father as to the ill-fate that would befall him if he married a non-Chinese girl; they threatened to disinherit him; and they even sent my father to China for a few months. But when my father was twenty-four years old and my mother was nineteen, they were married, with the blessings of Tutu (the Hawaiian grandmother). Unfortunately, Tutu died six months after the wedding, and so my parents were now entirely on their own.

She then describes some of the adjustments her parents had to make as a result of their differences in customs, food, and religion, but "today we eat a variety of types of racial dishes," and "today, our family is Episcopalian."

She attributes the fuller "Americanization" of her mother to her not having been fully accepted by either her Hawaiian or her Japanese playmates. "Consequently, this made my mother seek her friends from other nationalities who would accept her, or from other half-castes like herself." These friends encouraged her to seek higher education, which the girl's father agreed to finance. Her mother now teaches school and her father stresses education of the children.

It was seven years after my parents' marriage that my older brother, their first child, was born. By this time, my father's father had died, and his wife, my Popo, was our only living grandparent left. She is still living today. My brother was the first grandson to carry the family's surname. It was his birth that finally made my grandmother completely accept my mother into the family. It was also the fact that my grandmother finally realized that her children were Chinese only in blood but not in thoughts or actions. She consequently made herself become accustomed to American ways, and to the fact that her children were acquiring more modernized attitudes.

Then the girl speaks of the influence of this change on out-marriages in the family.

I believe my father's marriage to a non-Chinese made it easier for his other sisters and brothers to marry the mates of their choice, regardless of nationality. Of the nine children that remained then, six of them married someone of another nationality or of part-Chinese blood. Today, Popo calls her family all "chop-suey."

Another example of my parents' racial tolerance occurred when I was adopted into their family. My parents wanted another child badly, and so they adopted me, a Chinese, Hawaiian, Portuguese, and Irish child.

My parents are quite liberal about the nationality of the people we choose to date, and they have often said that it's up to us whom we marry.

I believe that our family, my Popo, aunts, uncles, cousins, etc., are truly an example of how different races can live in harmony with one another. So the next time I hear the phrase, "Hawaii, the melting pot of the Pacific," I'll inwardly be proud that my own family is fostering this ideal.

THE LOCAL COMMUNITY AND ITS CULTURE FOR THE MIXED AND UNMIXED

The "Pidgin Culture"

This chapter must end with something that all the peoples of Hawaii have developed in common and that holds them together. On other ethnic frontiers this has sometimes been referred to as "creole," but in Hawaii it is called "local," and I have come to think of it as "pidgin culture" and "pidgin society."

In Hawaii the word "local" is quite commonly used to refer to persons who are clearly "of" Hawaii, preferably by birth, by upbringing, and by a fundamental loyalty to and identification with Hawaii. A Haole so oriented would be called a "local" Haole. A "local" who is away from Hawaii will profess homesickness. When traveling, "locals" who may have little in common at home are often overjoyed at finding one another. I have been told that one reason more local non-Haoles do not occupy top positions in business and industry is no longer prejudice, for attempts have been made to discover talent among them, but the reluctance of local men to accept a transfer to the Mainland or elsewhere that would separate them from friends, relatives, and Hawaii's way of life.

The racial and class aspects of the concept "local" are subtle and hard to articulate. Primarily the term refers to persons who are not Caucasian and who may be mixed but more often are not. Persons of the blue-collar working class are most likely to be "local." A "local Haole" will qualify only if he is clearly, naturally, and unaffectedly at home with the other "locals" and they with him, and this attitude can and does cross class lines. Some Mainland Haoles can achieve this kind of assimilation more quickly than some local Haoles. If the non-Haoles detect any sign of standoffishness or lack of genuineness, it immediately arouses latent "anti-Haole" feelings that reflect the earlier domination of workers of all ethnic groups by the Haole elite in the days of the plantation era. The ability to switch easily into pidgin English, the "local dialect," the "fun" language of Hawaii,[14] is not essential. Mainland Haoles can be accepted if they show a genuine appreciation of local people. Again, knowing the local situation intimately, I wish to qualify this statement. Many local people, particularly young males, may deliberately set out to harass presumably defenseless Caucasians such as servicemen and, more recently, hippies. A young Haole in my class described how, as a teenager, he had participated in such harassment, joining local non-Haoles in their search for lonely Caucasians.

The term "pidgin culture of Hawaii" has struck me as felicitously describing this peculiarly "local" way of life which emerged on the playgrounds of the public schools, in the plantation communities, and in the urban working-class areas among persons of different ethnic backgrounds. It is in the language we call pidgin that a young man will court a girl, occasionally of an ethnic ancestry different from his own. If they marry it is in this dialect that the children will be reared, that affection is expressed, and that life goes on. To this culture are added the foods of many countries of origin, their superstitions, particularly those having to do with illness, which women exchange across back fences, and the forms of recreation on important family occasions.

The paradox is that this pidgin culture is so cosmopolitan, so tolerant, so urbane, yet so provincial. It is one important means by which the mixed peoples of Hawaii are becoming one people, somewhat differentiated from others, and exhibiting at times an extreme insularity. As against the world, they can be seen as becoming a new people, a new ethnic group, with quasi-ethnocentrism. Among themselves they show a decided cosmopolitanism. Gordon would call it both behavioral and structural assimilation.[15]

A further complication is the upward mobility—in the American pattern—which has influenced many families of various heritages and

---

[14] Elizabeth Carr, "Bilingual Speakers in Hawaii Today," *Social Process*, **25**, 53–57 (1961–1962). See also "The Sociology of Speech and Language," *op. cit.*, **24** (1960).
[15] Milton M. Gordon, *Assimilation in American Life: the Role of Race, Religion, and National Origins.* New York: Oxford University Press, 1964, pp. 70–71.

which starts with an emphasis on education. Orientals from peasant villages have come to realize that even in humble families a child can be educated to become a certified teacher, that highly respected vocation of *Sensei* among the Japanese, of *Sinsaang* among the Cantonese Chinese. Thus encouragement of higher education has pervaded the community. The schools and the university in turn have speeded the process of emancipation from immigrant ways, a sometimes unexpected consequence for the parents.

After several decades of affluence the work-and-thrift ethic, so reminiscent of the "Protestant ethic," which many peasant families brought with them, was transmuted to an orientation that emphasizes consumption, small families, home ownership, landscape gardening, and private school education, in which both husband and wife work and children are cared for by their retired grandparents. An ethnic pride may be replaced by a middle-class complacency, which rejects the pidgin culture and society. This, in turn, is being reacted against, as we have seen, by some members of the younger generation who have reached high school and college years. All this is very much in the pattern of the Mainland. So paradox follows paradox.

Hawaii's "Triple Melting Pot." In the process certain families are left behind or have refused to participate in the competitive struggle for higher status and greater income. These families are found in all ethnic groups—as are those that strive—but tend to be more common in some. If we were to delineate a "triple melting pot" for Hawaii, it would be much more difficult to do than Kennedy and Herberg found it for the eastern part of the United States.[16] In Hawaii mixing is at three socio-economic levels: first a pool of low academic achievers, the semiskilled, unskilled, and unemployed who tend to be from the Hawaiian, Samoan, Filipino, and Puerto Rican groups. A second pool mixes those more successful in school: skilled workers, retailers, service workers, again from all ethnic groups, but so far mainly Chinese, Japanese, Koreans, part-Hawaiians, and Portuguese. In the third pool are the businessmen and professional people, ethnically Caucasian, Japanese, and Chinese, with some participation, but on a smaller scale, of *all* the other ethnic groups. In

---

16 Ruby Jo Kennedy, "Single or Triple Melting Pot? Intermarriage Trends in New Haven, 1870–1940," *Amer. J. Sociol.*, **49**, 331–339 (January 1944). Cf. Will Herberg, *Protestant, Catholic, Jew, an Essay in American Religious Sociology.* Garden City, New York: Doubleday, 1960. Although Gerhard Lenski does not use the triple melting pot concept, he refers to four religious communities or subcommunities in Detroit: Protestant White, Protestant Negro, Catholic, and Jewish. See *The Religious Factor, a Sociological Inquiry.* Garden City, New York: Doubleday (rev. ed.) 1963, p. 35 ff.

each "pool" the groups are still to be differentiated, and the people in it show some mutual resentment. This resentment can be more easily expressed ethnically rather than in terms of class. So people in the first "pool" may discriminate against Japanese on one occasion, against Haoles on another, and Chinese on still another. People in the third "pool" can be heard to make disparaging remarks with ethnic labels against people in the other "pools" and against those in the same "pool" with whom they are competing.

Our statistics on intermarriage are not refined enough and our research not good enough to determine in which "pool" most mixing goes on. Schmitt's research inclined him to assert that it was in the blue-collar class.[17] However, much mixing also occurs in academic circles. Contrary to the religious melting pots that Kennedy and Herberg have referred to and contrary to the four religious communities Lenski identifies, the melting pots or communities of Hawaii are not markedly religious because Hawaii is not only an ethnic frontier, it is also a religious frontier. This means that movement has occurred among the major religions— Roman Catholic, Protestant (of various denominations), Mormon, and Buddhist (also of various denominations)—and interfaith marriages are not uncommon, although we have no statistics to bear them out.

Conclusion

It is clear that mixing in Hawaii started at the moment it lost its isolation two hundred years ago and that it continues at gradually accelerating rates. It is clear also that the offspring of these mixtures and their descendants cannot yet be categorized fully as a new people. It is not clear what the outcome will be, but there can be no question that the influence of island "isolation" and the interplay of many groups under rather peculiar historic circumstances have done more to break down ethnic barriers than to foster exclusive ethnocentricities. We may not be able to speak of all the people of these island communities as the mixed people of Hawaii, but they certainly are the *mixing* people of Hawaii.

SELECTED BIBLIOGRAPHY

Adams, Romanzo, *Interracial Marriage in Hawaii*. New York: Macmillan, 1938.

Adams, Romanzo, *The People of Hawaii*. Honolulu: Institute of Pacific Relations, 1923.

---

[17] Robert C. Schmitt, "Interracial Marriage and Occupational Status in Hawaii," *Amer. Sociol. Rev.*, **28**, 809–810 (October 1963). See also "Recent Trends in Interracial Marriage Rates by Occupation," unpublished, 1970.

Carr, Elizabeth, "Bilingual Speakers in Hawaii Today," *Social Process,* **25,** 53–57 (1961–1962).

Lind, Andrew, *Hawaii's People,* 3rd ed. Honolulu: University of Hawaii Press, 1967.

Lind, Andrew, *Hawaii's Japanese: Experiment in Democracy.* Princeton, New Jersey: Princeton University Press, 1946.

Lind, Andrew, *Hawaii, Last of the Magic Isles.* London: Oxford University Press (for the Institute on Race Relations), 1969.

Morton, Newton E., Chin S. Chung, and Ming-Pi Mi, *Genetics of Interracial Crossing in Hawaii.* Basel and New York: Karger, 1967.

Parkman, Margaret A., and Jack Sawyer, "Dimensions of Ethnic Intermarriage in Hawaii," *Amer. Sociol. Rev.,* **32,** 593–607 (August 1967).

Peterson, William, "Classification of Subnations in Hawaii," *Amer. Sociol. Rev.,* **34,** 863–867 (December 1969).

Rubano, Judith, *Culture and Behavior in Hawaii.* Honolulu: Social Science Research Institute, University of Hawaii, 1971.

Schmitt, Robert C., "Interracial Marriage and Occupational Status in Hawaii," *Amer. Sociol. Rev.,* **28,** 809–810 (October 1963).

Wittermans-Pino, Elizabeth, *Interethnic Relations in a Plural Society.* Groningen: Wolters, 1964.

Yamamura, Douglas, and C. K. Chang, "Interracial Marriage and Divorce in Hawaii," *Social Forces,* **36,** 77–84 (1957).

Donald Pierson

CHAPTER TWELVE

BRAZILIANS OF MIXED RACIAL DESCENT

Brazil is an enormous land, spreading out as it does over approximately half the South American continent. Only four countries in the world— China, the Soviet Union, Canada and the United States (after Alaska, but not before)—are larger. An immense store of natural resources only partly tapped makes it likely that Brazil will play an ever larger role in the international economy. The population, also virtually half that of South America and now approaching 93 millions, makes this nation the seventh most populous in the world. Whatever is happening here, has happened, or will happen has considerable meaning for us all.

A Statistical Aggregate

Brazilians of mixed racial origin constitute more a statistical aggregate than a group in the sociological sense, "clear to the observer but not so

Note. In addition to published sources, I have drawn on notes and personal knowledge obtained over many years as resident, researcher and director of research, professor, administrator, and editor during which I came to know at first hand several of the Brazilian states, including their interiors. For aid in bringing observations up-to-date, especially in the states of Pará, Paraíba, Pernambuco, Bahia, Espírito Santo, Rio de Janeiro, Guanabara, São Paulo, Minas Gerais, and Rio Grande do Sul, I am grateful to several former students and other friends in Brazil, in particular to Professors Cecilia Sanioto Di Lascio of Recife, Renato José Costa Pacheco of Vitória and Colatina, Hiroshi Saito of São Paulo, Haydee Guanaes Dourado of Brasília, Lavinia Villela Raymond of São Paulo and DePaul University; and also to Zacharias Pithon Barretto of Salvador, Anselmo Macieira of Niterói and Campos, Edulo Penafiel of Rio de Janeiro, Maria Aparecida Madeira Kerbeg, of São Paulo, and Rodrigo Octávio Coutinho Filho of Belo Horizonte. Obviously, I alone am responsible for any imprecision or inadequacy the reader may note.

clear to the observed," as careful investigators have found out.[1] They have no familial, religious, educational, political, or similar associations of their own; nor do they stand out against other units of the population as do the Cape Coloureds of South Africa or the Goanese in India. Instead, persons of mixed racial descent will be found in all groups to varying degrees, depending on other circumstances, and an individual may move out of the aggregate, socially, during his lifetime, thus giving it an amorphous, tentative, and unstable form.[2]

Miscegenation

In a quiet, unobtrusive way miscegenation has gone on in Brazil since the first contact of Europeans with native Amerindians in the early part of the sixteenth century and later with large numbers of imported Africans. In few areas of the world, perhaps, has miscegenation proceeded so extensively and so continuously in recent times.

The Beginnings. In the outline preceding Chapter 1 of a book on Brazil we read, with reference to Bahia, "Discovery, Settlement, Miscegenation,"[3] the three words being in that order. However, race mixture began nearly a half century before the first permanent settlement at Bahia in 1549, and even preceded the first impermanent settlement in 1531.[4]

The story of Diogo Alvares Correia, better known as "Caramurú," has often been told.[5] A Portuguese sailor who was shipwrecked or jumped

---

[1] See, for example, with reference to the colored population as a whole, Oracy Nogueira, "Relações raciais no município de Itapetininga," in Roger Bastide and Florestan Fernandes, Eds., *Relações raciais entre negros e brancos em São Paulo*. São Paulo: Editôra Anhembi, 1955, p. 546.

[2] Regarding the precise character of the subtle and rather complex Brazilian racial situation, there is some confusion in the literature, due especially to this subtlety and complexity, to certain semantic difficulties, and to the paucity of empirical studies. For a more extended account see Donald Pierson, *Negroes in Brazil: A Study of Race Contact at Bahia*. Chicago: University of Chicago Press, 1942. More specifically, see the "Introduction to This Edition" of the 1967 reprint (Carbondale: Southern Illinois University Press), and also consult the bibliographies given.

[3] Pierre Denis, *Brazil*. Translated from the French by Bernard Miall. London and Leipsic: T. Fisher Unwin, 1911, p. 27.

[4] Far to the south miscegenation preceded the coming of Martim Afonso to São Vicente in 1531 in that area and at intervening points along the coast.

[5] For a brief account in English see Donald Pierson, *op. cit.*, pp. 141–143; also Arthur Neiva, "Diogo Alvares, Caramurú e os francêses," *Revista da Academia Brasileira de Letras*, 1, No. 3 (1941); J. F. de Almeida Prado, *Primeiros Povoadores do Brasil*,

ship some time between 1509 and 1511 near the site where the city of Salvador later grew up, Caramurú lived for many years among the Amerindians and had numerous mixed-blood descendants. Perhaps not so well-known is the fact that some years before a number of European men had lived among the Tupinambás in this area and also to the north and south along the coast, including, then or later, Normans, Bretons, perhaps Spanish, and even English.[6]

Some of these men were factors—as Caramurú also may have been—working for French traders who carried on a clandestine commerce, taking back to Europe the much-prized dyewood for which Brazil is named, as well as native cotton and pepper. Some years earlier Pedro Alvares Cabral, after discovering Brazil in 1500 and having anchored for a week near the point at which Porto Seguro later was founded, left two deportees from Portugal to learn the language of the Amerindians and serve later as interpreters. Many, if not all, "took native women in the land," Soares de Sousa wrote in that century, "where they lived without any desire to return, like natives, with many women; from whose presence and that of those who came every year to Bahia and the Sergipe river in French caravels, the land filled up with mixed-bloods. . . ."[7]

Similar events occurred in other parts of Brazil, including São Vicente in São Paulo, to the south, and later in Minas Gerais, Goiás, and elsewhere in the interior. "As Diogo Alvares in Bahia, João Ramalho at Piratininga, and others had done," Handelmann has written, "the first isolated colonists soon were taking as they wished one or more Indian women as wives, giving rise to a numerous progeny of half-breeds."[8]

At the time of settlement and for many years thereafter the ratio of incoming European men to incoming European women was heavily in favor of the men.[9] At the same time, the leaders of the Portuguese state

---

1500–1530. São Paulo: Cia. Editôra Nacional, 1935, pp. 117–123; Thales de Azevedo, "Começa a Mestiçagem," and "Caramurú," in *Povoamento da Cidade do Salvador.* Bahia: Prefeitura do Município do Salvador, 1949, pp. 57–85.

[6] J. F. de Almeida Prado, *A Bahia e as Capitanias do Centro do Brasil, 1530–1626,* 2 vols. São Paulo: Cia. Editôra Nacional, 1945, I, p. 158.

[7] Gabriel Soares de Sousa, *Notícia do Brasil: Tratado Descriptivo do Brazil in 1587.* 2 vols. São Paulo: Livraria Martins Editôra, n.d., II, p. 289. Amerigo Vespucci, on his second visit to the Brazilian coast in 1501, remained, together with his sailors, for two months, "making repairs and resupplying the ship, during which time they frequented Indian women." (J. F. de Almeida Prado, *ibid.,* I, p. 33.)

[8] Gottfried Heinrich Handelmann, *História do Brazil.* Translation of *Geschichte von Brasilien* (Berlin, 1860) by the Instituto Histórico e Geográphico Brasileiro. 2 vols. Rio de Janeiro, 1931, p. 73.

[9] Away from the coast, this unbalanced sex ratio continued into the 18th century. Even as late as 1731, for instance, a captain-general wrote from Minas Gerais that "through-

were feeling a grave need for population to settle, and to hold against other nationals, the vast Brazilian coast in the midst of a severe drain on the limited population resources of the mother country, which simultaneously was seeking to carry on extensive colonial ventures in the east, where they held another irregular coastline some 1500 miles long. In a letter to the King in 1612 Diogo de Vasconcellos complained that unless the number of colonists were appreciably increased, "it will be very difficult to improve or even to settle so vast a Coast."[10]

A similar lack of European women led Francisco d'Almeida not only to accept the fact that intermixture already had occurred in the Indies but also actively to foster, as a definite policy of state, the union of Portuguese men with indigenous women. Similar unions also were being sponsored, simultaneously, by the Dutch in their colonizing ventures in Java and South Africa and later, for a time, by the English in India, a policy that in each case developed as a natural, and perhaps an inevitable, response to the actual conditions of settlement.

Miscegenation involving a darker race in Brazil may have been favored by other circumstances. It is probable, for instance, that many of the early colonists came from southern Portugal, where they and their forebears during the many centuries of Moorish occupation had become thoroughly familiar with a darker people and even had intermarried to some extent with them, a people also of a higher cultural level in whom, moreover, race consciousness reputedly was "weak."

Intermarriage. Although Caramurú may have lived with more than one Amerindian woman, he eventually took "the comely Paraguassú" to France, where they were married before returning to the Bahian coast. It is said that Thomé de Souza was much indebted to her, as also to Caramurú and their and his other children, for the eventual success of the first permanent settlement at Salvador. Of the four legitimate children and at least eight—perhaps more—natural children of Caramurú, the daughters all married into the nobility or near-nobility among incoming colonists, many of whom were impoverished and some of whom had been banished from Portugal by the Court, thus becoming the founders of important families among the landed aristocracy. With the passing of

---

out the mining area there are almost no (European) women to marry, and when there is, which is rare, the suitors are so numerous that the father is greatly embarrassed to choose among them." See *Revista do Arquivo Público Mineiro*, I, 1933; 350, *apud* Pedro Calmon, *História Social do Brasil*. 2d ed. 2 vols. São Paulo: Cia. Editôra Nacional, 1937: I, 95.

10 Manoel Bomfim, *O Brasil*. São Paulo: Cia. Editôra Nacional, 1935, p. 11.

time Caramurú has become, like João Ramalho and others elsewhere, a legendary figure to whom living descendants, including those of the "ancient and noble house" of Garcia d'Avila at Bahia, proudly trace their lineage. Although the scarcity of European women had largely disappeared by the seventeenth century, unions of European men and their descendants with Amerindian women were still observed by Zacharias Wagner at Recife to be frequent.[11]

After the first years of settlement, however, intermarriages probably were few. Although many incoming Portuguese colonists and adventurers entered readily into informal unions with Amerindian or part-Amerindian women, it appears that they tended to hesitate before marrying them. Apparently the Jesuits, in an attempt to curb excesses and normalize the situation from the Church's point of view, helped overcome this reluctance.[12] Intermarriage became not only legal as far as the Portuguese state was concerned but also "regularized in Christian marriage," thus receiving the powerful sanction of the Church, the chief guardian of the mores of the time.

By the time the Amerindians on the coast had been absorbed or expelled into the interior, Africans were being imported as slaves for the developing plantations, and race mixture continued. But now that the scarcity of white or near-white women was less acute, and also since marriages with slaves or persons of slave origin were under negative sanction, unions between Portuguese men and their descendants and African women ordinarily were extralegal. Yet at least a few marriages with African women apparently did occur, even in the colonial period.

Nevertheless, intermarriage probably then—as perhaps always after the first years—more often involved mixed-bloods. By the early nineteenth century Koster found unions of white men with mulatto women at Recife to be "not rare." Although commented on in intimate circles, remarks were made "without acrimony,"[13] and eventually such marriages came "no longer to be disdained as . . . formerly . . . ," Lacerda wrote in 1911,

---

[11] Alfredo de Carvalho, "O Zoobiblion de Zacharias Wagner," *Revista do Instituto Archeológico, Histórico e Geográphico de Pernambuco*, **11**, No. 4, 194–195 (1904). See also Gilberto Freyre, "Caraterísticas gerais da colonização portuguêsa do Brasil: formação de uma sociedade agrária, escravocrata e híbrida," Chapter 1 of *Casa Grande e senzala*, 2nd ed. Rio de Janeiro: Schmidt-Editor, 1936; English translation of the 4th ed. by Samuel Putnam, *The Masters and the Slaves*. New York: Alfred Knopf, 1946.
[12] Padre Manoel de Nobrega, *Cartas do Brasil, 1549–1560*. Rio de Janeiro, 1886, *apud* Gilberto Freyre, *ibid.*, p. 302.
[13] Henry Koster, *Travels in Brazil, 1809 to 1815*. 2 vols. London: Longman, Hurst, 1817: II, p. 178.

"now that the high position of the mulatto and the proof of his moral qualities have led people to overlook the evident contrast of his physical characters. . . ."[14]

At Bahia a generation later I found unions between whites and darker members of the community ordinarily to be extralegal, outside marriage. As the colors approached along the black-white continuum, however, intermarriage became more common; for instance, a son from a family with slight traces of African ancestry had married the daughter of a distinguished white physician and professor at the Faculty of Medicine (hence of the elite); a daughter of this family of mixed racial origin had married a descendant of the colonial aristocracy, an able lawyer, university professor and state deputy; another daughter had married into a quite wealthy white family with a palatial home in one of the more desirable residential areas of the city; and the three other sons had married "*brancas finas*" (white women of the "highest quality").

If, to light color, other status-enhancing personal or social characteristics were added, intermarriage tended to increase; in fact, marriages crossed color lines more often than class lines[15]; for example, I knew at Bahia a prominent and well-educated mixed-blood, quite dark, relatively wealthy and personally and occupationally competent, who had married into a distinguished white family. Of him, and others, it was said, "*Negro rico é branco, e branco pobre é negro*" (a rich black is a white, but a poor white is a black). Although this is to some extent an exaggeration, it does sum up, in a pithy and relatively accurate statement, the racial situation in Bahia—and Brazil. Non-European descent is only one of *several* personal and social characteristics, the patterning of which, in a given case, determines social rank. Although color undoubtedly plays a limiting role, it is far from absolute.[16]

According to data furnished by the State of São Paulo,[17] in the 10 years from 1948 to 1957 inclusive, even in this center of recent European immigration, 4553 marriages occurred between "whites" and mixed-bloods

---

14 Jean Baptiste de Lacerda, "The Metis, or Half-breeds, of Brazil," in *Papers on Interracial Problems,* G. Spiller, Ed. London: P.S. King & Son, 1911, p. 382.

15 Cf. also Felte Bezerra, *Etnias Sergipanas.* Aracaju: Livraria Regina, 1950, p. 251.

16 Thales de Azevedo reports a study at Bahia in 1943 of marriages among the lower and middle ranks. Of the 107 marriages of all colors sampled, about 21 percent were listed as intermarriages, the men being darker in 56 percent of the cases, the two partners approximately equal in color in one-fourth of the cases, and the women darker in only 18 percent. See Thales de Azevedo, "Um aspeto da mestiçagem na Bahia," *Revista do Arquivo Municipal* CI (São Paulo, 1945), pp. 45–57.

17 See Austin J. Staley, *Racial Democracy in Marriage: A Sociological Analysis of Negro-white Intermarriage in Brazilian Culture.* Unpublished Ph.D. dissertation, University of Pittsburgh, pp. 138–143.

and 811 between "whites" and blacks. These and other intermarriages,[18] however, constituted only some 3 percent of the total number of marriages in which color was specified, in a population given in the census as 86 percent "white." Yet in this region, in which plantation agriculture in the colonial era was lacking, intermarriage involving persons of African descent evidently has been considerable, even here, whereas that involving persons of Japanese origin is said to have increased markedly since about the middle of the last decade.[19]

In this connection one should emphasize the fact that intermarriage may produce family relationships of a relative permanence and continuity not always characteristic of informal unions.

Extent of Intermixture. The percentage of mixed-bloods increased with the passage of time. Pertinent statistical data are sparse and probably not always reliable. For what they are worth, however, it might be noted that even in the area that is now the state of São Paulo, in which St. Hilaire observed in the nineteenth century, "it is indisputable, that, excepting Missões, Rio Grande do Sul and Rio Negro . . . the least number of Negroes had been introduced," as early as 1797 mixed-bloods were given as 19 percent of the population.[20] In 1807 they were said to be 22 percent of the inhabitants of Bahia, whereas an estimate in the same year placed them at 18 percent of the population in the Brazilian Empire. The English physician, George Gardner, on visiting Penedo on the lower São Francisco river in Alagoas in 1837, found the mixed-bloods of the

---

18 There were 664 marriages between "whites" and "yellows," 14 between mixed-bloods and "yellows," and two between "blacks" and "yellows." Of the 4553 marriages between "whites" and mixed-bloods, 2588, or 57 percent, were of "white" women with mixed-blood men and 1965, or 43 percent, of "white" men with women of mixed blood. These constituted approximately one-fourth of all mixed-blood marriages but only 2.2 percent of all "white" marriages. Of the 664 legal unions between "whites" and "yellows," 69 percent were of "white" women with "yellow" men. These constituted 9.7 percent of all "yellow" marriages but only 0.3 percent of all "white" marriages. Of the 14 marriages between mixed-bloods and "yellows," 64 percent were of men of mixed blood with "yellow" women, whereas the two marriages between "blacks" and "yellows" were both of "black" women with "yellow" men. There were 21,235 cases in which color was not specified, or 9.7 percent of the total.

19 Endogamy still exists among a small segment of the upper class, involving, as formerly, certain families with unusual pride in pure European origin, as well as certain families which have sought to keep property undivided and, for this and other reasons, to resist the intrusion of individuals from outside the kinship group—including whites, both native-born and immigrant, as well as persons of color—an objective often accomplished by extensive marriage within the kinship group. Cf. Felte Bezerra, *op. cit.*, pp. 81–82.

20 See Samuel Harmon Lowrie, "O elemento negro na população de São Paulo," *Revista do Arquivo Municipal,* **48,** pp. 10, 11 (June 1938).

local *comarca* to be 37,225, or 45.1 percent of the inhabitants.[21] The first Brazilian census, or that of 1872, gave 3,801,722 mixed-bloods, or 39 percent of the total population. The federal census of 1890 indicated that the mixed-bloods were then 6.5 millions.

Soon, however, intermixture had proceeded to the point at which census takers and other public officials were beginning to admit that, with the possible exception of the category "caboclo" (see below), little if any attempt was being made to register racial distinctions but instead, and following popular usage, merely "color" differences.

The federal census of 1950, for instance, gave 26.6 percent of the Brazilian population as *pardo*; that is, intermediate between *branco* (white) and *prêto* (black). But, since all data in Brazil such as these reflect distinctions at times as much social as—if not more than—anthropological in character, perhaps no serious student of Brazil will doubt that the actual number of mixed-bloods was considerably greater than these statistics reveal. A study of 500 persons classified as *brancos* by public officials some years ago at Bahia, for instance, indicated that approximately a third showed quite evident intermixture, principally of African and, to a much lesser extent, of Amerindian or mixed Afro-Amerindian origin.[22]

At the time of writing no data regarding color from the 1960 federal census are publicly available, except for the state of Piauí, where the *pardos* were given as 64 percent, or approximately two-thirds of the total population. In the 1970 federal census *all attempts to distinguish even color were abandoned.* At the time of the 1950 census, then, or the last enumeration from which pertinent data are available, the division given for the entire country was *pardos,* 26 percent, *brancos,* 61 percent. The variation by states ranged from that in Pará, where the percentages were given as *pardos,* 65, *brancos,* 29; Pernambuco, *pardos,* 40, *brancos,* 49; São Paulo, *pardos,* 3, *brancos,* 86, both 89.

Terms for Mixed-Bloods

Some observers have considered the Portuguese and the Brazilians to be "color blind." This is a perceptive, but also an inaccurate, observation. It is perceptive in that color in Portugal or Brazil means less than in the

---

[21] George Gardner, *Viagens no Brasil.* São Paulo: Cia. Editôra Nacional, 1942, p. 95. Translation from the English, *Travels in the Interior of Brazil, 1836–1841,* 2d ed. London: Reeve, Benham, and Reeve, 1849.
[22] See Donald Pierson, *op. cit.,* p. 126.

United States, for instance, or South Africa. For one thing—but this is not all—"the somatic norm-image," in the phrase of Hoetink,[23] is darker. The observation is imprecise, however, in that neither the Portuguese nor the Brazilians are unaware of obvious physical differences. Quite the contrary: the appearance of a person—especially the color of the skin and, even more particularly, the texture of the hair—will be observed and occasionally referred to by persons of all ranks. A large number of terms have evolved to describe these variations.

I once collected at Bahia several of these terms, as did Thales de Azevedo more recently. In 1956 Diégues Junior listed 24 for mixed-bloods alone in various parts of Brazil; Hutchinson, Zimmerman, and Harris noted a considerable number in different parts of the state of Bahia; and, later, Harris and Kottak found 29 color terms in use in the "socially homogeneous, one-class" fishing village of Arambepe, on the northeast coast.[24]

A study of these terms is illuminating. First of all, they turn out to refer more to physical appearance than to racial descent; but they are only in part even referents to physical appearance, being arrived at in a far more complex way. For one thing, like all color categories in Brazil, they reflect the personal relationship of the speaker to the person spoken about and also the speaker's mood at the time. Even more importantly perhaps, they may reflect the possession of certain other criteria of status on the part of the person referred to, as is evident in the oft-quoted comment of Koster's servant at Pernambuco in the early nineteenth century. When asked if a certain man of high administrative position was a mulatto, he replied, "He was, but is not now; for how can a Capitam-mor be a mulatto man?" In other words, the achievement of a status-enhancing position had taken him out of the mulatto category. It also is revealed in certain cases of quite evident mixed-bloods today, some so dark that to a stranger they would at once appear to be *prêtos* (blacks) but who are

---

23 H. Hoetink, " 'Colonial Psychology' and Race," *Journal of Economic History*, 21, p. 1638 (1961). See also H. Hoetink, *The Two Variants in Caribbean Race Relations*. London: Oxford University Press, 1967.

24 See Thales de Azevedo, *As elites de côr: um estudo de ascensão social*. São Paulo: Cia. Editôra Nacional, 1955, pp. 25–32; Donald Pierson, *op. cit.*, pp. 135–140; Manuel Diégues Junior, *Etnias e culturas no Brasil*. Rio de Janeiro: Ministério da Educação, 1956, pp. 74–76; Harry W. Hutchinson, "Race Relations in a Rural Community of the Bahian Recôncavo," in Charles Wagley, Ed., *Race and Class in Rural Brazil*, 2d ed. New York: Columbia University Press, 1963; Ben Zimmerman, "Race Relations in the Arid Sertão," *ibid.*; Marvin Harris, "Race Relations in Minas Velhas, A Community in the Mountain Region of Central Brazil," *ibid.*; and Marvin Harris and Conrad Kottak, "The Structural Significance of Brazilian Categories," *Sociologia*, 25, 203–208 (São Paulo, 1963).

known in their communities as "whites"[25] or, more often, as *morenos* (see below).

Although space does not permit full consideration of the 29 terms for racial hybrids which my associates and I collected this year from different states in Brazil, one might note briefly a few of the more common. Apparently *mameluco* and *curiboca*, each of which is used to refer to a person of Amerindio-European origin, as well as *cafuso*, which is used to refer to a person of Afro-European descent, appear now only in books. Although *mestiço* literally means "mixed-blood," its meaning in some places is rather ambiguous and, in addition, its use is confined to intellectuals almost exclusively; it is not a popular term. *Mulato* is more commonly heard, especially in areas of heavy African importation. Originally referring to the first cross between European and African, it still does at times, but it may also refer to any degree of Afro-European intermixture and even, apparently to a mixed-blood of any origin. This category is often broken down into *mulato claro* (light) and *mulato escuro* (dark), and one hears other subcategories like *mulato aço* (with hair between brown and blond in color) and the diminutive, *mulatinho*. If given a certain intonation, *mulato* can carry pejorative, even offensive, meaning, although the feminine form (*mulata*) may, in some cases, reflect approval of a woman's physical beauty, with sexual overtones.

Moreno, which literally means "of dark color like that of the Moors," is an elastic, somewhat ambiguous term used to refer to anyone from brunette to deepest black. It is a more elegant reference, in many cases, to a dark mixed-blood and even to an unmixed, or relatively unmixed, descendant of Africans, especially if the one spoken about is a friend of the speaker or otherwise a person of prestige. It may be used by mixed-bloods and blacks to refer to themselves. If employed in the diminutive form (*moreninho*), it can express affection, but it can also be given at times, particularly if employed with a certain intonation, pejorative meaning. In Belém *moreno* is used to exalt those who possess "Brazilian color," as is said, although one also hears *caboclo* (see below) being employed there in that way. At Bahia, and elsewhere, the feminine *morena* is used of a brunette woman or girl, "from the dark of the *jacarandá*," as an informant once said, "to the lightest of the brunettes, with non-African

---

[25] See Charles Wagley, *Amazon Town: A Study of Man in the Tropics*. 2d ed. New York: Knopf, 1964, p. 134. Consequently the uncritical translation of the Brazilian *prêto* (and, to some extent also, *negro*) by the English "Negro," carrying as it does in this country a quite different connotation, does violence to any realistic conception of the Brazilian racial situation, just as also does, incidentally, the incautious identification of the effects of economic sifting with segregation (see Felte Bezerra, *op. cit.*, p. 256).

hair." She is considered the "ideal" type of feminine beauty, extolled in romance, poetry, and song.[26]

Caboclo at first apparently meant "Amerindian," but later it came to have at different times and in different places two additional meanings, namely, a mixed-blood of Amerindio-European origin or merely a rustic, often of some Amerindian descent. In certain areas or connections the term is valorized but in others it carries pejorative meaning.

Crioulo originally meant a native-born descendant of Africans, but it is now employed of any mixed-blood, usually of Afro-European descent. In some places it refers to a person somewhat lighter than a *prêto* (black); in others its meaning seems to be more or less identical with *prêto*, and in certain situations its use—as that also of *negro*—may reflect *carinhoso* treatment (a demonstration of kindness, tenderness, affection). A famous Brazilian soccer player, a man of quite dark color, refers to himself as a *crioulo*.

Pardo means, literally, "of dark color." It is used principally in official statistics to describe persons that census takers and other enumerators do not care to classify among the *prêtos, brancos* (literally, but not always genetically, whites), or *amarelos* (yellows).[27]

Perhaps this brief sketch will at least indicate the ambiguity involved in all these terms—and other similar ones—in Brazil.

Biological Function of the Brazilian Mixed-Bloods

Intermixture obviously reduces physical distance between the races in contact. If a variation in natural increase also favors one of these races, as apparently occurred rather extensively in colonial and later Brazil, the resulting population may move progressively toward that end of the color scale.

---

[26] See Donald Pierson, *op. cit.*, pp. 136–138. A study of 500 women classified as *morenas* in official archives at Salvador indicated that approximately a fourth were of relatively unmixed European origin, about two-thirds of Afro-European descent, and the rest mixed-bloods of Afro-European, Afro-Amerindian, or Afro-European-Amerindian origin. Costa Pinto considers the approval to be not of the beauty of the *morena* but of concubinage (see L. A. Costa Pinto, *O negro no Rio de Janeiro*. São Paulo: Cia. Editôra Nacional, 1953, p. 103).

[27] The category *amarelos* was added after the beginning of Japanese immigration in comparatively recent times. Although *pardo* is rarely heard in common speech, it is reported in one place in Brazil to refer there to a mixed-blood who is lighter than a *mulato* but darker than what is considered by some to be a *mulatinho*, in a scale for persons of color which ranges progressively, it is said, from lighter to darker, as follows: *mulatinho, pardo, mulato, prêto, crioulo, negro*. This apparently is rare.

Theodore Roosevelt once noted in Rio de Janeiro a painting of a black grandparent, a mulatto son, and a white grandchild, "the evident intention . . . being," as he wrote, "to express both the hope and the belief that the Negro was being absorbed. . . ."[28] Although the process involved obviously is not that rapid or simple, it does appear that Brazil has been gradually—but to all appearances inevitably—absorbing the two racial minorities of colonial times[29] into the mixed-blood portion of the population; the latter, in turn, may be turning progressively lighter and gradually disappearing into the "white" category, not surreptitiously, as occurs in the United States to a greater extent than is sometimes realized, but openly and with social approval.

At any rate, even in the areas of greatest African importation, such as Bahia, Sergipe, Pernambuco, Maranhão, Rio de Janeiro, and Minas Gerais, one finds the persistent belief that the population is gradually but irresistibly becoming more European in appearance. It is difficult adequately to test this rather general impression, since pertinent empirical studies are few.

Nevertheless, preliminary returns for the 1950 census convinced T. Lynn Smith that "it is possible to establish definitely the existence of a significant racial differential in the rate of reproduction in Brazil."[30] Some years ago, I noted that of 221 black mothers at Bahia, each of whom was observed with one of her children at a free medical clinic, a more European appearance in the child was clearly evident in approximately one-third of the cases; of 200 mixed-blood mothers observed at the same time a more European appearance in the child was evident in somewhat more than half the cases.[31] The wife of a prominent local physician, a woman of fair complexion and blue eyes, and everywhere considered a *branca* (white), had an African grandmother; a former governor, to all appearances white and so considered throughout the state and elsewhere, was only two generations removed from an African forebear; the grandmother of a prominent *branco* politician who held a responsible position in the federal government was a black woman who had worn on the streets of Salvador the distinctive and highly picturesque costume of African women and their descendants in Brazil.[32]

---

28 Theodore Roosevelt, "Brazil and the Negro," *Outlook*, **106**, p. 410 (Feb. 21, 1914).
29 Calmon (*op. cit.*, I, p. 163) maintains that at Bahia the pure black did not usually exist beyond the third generation, although this may be debatable.
30 T. Lynn Smith, *Brazil: People and Institutions*, rev. ed. Baton Rouge: Louisiana State University Press, 1963, pp. 102–103.
31 Donald Pierson, *op. cit.*, pp. 132, 133.
32 Cf. Felte Bezerra, *op. cit.*, pp. 225–226. For a description of the "whitening" process in Sergipe, *ibid.*, p. 234 ff.

From the biological point of view, then, the mixed-bloods in Brazil may constitute a traditional phase in an apparently extensive "whitening" process. There is still, however, a wide variation in physical characteristics. Amerindian traits in many places—but no no means in all—seem progressively less evident, whereas African traits, of course, given the relative numbers originally and other historical circumstances, are still of greater frequency.[33]

Although the fertility and mortality rates among the lesser favored ranks of the population, in which the darker portion has been, and is, concentrated, probably have for a long time favored this apparent "whitening" process, it may be that the mortality rate here is now lower than formerly, whereas the birth rate may be fairly stable. We need more evidence, but if this possible shift in natural increase is occurring and if it continues into the future the "whitening" trend at least will slow down. There would seem to be no question, however, that the process of miscegenation itself is likely to continue indefinitely into the future.

One corollary to these circumstances is that European physical characteristics tend to possess aesthetic value among all colors and ranks of the population, tempered by the fact that the "somatic norm-image," as we have seen, is considerably darker than that of some other countries.[34]

Occupational Roles

The economy during the colonial period was based largely on plantation —and some subsistence—agriculture, stock raising, placer mining in certain areas, handicrafts, and slavery. In the social order Vianna saw three distinct strata of rank.[35] Composing the upper tier were the *senhorial* class of landed proprietors, their immediate families and kinfolk, plus other persons closely linked to them, all of whom were almost exclusively European in derivation, although a few Amerindian mixed-bloods came

---

[33] Although there exists a popular belief that certain population types are emerging in the northeast and elsewhere, this possibility is disputed by some specialists. Adequate empirical data to resolve the problem would seem to be lacking. The study of Saldanha would appear to be based on certain debatable and otherwise questionable assumptions (see P. H. Saldanha, "Race Mixture among Northeastern Brazilian Populations," *Amer. Anthropol.*, **64**, 751–759 (August 1962)).

[34] Tempered also, to a far lesser extent, by an effort on the part of a comparatively few sophisticated, urban blacks, influenced principally by events in recent times outside Brazil, to valorize *negritude* (blackness), although their attitudes seem to be rather ambivalent.

[35] F. J. Oliveira Vianna, *Evolução do povo brasileiro*, 2d ed. São Paulo: Cia. Editôra Nacional, 1933, pp. 72–74.

to be included but rarely one of partial African descent. In the lower stratum were the slaves and, in between, the *rendeiros de domínio*, free persons linked to the landed proprietors by loyalty in exchange for protection in a system reminiscent of a feudal order. Included here were tenant farmers, artisans, a few small landholders and merchants, petty officials and other local functionaries, and unskilled workers.

At first this intermediate stratum also was nearly white, but as time went on and freedmen began to appear there were increasing numbers of mixed-bloods in it (as well as a lesser number of free blacks). In a subordinate role to the members of the *senhorial* class but also sharing largely their attitudes and values, this colonial pleb tended to cluster around them in a highly cohesive block.

Even in slave status mixed-bloods, particularly mulattoes, often were preferred by their masters for house servants, shoemakers, carpenters, cabinetmakers, potters, leather workers, basket weavers, and tailors, thus setting many of them apart from the field hands. Early in the colonial period, moreover, they tended to leave the slave stratum and this tendency increased markedly as time went on. At Maranhão in 1822, for example, there were four times as many *free* as slave mullatoes (whereas there were more than nine times as many *slave* as free blacks), and in Minas in 1835 out of 170,000 mulattoes three-fourths (but only one-sixth of the estimated 300,000 blacks) were free.[36]

Although public offices were denied to the mixed-bloods at first, and there were other discriminatory regulations, these restrictions were "more honored in the breach than in the observance," as Boxer has well noted.[37] Eventually mixed-bloods began to appear in the militia (for a time only in separate regiments) and, particularly among those nearer to the European in physical appearance, in the colonial bureaucracy and even the clergy. Many, especially those not recognized by their white fathers, often lived a precarious existence and even contributed to the ranks of lawless and predatory elements. With the development of the towns, however, and after the founding of the "Higher Academies" in the nineteenth century, new opportunities for employment in business, commerce, and the liberal professions opened to the mixed-bloods, especially those favored by fortuitous ties to the dominant group.

In Salvador in 1936, for instance, many had attained the upper occupational ranks, although usually, but not exclusively, they were those

---

[36] Pereira Lago, *Estatística histórico-geográphico da Provincia do Maranhão, 1822*, and Johann Moritz Rugendas, *Voyage pittoresque dans le Brésil*, apud Vianna, *op. cit.*, pp. 152–153.
[37] C. R. Boxer, *The Golden Age of Brazil, 1695–1750*. Berkeley and Los Angeles: University of California Press, 1962, pp. 166, 300.

lighter in color and otherwise more European in appearance. In general, but also with many exceptions, the darker mixed-bloods were still concentrated on the lower rungs of the occupational ladder. Of 5943 persons sampled at that time mixed-bloods were more numerous than whites among government functionaries, retail clerks, and army officers, constituting somewhat more than half the upper ranks of the latter. They were present also among priests, university professors, teachers, physicians, lawyers, politicians, and businessmen and their staffs. Four of the 18 members of an elective body which supervised the legal profession were mixed-bloods, as also were six of the 12 officials of the medical association, only three of whom were quite light. Six of the 14 aldermen were racially mixed, most of whom, however, gave evidence of only slight traces of non-European ancestry, and about a fourth of the members of the state legislature were racially mixed. In occupations of lesser prestige mixed-bloods constituted about one-half to three-fourths of the sample of barbers, streetcar conductors, bus and truck drivers, firemen, soldiers, police, and musicians, taxi drivers, and street sweepers, being in all cases, except among the barbers and police, predominantly medium-dark to dark mixed-bloods. Of those occupations in which blacks predominated there were sizable contingents also of persons of mixed racial descent, especially among streetcar motormen, cobblers, newsboys, street vendors, and domestics, with lesser percentages among stevedores, bricklayers, porters, baggagemen, and laundresses.

Today, mixed-bloods are to be found to some extent in virtually all occupations here and elsewhere in Brazil,[38] although the distribution varies from community to community, in keeping with the possibilities open to all competitors, and particularly the opportunity to develop skills. Many of the darker mixed-bloods are still buried in the less privileged groups. As Nestor Duarte has perceptively noted, however, this fact reflects an *economic* problem and should not be incautiously interpreted as evidence of a racial one per se.[39]

Since historical accident made Africa, not Europe, the source of slaves and Europeans and their descendants, not Africans and their descendants, proprietors of the plantations, mines, and pastoral lands of Brazil, economic inequality obviously followed color lines. Final abolition occurred only four generations ago, and, although manumission began early, in many cases freedmen had to start at the bottom of the economic ladder. Except in the case of those who have been aided by fortuitous circum-

---

[38] See, for example, Florestan Fernandes, "Do escravo ao cidadão," in Roger Bastide and Florestan Fernandes, Eds., *op. cit.*, pp. 55–56.

[39] Nestor Duarte, "A distribuição espacial de classes e raças na Bahia," *Revista do Arquivo Municipal*, **77**, pp. 171–172 (São Paulo, 1941).

stances, and particularly by the personal claims laid on former masters and their families or others of the dominant group, the economic struggle has been rugged under the realities of Brazil: the comparative lateness in which industrialization developed; the many difficulties in the way of acquiring land; a predominantly one-crop economy for a long period of time; the scarcity of capital in a preindustrial order; the low value placed on education in all classes of the population during the colonial period and even later, and the consequent lack for many years of educational opportunities except for some of the elite; plus the low value also placed on labor, a legacy of the slave era and reflected in the common saying, "work is for slaves and dogs."

Rise in Social Rank

Although the possibilities of rising in rank also varied from area to area and from time to time, in keeping with varying ecological and sociological circumstances, there were certain conditions that tended to favor the advancement of the mixed-bloods.

For one thing, the Brazilian ecological order was spatially mobile. Many of the Amerindio-European mixed-bloods of São Paulo, for instance, as others elsewhere, appeared among the *bandeirantes*, hardy penetrators of the Brazilian interior who explored vast areas previously unknown to Europeans and their descendants, while also raiding Amerindian villages for slaves. Many of these men subsequently settled in the interior and established cattle ranches, and some of them obtained a degree of wealth that a generation or two later, if not before, helped incorporate their families into the landed aristocracy on this sparsely settled frontier. "Many wished to be white," a colonial chronicler writes, "and some already were taken as such, since, by way of racial intermixture their origin had been forgotten. Such are many families of short genealogy."[40] Certain fugitive slaves, far from their places of birth, easily managed to pass for persons born of free parents.

The mixed-bloods also began life as members of an intermediate population group which lacked in many if not most cases certain physical characteristics that had become associated with a slave status while at the same time possessing certain other physical traits characteristic of the dominant group. Consequently they were often chosen, especially in the plantation areas, as we have seen, for those household tasks that brought

---

[40] See Oliveira Vianna, *op. cit.*, p. 163.

them into daily contact with the master and his family, where advantageous personal relationships might grow up and the culture of the upper status group also be more readily taken over.

Even though not always genetically related to his master, many a mixed-blood received his name, was baptized, and sometimes married under legal and ecclesiastical sanctions so that he was able to set up a legitimate family and establish family traditions like those that aided the rise of free Negroes in Charleston and elsewhere in the United States.

Especially in plantation areas, but not limited to them, certain other circumstances tended to favor the development of these most important personal relations to the whites. Included was the system of *creação*, by which many children, whether or not they were related to the head of the family by descent, were reared inside the large patriarchal group, and the system of godparentship, which brought many other mixed-bloods into closer personal relations with members of the elite. By way of these associations many were able to develop certain occupational and other skills, including, at times, the ability to read and write, an accomplishment not ordinarily characteristic in the colonial and subsequent periods even of white children of most of the elite.

Moreover, the few opportunities for instruction open to any child in colonial Brazil apparently never were closed to the mixed-bloods. In the Jesuit schools at Bahia, for instance, even in the sixteenth and seventeenth centuries, Amerindian, mixed-blood, and Portuguese children were accepted with equal favor and educated together. In 1774 a law opened to those of mixed racial descent legal access "to all offices, honors, and dignities, without discrimination on account of differences of color."[41]

The mixed-bloods, as we have seen, also began to be liberated from a servile status more frequently and earlier than the blacks, sometimes by reason of personal attachments to members of the master's family, sometimes at the urging of the clergy. In addition, the development of the towns and also of the "Higher Academies," as Freyre has outlined in detail,[42] increased the possibilities for the economic advancement of individuals who possessed, or could obtain, the necessary skills. In the meantime the return of young Brazilians who had been trained in Europe for the professions enhanced the prestige of the rising professional classes into which mixed-bloods had been admitted.

---

[41] *Annaes da Biblioteca Nacional, 37*, p. 85 (1913).

[42] For this and other pertinent information see Gilberto Freyre, "Ascensão do bacharel e do mulato," Chapter 7 of *Sobrados e mucambos*. São Paulo: Cia. Editôra Nacional, 1936; English translation by Harriet de Onís, *The Mansions and the Shanties*. New York: Alfred Knopf, 1963.

This rise was further favored by the slow rather than catastrophic character of the emancipation process in Brazil, which released the slaves, including the remaining mixed-bloods among them, from a servile status *gradually* and under circumstances that favored the continuance of intimate personal ties built up during slavery, especially in the plantation areas. Nor should the roles of sex and romantic love be overlooked, including the myth of the sexual potency of the hybrid, both male and female.

By these and other means many mixed-bloods, particularly if light in color, gradually rose in rank until they reached, penetrated, and eventually were absorbed into the middle and even to some extent the upper ranks of the social order. In 1936, for instance, among the "10 most important Bahians," chosen by students in the law school at Salvador were two men with slight traces of mixed racial descent, a somewhat darker mulatto, and a very dark mixed-blood, referred to locally as a *prêto*. In other words, of these 10 two-fifths were mixed-bloods. Students at the local normal school chose among the 10 "most important" two men with slight traces of African origin and three darker mixed-bloods; that is, half the group.

It should be emphasized, however, that this rise of the mixed-bloods in Brazil has been accomplished by people as individuals and not as a group, whether suddenly torn en masse from a servile status as an incident of armed strife or acting as a self-conscious majority fighting for demanded "rights." Since the slave revolts of the early nineteenth century (which perhaps were as much, if not more, culturally than racially inspired), conflict by reason of color has rarely been obvious but relatively subdued and subtle.[43]

In their attempts to rise in rank, however, the mixed-bloods definitely have been handicapped by those physical traits that centuries ago became identified with a slave condition and that have long been so identified, at times perhaps unconsciously but none the less positively.

Nevertheless, this restraining influence varies directly with the observable degree of African influence in physical characteristics, being attenuated or even virtually absent in the case of thousands of the lighter mixed-bloods. What is more important, it is only a predisposing and not a *determining* circumstance when ascribing rank. It is only one of several personal and social characteristics, some of which are of as great or perhaps even greater importance: occupational competence, educational achievement, affiliation with a family of prestige, the accumulation of wealth, "good" manners, beauty, poise, bearing, "charm," perhaps others,

---

43 Cf. Thales de Azevedo, *ibid.*, p. 195.

the patterning of which, in a given case, determines, maintains, or alters status.[44]

Prominent Mixed-Bloods in Brazil's Past

In fact, if some giant hand had sifted out all those mixed-bloods who have played significant roles in Brazil's past, a considerable portion of her intellectual, artistic, and political history would be wiped out. Although mention of more than a few of the more prominent is impossible here,[45] we should not fail to recall the famed Jesuit of the sixteenth century, Padre Nobrega; the noted politician and diplomat of the Second Empire, Barão de Cotegipe; and Floriano Peixoto, of partial Amerindian descent,[46] who became a *marechal* in the Brazilian army, helped set up the Republic, was elected its first vice president and, following on the resignation of Deodoro da Fonseca, became the second president of Brazil.

Nilo Peçanha became a partisan of the proposed Republic, a deputy in the Constitutional Assembly of 1890 and in the first Brazilian Congress, to which he was re-elected several times before becoming a federal senator. Chosen vice president in the administration of Affonso Penna, he became, on the latter's death, the seventh president of Brazil. Subsequently elected again to the Senate and, later still, governor of his native state, he also served as minister of foreign affairs in the administration of Wenceslau Braz. Of considerable political prestige also were his brother, Alcebiades Peçanha, Domício da Gama, and, more recently, the able brothers, João and Octavio Mangabeira. José do Patrocínio, a journalist and lecturer of humble origin, became the foremost leader of the abolition movement which, in the second half of the nineteenth century, dominated the public mind. Luiz Gama, son of the noted African slave, Luiza Mahin of Bahia, became a polemical journalist, lawyer, defender of slaves in court, and a vigorous supporter of the Republican Congress of 1872 in São Paulo at a time when few other Brazilians, it is said, dared actively to sponsor so dubious a movement.

André Rebouças, a quite dark mixed-blood, distinguished himself

---

[44] Cf. Charles Wagley, "Race and Social Class," in *An Introduction to Brazil*. New York: Columbia University Press, 1963, pp. 132–147.

[45] For a more complete discussion in English, see, particularly, Arthur Ramos, *The Negro in Brazil*. Washington, D.C.: The Associated Publishers, 1939, *passim*. See also Freyre, *loc. cit.*

[46] See Antonio Austregesilo, "A mestiçagem no Brasil como fator eugênico," in Gilberto Freyre e Outros, *Novos estudos Afro-brasileiros*. Rio de Janeiro: Civilização Brasileira Editôra, 1937, p. 333.

as a military engineer in the Paraguayan War, became professor at the engineering school in Rio de Janeiro, and helped work out problems of urban housing, marital law, and the redistribution of seats in the federal Congress. One often hears in Brazil of the court ball at which Princess Isabel, heir to the Brazilian throne, danced with him. Theodoro Sampaio, another dark mixed-blood, whom I knew as the highly respected and distinguished-appearing president of Bahia's principal scholarly institute, was at that time a member of 12 engineering or literary organizations, including the prestigious Bahian Academy of Letters. As a younger man he had participated in engineering projects with other noted engineers, both national and foreign, served on several commissions of the Imperial Government, published approximately a score of books or extended articles in engineering and other fields, and was briefly a federal deputy. Juliano Moreira became a pioneer in the treatment of mental abnormality, his prestige extending, it is said, even to Europe.

It was perhaps in literature and the arts that the mixed-bloods obtained their earliest recognition. The poet, José de Natividade Saldanha, educated at Coimbra in Portugal, also taught in Europe and the United States. Antonio Gonçalves Dias, often referred to as "a poetic genius," also was educated at Coimbra, where he became quite well known, later publishing dramatic works and a dictionary. Castro Alves, "the poet of abolition," although he died at the early age of 24, left "a very considerable mark . . . on his generation," as Ramos writes, "reflected in Brazilian letters down to the present day."[47] Machado de Assis, perhaps Brazil's greatest novelist, the son of a black painter and his Portuguese wife, became a typesetter, proofreader, journalist, poet, and writer of short stories. He is best known, however, for his realistic novels which broke sharply with the romantic mood of the time and are also noted for their social awareness, psychological insight, and ironic wit. He was elected president of the Brazilian Academy of Letters. Olavo Bilac was the principal poet of the "Parnassian School" and noted for the elegance and sensual richness of his poetic style. Around Mario de Andrade, who has been called "the leading figure of the modernist movement in Brazilian literature," strong currents of intellectual life flowed, his interests covering a wide range, in the European manner. He became famed as a novelist, poet, essayist, critic of letters and the arts, musicologist, and folklorist.

Father José Mauricio is said to have "dominated" the Brazilian musical world during his adult life in the colonial period. Without formal

---

[47] Ramos, *op. cit.*, p. 79.

instruction but gifted with a prodigious memory, he learned to play the violin, harpsichord, and organ, became choir master at the Cathedral in Rio de Janeiro (where the emperor, João VI, held him, it is said, in high esteem), composed and taught music, and founded the first school of music in Brazil. Domingos Caldus Barbosa, perhaps the first outstanding singer of popular Brazilian songs, carried them into the salons of Europe. Today mixed-bloods are well represented in orchestras, philharmonic societies, and military and civil bands and are numbered among the singers, composers and instrumentalists of national radio and television.

The work of the eighteenth-century sculptor Antonio Francisco Lisboa, popularly known as Aleijadinho, the son of an African woman and a Portuguese architect in Minas Gerais, was considered by the noted critic Mario de Andrade to be "the culminating expression of three centuries of colonial architecture." Sylvio Romero was an assiduous collector and annotator of Brazilian folklore, to whose largely self-taught proficiency scholars are much indebted. Oliveira Vianna, although self-taught, became one of the more able students of Brazilian social history.

What Others Think of Racial Hybrids

The Brazilian mixed-blood has been painted by Candido Portinari[48] as a smooth-skinned, thick-lipped, muscular, powerfully built male, with wavy hair. In the exaggerated style of this famed Brazilian artist, the undraped torso gives an impression of a vigorous, exceedingly healthy, self-confident man, with herculean neck, shoulder, and arm muscles, and fingers of firm grip. He is focused against massive works of construction of similar strength, solidity, and promise of endurance.

Conceptions of mixed-bloods and attitudes toward them probably have run the gamut from this and other appreciation and acceptance to depreciation and rejection, largely in keeping with the personal relationship to the mixed-blood in question and the latter's personal and social characteristics. Certain adverse attitudes toward all mixed-bloods have existed, in varying degree at different times and places and even at first including discriminatory legislation, which undoubtedly have played their roles. In literally thousands of cases, however, such attitudes have been altered as evidence appeared that the mixed-blood in question possessed one or more of the other determinants of rank.

Thus a stranger to Brazil may not know, without inquiry or some

---

[48] See the photograph in Freyre e Outros, *op. cit.,* facing p. 330.

research, when he hears Floriano Peixoto, the Barão de Cotegipe, Machado de Assis, or Juliano Moreira referred to or notes streets named for them that they were mixed-bloods.

The fact of mixed racial descent has a low order of value in the Brazilian culture. Cases similar to that of a Bahian white who casually remarked of an unusual woman of predominantly European appearance, known everywhere as a *branca* (white), and whose personal competence had carried her "ahead of her time" into the state legislature, "I saw a picture of her grandmother the other day: she was as black as coal," can be cited indefinitely. This discovery, however, led to no alteration in the woman's status.

Courtesy, tact, and the avoidance of giving offense are highly valorized in the Brazilian social order. To call a person to his face, or in the hearing of one of his friends, a "mulatto" or a "black" is a definite breach of etiquette. Moreover, in this social order, and especially in the centers of heavy African importation, references like these must be made with care, for if rigid distinctions were to be drawn between those persons who appear to be entirely European in descent and those who show some other lineage the dividing line would often pass directly through family groups.[49]

The attitudes toward mixed-bloods depend to some extent also on the relative security of a person's own social position; that is, they are similar to attitudes that arise out of a struggle for position in any social order. The newly arrived and those engaged in elbowing their way up are resented. For a mixed-blood who possesses these traits the term *mulato pernostico* has come into rather general use. The criticism implied in this phrase, however, as Thales de Azevedo has perceptively observed,[50] is not directed at the mulatto as a member of a group but instead at an *individual* social climber, and, as he also notes, it is used with equal force against a *white* or anyone else in similar circumstances. "We like a person to be modest," a Bahian once remarked. "If he is aggressive or self-assertive, we tend to push him back a bit."

Beginning at least in the nineteenth century among intellectuals, and probably reflecting attitudes of European or United States origin, there has been some concern in Brazil over the presumed cultural inferiority of the African. Nina Rodrigues, for instance, "a prisoner of the conceptions of his time," as Ramos has said, observing at Bahia the continuance of

---

49 Cf. Emilio Willems, "Race Attitudes in Brazil," *Amer. J. Sociol.*, **64,** p. 407 (March 1959); Felte Bezerra, *op. cit.,* pp. 218–219; and, in the middle of the nineteenth century, Thomas Ewbank, *Life in Brazil.* New York: Harper, 1856, p. 130.
50 Thales de Azevedo, *As elites de côr,* p. 60.

African cultural forms[51] in the last years of the nineteenth century, wondered if the African and his descendants ever could become completely assimilated. More recently the able scholar Oliveira Vianna, failing to distinguish between the biological and the cultural determinants of mental functioning and personality, and thus confusing racial potentiality with cultural achievement, forcefully maintained for many years that the black is inferior. Similar doubts also troubled the journalist Euclydes da Cunha and the poet Jorge de Lima.

As a corollary to these considerations there has been some concern regarding the possible biological, social, or cultural inadequacy of mixed-bloods. Evidently the highly fruitful work of Gilberto Freyre in revealing, in intimate detail and with the insight of a poet, the actual racial situation in Brazil was stimulated by doubts raised in his youthful mind while observing a group of Brazilian racial hybrids and recalling a tactless phrase about "mongrels" from a book written by a visitor from the United States.[52] Of considerable significance in this connection, however, is the fact that most, if not all, the writers whose comments have appeared in recent times *attack* the contention that race mixture leads to degeneracy. Roquette-Pinto, Gilberto Freyre, Arthur Ramos, and several other competent men have marshaled evidence to refute any belief that Brazil is prejudiced by reason of miscegenation, contending, instead, that malnutrition, illiteracy, and the widespread disrespect for manual labor which slavery left in Brazil—and not inherent racial inferiority or miscegenation—are responsible for any possible deficiency. The purely academic character of this debate is borne out by the fact that Freyre is white, as also were Roquette-Pinto and Ramos, whereas Oliveira Vianna and Jorge de Lima were mixed-bloods.

What Racial Hybrids Think of Themselves

Although we need further study of the question, especially of an empirical character and with particular reference to stratification and racial origin, it is probable that on the whole the mixed-bloods of Brazil spend little time thinking about themselves as racial hybrids.

Perhaps many largely ignore the matter, especially those of only slight mixture and those who occupy the less privileged ranks in which they share, rather unselfconsciously, a common life with hundreds of thousands of less privileged whites (and blacks). Those too negroid for

---

[51] See, for instance, Donald Pierson, *op. cit.*, Chapters 9 and 10.
[52] Freyre, *Casa Grande e Senzala*, pp. x–xi.

the symbols of servile origin to be readily overlooked by reason of other status-enhancing characteristics may feel, at times at least, depreciated, but, although they tend "to look upon themselves as ugly and inferior, and to feel shame regarding their African origin," as Virginia Bicudo has observed, "they still identify with the *brancos*, showing friendliness toward them and antipathy toward the blacks."[53] Because of the local prestige pattern which has been taken over, with the limited exceptions noted above, they tend to valorize that portion of their origin which is European and to emphasize it.

As the passage of time adds a romantic tinge to colonial happenings and perhaps because of the popular (and somewhat inaccurate and unjust) belief that the African—but not the Amerindian—would submit to slavery, some families look back with pride on having had one or more Amerindian ancestors. This attitude, apparently to be found in all classes, would seem to be more characteristic, however, of those areas in which the Amerindian has been absorbed. At least it is not so evident, we understand, in areas like Pará.

At least some mixed-bloods tend to look on themselves as transitional in an inevitable "whitening" process (see above). In Bahia I have often heard a. mother whose child appeared whiter than she did say, "Estou limpando a minha raça" (I am improving the stock). In fact, many mixed-bloods consider intermixture desirable and inevitable. "Race mixture obviously is no new thing," Theodoro Sampaio once remarked. "It has had a long history. Greece, Italy, and the Mediterranean Isles early mingled their blood with that of Africa. Wherever the conquering Romans went, intermixture occurred. For centuries Spain and Portugal interbred with the Moors. How natural, then, that the races in Brazil should blend and we Brazilians become one people." Another racial hybrid, Antonio Austregesilo, a professor at the Rio de Janeiro medical school, writes that "I am certain . . . miscegenation has brought . . . us more benefit than evil. It is not Aryan descent but race mixture that has given birth to . . . the creative capacity of the Brazilian people."[54]

Nevertheless, as they rise in socal rank many racial hybrids, like all those who recently have climbed or are in the process of climbing from one class to another within a comparatively brief period, tend to be threatened, at least intermittently, by feelings of insecurity, inadequacy, and inferiority. Some become ashamed of and seek to hide, as far as

---

[53] Virginia Leone Bicudo, *Estudo de atitudes raciais de prêtos e mulatos em São Paulo.* Unpublished M.A. thesis, Escola de Sociologia e Politica, São Paulo, 1945. See also Virginia Leone Bicudo, "Atitudes racaias de prêtos e mulatos em São Paulo," *Sociologia,* 9, pp. 195–219 (São Paulo, 1947). Cf. Felte Bezerra, *op. cit.,* p. 262.

[54] Austregesilo, *op. cit.,* pp. 330, 332.

possible, obvious evidence of lower status origin like their relationship to a darker and less "refined" relative. "Of his white father whom he never knew," João Varella writes, "he has a picture in the parlor; but of the black woman who gave him birth he has no picture, nor does he even speak of her."[55]

Quite naturally this sense of shame is resented by the darker members of the community. A *prêta*, for instance, although herself of mixed Amerindian and African descent, on becoming enraged over an incident involving a person lighter than she, burst out, "Listen, wise fellow, you're just a mixed up one! You don't even belong to a pure race!"

Some persons of mixed origin, especially certain intellectuals who are aware of events of racial importance outside Brazil and who are particularly ambitious, highly sensitive, or unusually given to introspection, have become obsessed with a repugnance for certain of their own physical traits that link them to a group of servile origin. This repugnance may at times reach even exaggerated form. Thus Gonçalves Dias, in spite of his obvious accomplishments and the prestige they had brought him, had, we are told, "a wound always bleeding, although hidden under the cloak of a *doutor* (a title of prestige), sensitive to his inferior origin, to the stigma of his color, to his negroid features always shouting at him from his mirror, 'Remember, you are a mulatto!' "[56] A similarly sensitive poet, Cruz e Sousa, may even have been pathological.[57]

These feelings, however, appear to have been generated internally rather than by external conflict, and, at least to any noticeable extent, they appear to have been lacking in many less sensitive racial hybrids; for example, André Rebouças, Nilo Peçanha, and Machado de Assis. Certainly, "there was no segregated colored group with which they could be identified," as Frazier has well observed, in order to become marginal men.[58]

It would seem that Anselmo Macieira,[59] referring to the old sugar center of Campos in the state of Rio de Janeiro, which he has known all his life, has well described the actual situation there and elsewhere in Brazil.

A mixed-blood here who is "cultured" and has completed the course in a profes-

---

[55] From an unpublished manuscript, "O Africano na Bahia."

[56] See Freyre, *Sobrados e mucambos*, p. 320.

[57] Emiliano Pernetta, *Cruz e Sousa*, p. 3, *apud* Octavio Ianni, *As metamorfoses do escravo*. São Paulo: Difusão Européia do Livro, 1962, p. 264.

[58] See E. Franklin Frazier, "A Comparison of Negro-White Relations in Brazil and in the United States," *Trans. N.Y. Acad. Sci.*, **II**, p. 265 (1944). Cf. Felte Bezerra, *op. cit.*, p. 264.

[59] In a letter to the author.

sional school may seek to marry a white wife. At any rate, he will behave like a white, avoiding all reference to that part of his origin which is black. At this flight from obvious evidence of miscegenation, the whites will smile discreetly but without malice; and no hostile act will be directed at one who is "making progress," even if he is dark enough to be called a black by those who do not know him well. It will be said of him that he is an *intelligent* mulatto; that he is hard-working, courageous, very *direito* (upright, virtuous, sincere). And, with the passing of time, this mulatto-branco will become accepted without reservation, the irrelevant detail of his mixed racial origin being largely overlooked.[60]

SELECTED BIBLIOGRAPHY*

Frazier, E. Franklin, "A Comparison of Negro-White Relations in Brazil and the United States," *Trans. N.Y. Acad. Sci.* **II**, 6, 251–269 (1944).

Harris, Marvin and Conrad Kottak, "The Structural Significance of Brazilian Categories," *Sociologia*, **25**, 203–208 (São Paulo, 1963).

Freyre, Gilberto, "The Rise of the College Graduate and the Mulatto," in *The Mansions and the Shanties*, translated by Harriet Onís from *Sobrados e mucambos*. New York: Knopf, 1963, pp. 354–399.

Freyre, Gilberto, *The Masters and the Slaves*, 2nd rev. ed., translated by Samuel Putnam from *Casa grande e senzala*. New York: Knopf, 1963.

Lacerda, Jean Baptiste de, "The Metis, or Half-breeds, of Brazil," in *Papers on Interracial Problems*, G. Spiller, Ed. London: P.S. King & Son, 1911, pp. 377–382.

Lowrie, Samuel Harmon, "Racial and National Intermarriage in a Brazilian City," *Am. J. Sociol.*, 44, 684–707 (March 1939).

Nogueira, Oracy, "Skin Color and Social Class," in *Plantation Systems of the New World*, Vera Rubin, Ed. Washington, D.C.: Pan American Union, 1959, pp. 164–179.

Pierson, Donald, "Race Relations in Portuguese America," Chapter 19 in *Race Relations in World Perspective*, Andrew W. Lind, Ed. Honolulu: University of Hawaii Press, 1955, pp 433–462.

Pierson, Donald, "Race Mixture and the Crumbling of the Color Line" and "The Rise of the Mixed-Blood," in *Negroes in Brazil: A Study of Race Contact at Bahia*. Carbondale: Southern Illinois University Press, 1967, pp. 111–140, 159–176.

---

[60] See also Aluizio de Azevedo, *O Mulato*, 5th ed. Rio de Janeiro: Livraria Gardner, n.d.; Florestan Fernandes, "A ascensão social do negro e do mulato," Section 2 of Chapter 5, in *A integração do negro à sociedade de classes*. São Paulo: Universidade de São Paulo, 1964; Samuel Harmon Lowrie, "Racial and National Intermarriage in a Brazilian City," *Amer. J. Sociol.*, 44, pp. 684–707 (March 1939); Viuva Juliano Moreira, "Juliano Moreira e o problema do negro e do mestiço no Brasil," in Freyre e Outros, *op. cit.*, pp. 146–150; Pierson, *Race Mixture and the Crumbling of the Color Line*, Chapter 4, and *The Rise of the Mixed-Blood*, Chapter 6.

* Most of the more pertinent—and more reliable—data are in Portuguese. Translations into English are few and, like all such efforts, not always precise, even as to titles. A few publications of general character are included here, to aid in gleaning information on this specific subject. For extended bibliographies, see Donald Pierson, 1967.

Ramos, Arthur, *The Negro in Brazil*. Translation by Richard Pattee of a manuscript prepared especially for publication in the United States. Washington, D.C.: The Associated Publishers, 1939.

Wagley, Charles, Ed., *Race and Class in Rural Brazil*, 2nd ed. New York: Columbia University Press, 1963.

Wagley, Charles, "Race and Social Class," in *An Introduction to Brazil*. New York: Columbia University Press, 1963, pp. 132–147.

Willems, Emilio, "Race Attitudes in Brazil," *Amer. J. Sociol.* **54,** 402–408 (March 1949).

Peter A. Munch

Southern Illinois University

CHAPTER THIRTEEN

RACE AND SOCIAL RELATIONS IN TRISTAN DA CUNHA

The community of Tristan da Cunha, settled in a village on the northwest shoreline of an isolated volcanic island in the middle of the South Atlantic (population 1970: 275), is racially mixed.[1] It was founded in 1817 as a utopian community based on the principles of equality and anarchy and with communal operation in the economic field.

Situated about midway between South Africa and the eastern coast of South America, the island was uninhabited when first discovered by European seafarers. The huge, apparently extinct volcano, rising almost 7000 feet above sea level, was sighted in 1506 by the Portuguese Admiral Tristão da Cunha, who named it after himself. With its precipitous cliffs, the almost circular shoreline offering no shelter for seagoing craft, the island did not seem well suited for human settlement, and it remained uninhabited for more than 300 years after its discovery. Only a few hardy

---

[1] I spent four months on Tristan da Cunha as a member of a Norwegian scientific expedition in 1937–1938. In 1961 the island was evacuated because of a volcanic eruption, and I spent two months with the exiled islanders in England during the summer of 1962. In 1964–1965, after the islanders' return to Tristan, I revisited the island for a stay of six months. A shorter period was spent with emigrated Tristan islanders in England during the summer of 1967, and in 1968 contacts were made with old emigrants from Tristan in New London, Connecticut. Archive studies were made in Cape Town in 1937, in London and Cape Town in 1964, in London in 1965 and 1967, and in New England in 1968. Financial assistance from the National Science Foundation, the Social Science Research Council, the American Philosophical Society, and Southern Illinois University is gratefully acknowledged.

seal hunters would occasionally spend some months on the island during the mild southern summer, attracted by the abundance of fur seal and sea elephant that once crowded the narrow beaches.

The founder of the present community was a Scot named William Glass who had enlisted in the Royal Artillery and became a member of a British garrison that was placed on Tristan da Cunha in 1816 in connection with the annexation of the island by Britain. The following year, when the island was abandoned and the garrison removed, Glass and two companions decided to stay. They drew up a short document of agreement, stipulating among other things, "That in order to ensure the harmony of the Firm, No member shall assume any superiority whatever, but all to be considered equal in every respect."[2]

While stationed at the Cape Colony Glass had married a young "Cape Creole" of Dutch ancestry, and he brought her and their infant son with him to Tristan. Before the garrison left they also had a daughter. The other two members of the "firm" were bachelors, and they did, in fact, not stay long, but Glass and his rapidly growing family were soon joined by others, mostly sailors and navy men. In 1827 five women from Saint Helena were persuaded to join the company on Tristan in search of husbands. Soon American whale ships began to call at the island for fresh supplies, and a few of the whalers settled down and married Tristan girls. When William Glass died in 1853, at the age of 66, he was the father of 16, the grandfather of 25 or more, and the more or less recognized patriarch of a community of 83 people in 10 households.

In the literature about Tristan da Cunha there is a widespread notion, which I also accepted at first, that William Glass's wife was a Cape Coloured woman and that this may have been the main reason why the couple remained on Tristan rather than return to a world in which such a "mixed" marriage would be an embarrassment or worse. The notion may, in fact, stem in part from a general statement in a report by Captain Denham, H.M.S. *Herald*, who visited the island in 1852: "The young women were of the mulatto caste, but among the children, forming the second generation, there were handsome brunettes of a strikingly fine figure."[3] Accordingly, in a report from Captain M. S. Nolloth, H.M.S.

---

2 For a short history of Tristan da Cunha, see Peter A. Munch, *Sociology of Tristan da Cunha* (Results of the Norwegian Scientific Expedition to Tristan da Cunha 1937–1938, No. 13), Oslo: Det Norske Videnskaps-Akademi, 1945, pp. 13–47. A more comprehensive history of the island and its settlement is given by Jan Brander, *Tristan da Cunha, 1506–1902*, London: George Allen and Unwin, 1940. Cf. Peter A. Munch, *Crisis in Utopia: The Ordeal of Tristan da Cunha*, New York: Thomas Y. Crowell, 1971.

3 Quoted from Brander, *ibid.*, p. 150.

Frolic, who visited the island four years later (after Mrs. Glass had left the island), we find one of the Glass daughters described as a "light-coloured mulatto."[4] I have, however, been unable to trace an original document that would confirm Maria Glass's mixed racial background. On the contrary, the most reliable sources—the English artist Augustus Earle and the Reverend William F. Taylor, both of whom spent an extended period of time on the island, and both of whom knew Mrs. Glass personally—agreed to describe her as a "Cape Creole."[5] The term "creole" has certainly taken on a variety of meanings, including that of various racial mixtures. Originally, however, the term clearly denoted a person born in the colonies of European parents, and this is obviously the sense in which the term is used by Earle and Taylor, as opposed to "half-caste," which is the term they use for persons of mixed race. From Maria Glass's maiden name, Leenders, we may conclude that her parents were Dutch.

The five women from Saint Helena, however, were of mixed but undetermined racial origin. Another "traditional" view in the literature about Tristan da Cunha is that one of the women was a "negress," whereas the rest of them were "mulattoes." The "negress" is supposed to be the one who became the wife of Thomas Swain, a navy man who had settled down on Tristan only the year before the women arrived. However, in the Rev. W. F. Taylor's carefully kept census of the island population Thomas Swain's wife is expressly described as having an "English father," and another woman from Saint Helena is claimed to be of "English parents," that is, white.[6]

Today the islanders' mixed racial background is evident from a great diversity of facial types and skin pigmentation. In accordance with the numerical predominance of Caucasians among their ancestors, most of the islanders look quite European—weather-beaten, to be sure, from a lifelong exposure to sun, wind, and salt sea, but no darker than can be found on the coasts of Norway, Scotland, or Holland. There are blue-eyed blonds among them, as well as freckled redheads. Some carry the more swarthy Mediterranian looks inherited from an Italian sailor who was

---

[4] *Ibid.,* 165.

[5] Augustus, Earle, *A Narrative of a Nine Months' Residence in New Zealand in 1827, Together with a Journal of a Residence in Tristan d'Acunha, an Island Between South America and the Cape of Good Hope,* London: Longmans, 1832. William F. Taylor, *Some Account of the Settlement of Tristan d'Acunha, in the South Atlantic Ocean,* London: Society for the Propagation of the Gospel, 1856.

[6] The original documents from the Rev. Taylor's stay on the island are now in the archives of the United Society for the Propagation of the Gospel at its headquarters in London.

shipwrecked on the island in 1892, and a few show definite negroid or Malayan traits.

Throughout the history of this community anarchy and equality prevailed as the most prominent social values, which crystallized into firmly established social codes demanding dignity, kindness, and generosity in all conduct and behavior. These are among the most important virtues instilled in every Tristan islander from childhood. Social differentiation was never pronounced, and in spite of the absence of any governmental institution or authority visitors have been unanimous in pointing to the apparent harmony and peace of the community.

My own observations during a four months' stay on the island in 1938 confirm these impressions. I found a community of 188 persons, with no institutional form of government or leadership (except what English missionaries had imposed on them, which was generally ignored by the islanders), and with no laws and law enforcement. Yet the most serious crime that occurred was a rare case of petty theft. There had never been a fight within the memory of the oldest people, and ill-natured quarrels were rare. Personal animosities never seemed to go beyond the stage at which the parties would not speak to one another, and even this mild form of hostility appeared to be such a mental effort to the peaceful islanders that it could never be kept up for long.

In this highly mixed community, peaceful and to all appearance completely integrated as it is, there seems to be no social barrier on the basis of race. Nevertheless, there is evidence of some mild structural tensions, which appear to have their roots in certain cultural, ethnic, and even racial differences among the original settlers. Most of the time in the history of the community these tensions remained latent, repressed as they were by the demands for nonoffensive behavior and conduct. On certain rare occasions, however, when the traditional values of the Tristan community were challenged by changes in the composition of the population or by influences from outside, the structural tensions came to the surface and in one or two cases resulted in what amounted to a fission of the community along the existing lines of structural differentiation.

"Whites" and "Blacks"

By the time of William Glass's death in 1853 important changes had taken place in his utopian dream as well as in its realization. It appears that some of the sailors and navy men who had joined the party had been more attracted by the prospects of equality and anarchy than by communal ownership and management. Anyway, Glass appears to have had difficulties making the newcomers "perform their proportion of labour" according to the letter of agreement, and only four years after the establishment of the egalitarian commune a new document was drawn up which not only placed William Glass "at the head of the firm" but also pronounced that "it is at the same time to be understood that the whole of the Land, Stock, &c &c is the sole and joint property of Wm. Glass and John Nankevile"—Nankevile being the one remaining original companion of Glass. Nankevile soon left the island, and Glass presumably became the master and sole proprietor of the whole outfit, including the land. A few years later he even drew up a last will and testament, witnessed by a sea captain and a passenger from a passing ship, in which he assigned one third of his property to his eldest son, the rest to be distributed among his other children.[7]

It appears that William Glass had all but abandoned the lofty principles of equality and anarchy as well as the utopian dream of a communal enterprise in harmony and concord. Instead we have a private corporation presumably owned, operated, and completely controlled by the Glass family, in which the other settlers were little more than hired hands working for their keep. Yet the enterprise was still conceived as a working whole, and the revised agreement of 1821, which was presumably signed by the 11 men then residing on Tristan da Cunha, still contained the provisions "That whatever profit may arise from the sale of Oil, Skins, &c shall be equally divided between all Hands" and that "Every thing that arises from the produce of the Land, shall be equally divided in the like manner, as long as the People continue to Work at the same."

During the following three or four decades the traffic of sailing ships in the waters around Tristan da Cunha was lively and barter with passing ships became an important part of the island's economy. Sailors continued to come and go. Of the 11 men listed in the revised agreement only one besides Glass stayed for the rest of his life. The others left, but new settlers soon took their places. Among those who stayed were Alexander Cotton and Thomas Swain, two salty sea dogs with boisterous navy careers behind them. They were among the five men who in 1827 persuaded a ship's captain to bring them five women from Saint Helena. The two chosen by Cotton and Swain were sisters. A decade later, in

---

[7] The documents pertaining to the early history of the Tristan community were discovered in 1932 in the possession of a granddaughter of William Glass residing in New London, Connecticut, and are now in the British Museum. The story of their discovery as well as the text of most of the documents can be found in Douglas M. Gane, "Early Records of Tristan da Cunha: The Discovery in New London," *United Empire*, 589–598, 651–658, 709–713 (1933).

1836, a Dutchman named Pieter Groen was shipwrecked on the island. He decided to stay, changed his name to Peter Green, and took for his companion a daughter of Thomas Swain's woman, who as a little girl had arrived with her mother.

As it appears, although the new arrivals probably recognized William Glass as the founder of the community, they largely ignored his claims to exclusive property and leadership. Clearly they had not settled down on the island to help build an empire for the Glass family, and together with the few older settlers who remained they strongly embraced the original principles of freedom, equality, and anarchy. It was during the next few decades that the community developed its present atomistic structure as each newcomer established his own independent household, cleared his own piece of land, and even acquired some cattle and sheep. It is not known whether Glass resisted or even resented the development. A certain social distance, however, and perhaps a slight tension seems to have developed between the well-mannered landlubber Glass and his family on the one hand and his company of fiercely independent sea dogs on the other, a distance that was accentuated by the arrival of American whalers on the scene.

The first American whaler appeared offshore in Tristan da Cunha in 1828. American whaling was then just developing, but it grew rapidly during the following decades to become one of the most important industries of the New England coast. The fisheries were carried on all over the Atlantic and Pacific Oceans. As the ships often kept to the sea for two or three years before returning to home port, they were in need of refitting, and Tristan da Cunha became one of the most frequently visited fitting stations of the New England whaling fleet, where ships would heave to for fresh supplies of water, vegetables, and meat. The traffic reached its peak during the 1840's, when more than a hundred ships must have visited the island each year, and slowly diminished until the last American whaler called at Tristan in 1913.

During the first two decades of American whaling off Tristan a particularly close relationship developed between the Glass family and the Americans. In fact, most of William Glass's children got involved with whalers and whaling. Five of his eight daughters married Americans, four of them whalers. Some of his whaler sons-in-law settled down for a while, one of them for the rest of his life. There were also three or four illegitimate grandchildren by whalers. One of Glass's eight sons died in infancy. Of the seven who grew up at least six went whaling in American ships and soon made their homes in far-away New London. Two of the remaining daughters also settled in New England.

From all this the other settlers were almost totally excluded. Only two of their numerous children sought or found mates among William Glass's children, and not one of their daughters married a whaler. Two or three of the boys went whaling, but they did not ship out in American whalers. They went to South Africa, where they were engaged in whaling from established land bases, and most of them eventually returned to Tristan.

It is not quite certain who was keeping aloof from whom in this apparent gap between the Glasses and the rest of the community. All the other settlers were sailors, with the seafarers' pride and proverbial lust for independence. It is well known that in the days of the windjammers a typical sailor would look with benign contempt at the landlubber, but for the whaler he had nothing but scorn. Cotton, Swain, and Green have been described as rather thorough mariners and man-of-war's men, and the strong ties of common traditions and common spirit that united them were apparently reinforced by the close kinship of their Saint Helena women. The relationship was further strengthened by extensive intermarriages between the three families in the second generation. Three of Peter Green's four sons married daughters of Alexander Cotton, and when Cotton's fourth daughter married Thomas Swain's oldest son, her cousin, an intricate network of socially recognized and significant relationships was established between the three sailor families to the complete exclusion of the Glasses and their whaler friends, at least for the time being.

Anyway, somewhat later there is evidence of a certain tension within the Tristan community along the line of sailor versus whaler. In 1884 the old salt Peter Green, who had become the "grand old man" of Tristan da Cunha after Glass's death, wrote to the British authorities expressing hope that "the three whaling boys" could be removed from the island, since they had "brought a very small stock of knowledge back to Tristan, and that is of a very vulgar kind."[8]

On the other hand, it is conceivable that the apparent tension in the Tristan community also had a racial background. There is no direct evidence of racial conflict on the island. It is a striking fact, however, that the apparent split in the community occurred almost exactly along racial lines. William Glass's family was all white, and so, apparently, were the American whalers. All the other settlers, although themselves white, were engaged in common-law marriages to women from Saint Helena, of whom only one presumably was white—she was the one whose

---

[8] *Correspondence Relating to the Island of Tristan d'Acunha*, Imperial Blue Book C. 4959. London: Printed for Her Majesty's Stationery Office, 1887, p. 35; see also Brander, *op. cit.*, p. 263.

daughter by her Tristan man was married to one of William Glass's
whaler sons. The others were of an undetermined racial mixture and
were described by outsiders as "half-castes."

Obviously the genetic heritage of the Saint Helena women must
have been evident in their children, as it is evident in a large part of the
Tristan population today. That this racial appearance played a part in
the development of a slight differentiation in the Tristan community
between the Glasses and the rest is indirectly confirmed by the fact that
in later years the Glasses have been known to regard themselves as white,
at least as "more white" than the rest of the community, a thing they
would whisper only among themselves.

It is not known whether this structural tension in the Tristan community caused an open conflict or even a noticeable friction during
William Glass's lifetime. Apparently, in spite of his possible racial prejudices, William Glass was a gentle man, and it seems that the social
codes of dignity, kindness, and generosity, for which the Tristan community has been known over the years, were already then well established. A look at the marriage records, however, seems to indicate that
the tension was deep and tenacious. There was never in the history of
the community a marriage between a Cotton and a Glass, and the first
marriage between a Glass and an agnatic descendant of Peter Green was
contracted in 1939.

In any case, after the founder's death in 1853, the split appeared to
be deep enough to cause the first great fission of the community. In 1856
nearly all the family of William Glass, including his widow, left Tristan
da Cunha in two whale ships bound for New London, and perhaps for
a couple of decades the name Glass was not found among the settlers of
the island. About a year later another large group left for South Africa,
thus reducing the population to less than half its former size. The second
group of emigrants included one of the two remaining sons-in-law of
William Glass, with his family, and the white woman from Saint Helena
with her man (now duly married by the Rev. Mr. Taylor, the first resident minister on the island) and their children.

Skin Color and Prestige

The possible racial tension in the Tristan community was practically
removed with the departure of the all-white Glasses in the 1850's. There
were now only four families left on the island, and the situation was
completely dominated by the three "sailor" families of Green, Cotton,
and Swain with their colored Saint Helena women and presumably choc-

olate-colored children. Only one all-white family of the Glass set remained, the family of Andrew Hagan, a whaling captain who in 1849 had abandoned his ship, settled down on the island, and married one of William Glass's daughters. This family apparently became the source of some continued tension between "sailors" and "whalers," especially since Hagan received the support of two members of the Glass family who had returned from whaling. Those were the "three whaling boys" whom Peter Green wanted removed from the island, but the "color bar" (if it ever existed) was broken by the marriages of the two returning Glasses to daughters of Thomas Swain and his Saint Helena woman. The community was then almost totally integrated racially, and there is no evidence that race at that point had any social significance—except in relation to outsiders.

There is no doubt that outsiders visiting the island—officers of naval ships and missionaries—regarded the whole population of Tristan da Cunha as "colored," but racial appearance and background were seldom mentioned in the official reports. We have already noted that Captain Denham, in 1852, described the women of Tristan as being "of the mulatto caste" and their young daughters as "handsome brunettes of a strikingly fine figure." In another instance Lieutenant Watts-Jones, who visited the island in 1903 as Commander of H.M.S. *Thrush*, makes the following statement:

> The majority of the islanders, though rather sunburnt and weather beaten, are practically "white." Some, however, show, by more or less distinct negroid characteristics of feature or colour, their descent from Cape or St. Helena women. This is chiefly to be found in the Green and Swain families, especially among the older members, Henry Green being but little removed from a Kaffir in appearance.[9]

This, of course, cannot be regarded as an accurate statement of the physical anthropology of the Tristan people, but it reveals something about the attitude of outsiders to the islanders, which is the social fact of interest in this context.

About 30 years earlier Captain G. Stanley Bosanquet, Commander of H.M.S. *Diamond*, who greatly admired the anarchical order of the community and "was unable to see any need for establishing rules for their future guidance," described the situation as follows:

> They have certain rules of their own, and the present senior male member of the community, Peter Green, is made their referee if necessary. This position

---

[9] *Further Correspondence Relating to the Island of Tristan da Cunha*, Imperial Blue Book Cd. 1600. London: Printed for His Majesty's Stationery Office, 1903, p. 13.

has been conceded to him, not alone from his superiority in years, but also from having greater force of character, being a European, than the rest of the community, who are half-castes, and of more plastic materials. . . .[10]

A similar opinion was expressed by the Rev. E. H. Dodgson, who served as a minister on the island from 1881 to 1884 and again from 1886 to 1889. During his first visit to the island he sent home a report in which he had a few not very flattering words to say about the people of Tristan, comparing them with a "missing link" in the Darwinian chain between man and ape, apparently to demonstrate that they were physically and mentally inferior and unfit to survive on their own (he was advocating a complete evacuation of the island).

Obviously Peter Green did not accept the idea of the superiority of the "European" race as valid—"I consider that me or mine claim no more of the monkey than Mr. Dodgson," he wrote. It was inevitable that this attitude on the part of prestigious outsiders should sooner or later have an effect on the islanders' self-image.

The Tristan islanders, especially the sailors and navy men among them, had always looked on themselves as the most loyal subjects of the British Crown, which was represented in their own experience mainly by the Admiralty and the British men-of-war that occasionally visited the island. To visiting officers they always showed the greatest and most devoted reverence. With other sailors, whether from a navy ship or from a merchantman, they seem to have communicated on an equal footing, while they probably continued to look down on the whalers.

Around the turn of the century, however, as the sailing ships gradually disappeared from the oceans, Tristan da Cunha fell into a situation of increasing isolation. A new generation of Tristan islanders grew up with vaguer ideas about authority and outside power. By the 1930's the whole of the "outside world" had grown into a single, undifferentiated "superculture," mysterious and remote, which made sporadic and intermittent appearances in the form of a passing ship, a resident missionary, or a visiting dignitary.[11] In this world the "Admiralty," the "Colonial Office," and the "S.P.G." had merged in the islanders' minds with everything else from the outside into a single, vaguely conceived superpower vested with awesome authority emanating like rays of mana from the Crown, and every stranger visiting the island was somehow believed to be a part of it and was addressed with a humble "Sir," whether

---

[10] *Correspondence Relating to the Island of Tristan d'Acunha*, Imperial Blue Book C. 1445. London: Printed for Her Majesty's Stationery Office, 1876, p. 6.

[11] Peter A. Munch, "Culture and Superculture in a Displaced Community: Tristan da Cunha," *Ethnology*, 3, 369–376 (October 1964).

an Admiral of the Royal Navy or a coalheaver from a passing freighter. This was the time when the self-image of the Tristan islanders reached its lowest ebb and they developed that deep respect, to the point of deference, for the "outside world," which seems so peculiarly incongruous with their spirit of anarchical independence. In relation to this mysterious "outside world" they themselves were "only low and poor people," and this most humble spirit was as much part of the dignity of being a "Trisst'n" as the cheerful generosity, the unselfish kindness, and the modest frugality they were taught as children.

Awareness of their own increasing poverty during this period of isolation, reinforced by patronizing efforts on the part of sympathetic and well-meaning outsiders to bring charity to the island, was undoubtedly at the root of this attitude of humility. Lack of knowledge about the real conditions on the outside was also a factor. Whatever the reason, the islanders were now ready—and willing—to accept the notion that they were "low and poor people," not only because of their poverty but also because they were "black," which was indeed part of their self-image at the time of my first visit to Tristan in 1938.

Once the notion of inferior status is accepted by a people the symbols of inferiority may take on added social significance, even in their internal relationships. This is what happened in Tristan da Cunha when skin color became a symbol—and perhaps a criterion—of relative prestige *within* the community, although it was never the only or even the most important one.

The social structure of the Tristan community could be described as highly "atomistic" in the sense that the islanders "recognize only individual allegiances" and "lack the social forms necessary for group action."[12] Each household is in principle independent of the rest. Like most agrarian and fishing communities anywhere in the world, however, the Tristan community is tied together by a network of cooperation and mutual aid, which in this case takes the form of a system of selective reciprocity between individuals. In accordance with the basic principle of "equality in every respect," there is no distinction of established rank or social class. Prestige and social status as well as selective associations are in principle strictly individual matters and are based primarily on personal performance and conformity to the values and norms of the community.

---

[12] On "primitive atomism" see William Graham Sumner and Albert G. Keller, *The Science of Society*. New Haven: Yale University Press, 1927, Vol. I, pp. 16ff Vol. IV, pp. 1ff. The term was apparently picked up by Ruth Benedict and used in her unpublished Bryn Mawr lectures, quoted by John J. Honigmann, "Interpersonal Relations in Atomistic Communities," *Human Organization*, **27**, 220-229 (Fall 1968).

Economic factors play a part in this. As in most human communities, one source of prestige is a secure economic status. At least before the introduction of modern industry, however, there was no opportunity to secure economic status except by one's own manual work. The subsistence of the Tristan community was based on the production of potatoes, which formed the staple diet of the islanders and far exceeded any other economic resources in importance; and, since there was no private property in land, no division of labor (except that between sexes and age groups), no employment of wage labor, no currency, and no regular trade, the only way a man could secure his economy was to work diligently on his allotted potato patches. High prestige, accordingly, was attached to work, which was taken as an indication of a strong sense of responsibility. On this basis the Tristan islanders did distinguish between two categories, or "social types," namely, "those who work" and "those who don't work," and there was even an incipient social stratification because the upper stratum of "those who work" tended to become somewhat exclusive in their selective reciprocal relations. Since work and diligence are strictly individual qualities, the incipient class system remained completely open.

There are indeed indications that racial appearance may have played a minor part in this incipient social stratification. As the islanders accepted the notion of their own low status in relation to outsiders because they were "black and poor," it appears that a dark skin became an undesirable trait, even in their own internal relations. In 1938—which was toward the end of the period of extreme isolation—it was generally recognized among the islanders that fair girls had a better chance of getting a laborious husband of relatively high prestige than the dark ones, and this seemed to be confirmed by the fact that the greater number of dark-skinned women were indeed married to men of inferior industry and status. Certainly the prejudice against a dark skin was not so strong that zeal and industry could not substantially overcome it. In fact, there were some very dark-skinned older people among the upper stratum of "those who work," and they were fully accepted in that group. Of the younger generation, however, none of the conspicuously dark-skinned men was found in this upper stratum of influence and prestige. This, of course, could be due to mere chance since we are dealing with a small population. It is hard to free oneself from the impression, however, that there was, even in this egalitarian community, a slight racial prejudice, obviously stemming from the attitude of outsiders to the population as a whole.

This worked to the advantage of the Glasses. Not only was the whaler Tom Glass, the returned son of William Glass and Maria Leenders, an all-white man, although he had crossed the color bar by marrying a daughter of Thomas Swain, but the predominantly Caucasian background of the Glass family was strongly reinforced when two of Tom Glass's sons brought home all-white Irish wives, who produced a proportionately large number of fair, blue-eyed individuals in the next generation. The Glasses were no doubt conscious of the fact that they had more white "blood" than most of the islanders.

To the Swains, however, it was a disadvantage. One of the second generation Swains had gone whaling, had brought home a colored wife from Saint Helena, and had raised a large family with her. This, of course, strongly reinforced the Saint Helena racial background in this family. Moreover, there was extensive intermarriage in the third generation within this particular family, with numerous first-cousin alliances, which even included another returned Glass (whose mother was a Swain) and a few others who married Swain girls and thereby became engaged in these intricate in-law relationships. Whether this was entirely by choice is impossible to say, but it seems that the slight prejudice against a dark skin had already started to make itself felt. Although the group was comparatively large, constituting about half the population of fewer than a hundred at the time, it appears to have been a rather close-knit group and rather exclusive in their selective reciprocities. It is perhaps an indication of the cohesiveness of this group that two of the four longboats in existence around the turn of the century were exclusively owned by "Swains," as the group was soon identified, since that name was preponderant among them.

In 1938 the "Swains" were still quite visible as a separate social set, tied together by numerous established reciprocal relationships. A general notion among the islanders was that the "Swains" had acquired a particular group character of their own, which was stereotyped in a negative way in the island thoughtways. The "Swains" were generally regarded as poor workers and imprudent managers, as people who would not live up to the island standards of dignity and self-respect in grooming and housekeeping, and on the whole as rather "worthless" individuals with limited skills and little sense of responsibility. Some of them were considered downright lazy—and perhaps some of them were because this is what was expected from them as "Swains."

It is significant to note that this low image of the "Swains" as a social type was in fact confirmed by their own behavior in various ways. In general, they really kept their houses in a poorer shape than the others, their clothes were more often dirty and untidy, their boats sloppily built and more often out of repair, and they regularly ran short of potatoes because they did not keep their potato patches weeded. Even their donkeys were not well trained and were generally considered as "worthless" as their masters. Also, their moral code, particularly in regard to sex, appeared to be laxer than that of the rest of the community. It is at least a striking fact that all but one of the eight illegitimate births that occurred in the community from 1870 to 1955 were produced within the social set of the Swains, including four or five suspected cases of incest involving two pairs of brothers and sisters and two possible cases of father-daughter relationships.[13]

On the whole it was evident in 1938 that most of the "Swains" belonged to "those who don't work" and that the group held relatively low prestige. There can be no doubt that this was related to the racial background and appearance of this particular group, which was still conspicuous in the fourth and fifth generations and had, in fact, become a part of their general image among the islanders as a distinguishing "typical" characteristic. It is impossible to say which is "cause" and "effect" in this relationship between racial appearance, prestige, and character traits. It seems that even the egalitarian community of Tristan da Cunha was caught in a vicious circle of race prejudice in which the rejection of an indelible racial trait appears to lower the incentive among the victims to live up to the ethical and esthetic standards of the dominant group, thus leading to the development of certain "undesirable" character traits and in turn, confirming the prejudice.

The more remarkable is the fact that in later years the Tristan islanders appear to have abandoned these internal discriminations entirely.

A New Self-Image

Shortly after World War II the long period of extreme isolation of the Tristan community came to an end. Modern industry, based on commercial fisheries, was established on the island. A factory was built and began processing crayfish tails for export. Two small fishing ships were operating in the adjacent waters. Not only did this bring a new affluence to Tristan that had never been seen before, but even more important is the fact that it pulled the Tristan community back into the commerce of the modern world, establishing regular connections by ship and radio with Cape Town and the world at large and a permanent colony of

---

[13] Not included in the number of illegitimate births are the relatively few cases in which a child was born to an engaged couple who subsequently married. Such cases carry almost no stigma on Tristan.

outsiders and their families living at the "station" just below the village.

An even closer contact with modern civilization was in store for the islanders. In 1961 the volcano—long believed to be extinct—erupted near the settlement, forcing the evacuation of the island. The islanders were taken to England and settled near Southampton, where they became part of the labor force of an industrial society and spent two years fighting disease, mental depression, and reluctant authorities before they were allowed to return to their island.

In this new situation some interesting things happened to the islanders' self-image and social structure. In the first place the presence of a permanent colony of outsiders and extended contacts with the outside world gave them a new awareness of their own collective identity as "Trisst'ns" or "islanders," as opposed to the "stations" as well as to the ships' officers and the South African fishermen and sailors who worked the ships. In relation to this new collective identity it seems that internal social differentiations had lost most of their significance and meaning, and the incipient stratification between "those who work" and "those who don't work," whether based in part on racial appearance or not, was halted in its development.

During the exile in England, under the spotlight of press, radio, and television, and confronted with a strange society full of stress, worries, and crime, the new collective self-awareness of the Tristan islanders emerged. Desperate to get back to their island, but abandoned by the authorities in the hope that they would "adjust" to modern ways, this atomistic community of rugged individualists, who had never submitted to any internal authority, abandoned their high ideals of anarchy and individual integrity and consolidated into a unified group, with a common purpose and a common goal, under the firm leadership of "Chief" Willie and the other Repettos. Confronted with this unanimous spirit, the authorities had no alternative but to return the islanders to Tristan.

As it turned out, the consolidation of the Tristan community was temporary. After resettlement on the island the islanders immediately reverted to their traditional atomistic structure with its intricate network of personal obligations and allegiances and with complete freedom from any collective obligations to the community as a whole. But the experience had left a residue of pride, almost aggressive arrogance, in relation to outsiders, which stood in sharp contrast to the humble deference I knew in 1938.

There may have been a number of factors involved in this radical change in the islanders' attitudes. When they came to England and had to fight even the authorities of the Crown to save their own identity and way of life, they did not come entirely unprepared. For one thing, 10 years

of close contact with modern civilization through the fishing industry
and the local British administration, which was established in that connection, had taught them once more what they had apparently forgotten
during the long period of isolation, namely, that the outside world
was not an undifferentiated body of awesome authority, in relation to
which they themselves were only "low and poor people." They discovered
that in contrast to their own atomistic and relatively egalitarian community
there were hierarchies of power and influence which sometimes put
serious limitations on what a man could or could not do. In other words,
they learned again to distinguish between "important" and "unimportant" people (to use their own expressions). Above all, they learned that
a Tristan islander is not necessarily inferior to *everybody*, perhaps even to
none (except the Queen).

The new self-awareness of the islanders was strongly confirmed, if not
fostered in part, by the privileged position they enjoyed on board the
fishing ships, where some of them worked as fishermen. Here the line of
command, which is always in evidence on a ship, was greatly emphasized
by the conspicuous social distance between the "European," that is, the
white officers and the Cape Coloured and African crew. Here the islanders
saw really "black" people for the first time at close range and found that
they themselves, in comparison, resembled the white officers much more
than the crew in appearance, language, and the general social conduct. So
they happily took—and were accepted in—an intermediate position in
the racial caste system of the South African ships, but one much closer
to the officers. When serving on board the ships, the islanders demanded,
and were given, separate quarters from the rest of the crew. They were
always on a first-name relationship with the officers, and when off duty
the islanders might go to the bridge for a friendly visit or drop in on an
officer in his cabin for a drink (even though alcoholic beverages were
strictly forbidden to the Africans). The relationship was a mutual one.
When officers went ashore, they were more often seen visiting in the
village than at the station. In some cases warm personal friendships developed.

The ability of the islanders to take this social position so close to the
white officers of the fishing ships was obviously based primarily on their
incredible skill as boatmen and on their superior knowledge of beaches
and weather conditions around the island. The officers often relied on
the islanders' judgment before deciding where to fish or whether to put
the fishing dinghies "over the side" at all. When it came to landing a boat
through the surf of the open beaches of Tristan, they were completely
dependent on the islanders.

All this, of course, meant a great deal to the islanders' self-esteem.

The pride taken in their homemade canvas boats and in their own boat-manship has always been great. In that element they were the masters, and they knew it. Here they were for the first time associating as friends and equals with people who, as professional seamen, really could recognize and appreciate their superior skills. It was in these associations, above all, that the islanders learned to raise their heads, to abandon their traditional deference to outsiders, and to say with pride: "I's an Islander." No more did they look on themselves as "low and poor people."

The most remarkable thing in this connection is perhaps the fact that, in the process of developing this new self-image, the islanders also abandoned the notion of being "black." This was demonstrated in striking fashion shortly after I arrived in England in the summer of 1962 to visit the evacuated islanders. I had not seen them for 24 years and was not at all sure that I would remember everybody. Recognizing one islander waiting for a bus, I went over and talked to him. It happened to be one of the darker "Swains," with conspicuous pigmentation of the skin. In 1938 this man had held a position near the very bottom of the prestige scale. While we were talking a colored woman passed by, certainly not any darker than my companion, and wondering if it was somebody I ought to have recognized I asked him if she was one of his people. "No," was the answer, "here in England, you see a lot of those colored people around."

SELECTED BIBLIOGRAPHY

Blair, James P., "Home to Lonely Tristan da Cunha," *National Geographic Magazine*, 125, 60–81 (January 1964).

Brander, Jan, *Tristan da Cunha, 1506–1902*. London: George Allen and Unwin, 1940.

Munch, Peter A., *Sociology of Tristan da Cunha*. Oslo: Det Norske Videnskap-Akademi, 1945.

Munch, Peter A., "Cultural Contacts in an Isolated Community: Tristan da Cunha," *Amer. J. Sociol.*, 53, 1–8 (July 1947).

Munch, Peter A., "Culture and Superculture in a Displaced Community: Tristan da Cunha," *Ethnology*, 3, 369–376 (October 1964).

Munch, Peter A., "Traditional Songs of Tristan da Cunha," *J. Amer. Folklore*, 74, 216–229 (July-September 1961).

Munch, Peter, *The Song Tradition of Tristan da Cunha*. Folklore Institute Monograph Series 22. Bloomington, Indiana: University of Indiana Press, 1970.

Munch, Peter A., "Economic Development and Conflicting Values: A Social Experiment in Tristan da Cunha," *Amer. Anthropol.*, 72, (December 1970).

Wheeler, Peter F. J., "Death of an Island," *The National Geographic Magazine*, 121, 678–695 (May 1962).

Whiteside, Thomas, "Annals of Migration: Something Wrong with the Island," *The New Yorker*, 154–207 (November 9, 1963).

GENERAL BIBLIOGRAPHY

The intention of this general bibliography is to provide the reader with reference material less limited in scope than that in the selected bibliographies following each chapter. With some exceptions, most of the texts listed below deal with the global issues of race relations, prejudice and discrimination, minority stratification, and mixed-race marginality.

Allport, Gordon W., *The Nature of Prejudice*. Cambridge: Addison-Wesley, 1954.

Banton, Michael, *White and Coloured*. New Brunswick: Rutgers University Press, 1960.

Banton, Michael, *Race Relations*. New York: Basic Books, 1967.

Barron, Milton L., *People Who Intermarry*. Syracuse: Syracuse University Press, 1948.

Berry, Brewton, *Race and Ethnic Relations*, 3rd ed. Boston: Houghton-Mifflin, 1965.

Blalock, Hubert M., Jr., *Toward a Theory of Minority Group Relations*. New York: Wiley, 1967.

Frazier, E. Franklin, *Race and Culture Contacts in the Modern World*. New York: Knopf, 1957.

Gordon, Milton M., *Assimilation in American Life: The Role of Race, Religion, and National Origin*. New York: Oxford, 1964.

Handlin, Oscar, *The Uprooted*. Boston: Little, Brown, 1951.

Herberg, Will, *Protestant-Catholic-Jew*. Garden City, New York: Doubleday, 1956.

Hughes, Everett C., and Helen McGill Hughes, *Where Peoples Meet: Racial and Ethnic Frontiers*. New York: The Free Press, 1952.

Katz, Irwin, and Patricia Gurin, Eds., *Race and the Social Sciences*. New York: Basic Books, 1969.

Kennedy, Ruby Jo Reeves, "Single or Triple Melting Pot: Intermarriage Trends in New Haven, 1870–1940." *Amer. J. Sociol.*, **49**, 331–339 (January 1944).

Kramer, Judith R., and Seymour Leventman, *Children of the Gilded Ghetto*. New Haven: Yale University Press, 1961.

Lenski, Gerhard, *The Religious Factor*. New York: Doubleday, 1961.

Lind, Andrew W., Ed., *Race Relations in World Perspective*. Honolulu: University of Hawaii Press, 1955.

Locke, Alain, and Bernhard J. Stern, *When Peoples Meet: A Study in Racial and Culture Contacts*. New York: Hinds, Hayden, and Eldredge, 1946.

Masuoka, Jitsuichi, and Preston Valien, Eds., *Race Relations: Problems and Theory*. Chapel Hill: University of North Carolina Press, 1961.

Patterson, Sheila, *Dark Strangers*. London: Tavistock, 1963.

Park, Robert E., *Race and Culture*. New York: The Free Press, 1950.

Salzano, F. M., "Race Mixture," *Intern. Soc. Sci. J.*, **17**, No. 1, 135–138 (1965).

Shibutani, Tamotsu, and Kian M. Kwan, with Robert H. Billigmeier, *Ethnic Stratification: A Comparative Approach*. New York: Macmillan, 1965.

Simpson, George E., and J. Milton Yinger, *Racial and Cultural Minorities: An Analysis of Prejudice and Discrimination*, 3rd ed. New York: Harper and Row, 1965.

Thomas, W. I., and Florian Znaniecki, *The Polish Peasant in Europe and America*, 5 vols. Boston: R. G. Badger, 1918–1920.

Thompson, Edgar T., and Everett C. Hughes, Eds., *Race: Individual and Collective Behavior*. New York: The Free Press, 1958.

van den Berghe, Pierre L., "Hypergamy, Hypergenation, and Miscegenation," *Human Relations*, **13**, 83–91 (1960).

van den Berghe, Pierre L., *Race and Racism*. New York: Wiley, 1967.

van den Berghe, Pierre L., *Race and Ethnicity: Essays in Comparative Sociology*. New York: Random House, 1970.

Vander Zanden, James W., *American Minority Relations*. New York: Ronald, 1963.

Wagley, Charles, and Marvin Harris, *Minorities in the New World: Six Case Studies*. New York: Columbia University Press, 1958.

Williams, Robin M., Jr., *The Reduction of Intergroup Tensions*. New York: Social Science Research Council, 1947.

Williams, Robin M., Jr., et al., *Strangers Next Door: Ethnic Relations in American Communities*. Englewood Cliffs, New Jersey: Prentice-Hall, 1964.

INDEX

Adams, Romanzo, 214, 235
Amalgamation, *see* Race mixing
American Mestizos, 18, 20–21, 191–212
   discrimination against by whites, 198–
      200, 205, 206, 209–211
   distribution of in United States, 191–192
   education of, 208–211
   future prospects of, 210–211
   identity of, 200–204
   life styles of, 204–211
   migration of, 197
   nomenclature of, 192–194, 206
   occupations of, 205–206
   origins of, 194–197
   political behavior of, 207
   race mixing of, 193–200
   racial classification of, 193, 200–204,
      206, 208
   relations with whites and blacks, 198–
      200
   religion of, 207
   slavery, 192, 195, 196
Anglo-Indians of India, 18, 19, 39–59
   attitudes, images, and stereotypes of,
      47–51
   attitudes of Anglo-Indians, toward
      others, 50
    toward the British, 51
   attitudes of others toward Anglo-Indians,
      48–50
   colonialism, 39–41
   demography of, 42
   education of, 53–56
   future prospects of, 58

history of, 40–41
identity of, 43–44, 47, 56–57
intermarriage of, 40, 45–46
marginality of, 44–47
migration of, 57–58
nomenclature of, 41–42
occupations of, 52
organization of, 44
political behavior of, 43–45
race mixing of, 39–40
religion of, 40
seepage and infiltration of, 51–52
transition to independent India, 42–43
vertical mobility of, 52–53
Anthony, Frank, 44, 54, 56, 58
Antonovsky, Aaron, 12, 14, 23
Apartheid, 25, 32–33
Attitudes, images, and stereotypes, of
     Anglo-Indians, 47–51
  toward others, 50
  toward the British, 51
  of Anglos toward Mexican-Americans,
     184–185
  of Durban Coloureds, 36–38
  of Dutch toward Eurasians, 99–100
  of Indonesians toward Eurasians, 100–101
  of Mexican-Americans, 185–186
  of mixed Brazilians, 257–259
  of others, toward Anglo-Indians, 48–50
    toward Durban Coloureds, 34–36
    toward mixed Brazilians, 259–262
  of Tristan da Cunhans, 272–281
  of whites and blacks toward American
     Mestizos, 198–200

285